THE LEGEND OF
JOHN WILKES BOOTH

WITHDRAWN

CultureAmerica

Karal Ann Marling

Erika Doss

SERIES EDITORS

WITHDRAWN

THE LEGEND of JOHN WILKES BOOTH

Myth, Memory, and a Mummy

C. WYATT EVANS

CONTRA COSTA COUNTY LIBRARY

UNIVERSITY PRESS OF KANSAS

3 1901 03709 7633

© 2004 by the University Press of Kansas

All rights reserved

Published by the University Press of Kansas
(Lawrence, Kansas 66049),
which was organized by the Kansas Board of Regents
and is operated and funded by Emporia State University,
Fort Hays State University, Kansas State University,
Pittsburg State University, the University of Kansas,
and Wichita State University

Library of Congress Cataloging-in-Publication Data
Evans, C. Wyatt.
The legend of John Wilkes Booth : myth, memory, and a
mummy / C. Wyatt Evans.
    p.   cm. — (CultureAmerica)
Includes bibliographical references and index.
ISBN 0-7006-1352-8 (alk. paper)
1. Booth, John Wilkes, 1838–1865—Legends—History and
criticism.   2. Assassins—United States—Biography.
        I. Title.   II. Culture America.
        E457.5.E85   2004
    973.7′092.—dc22   2004019564

British Library Cataloguing-in-Publication Data is available.

Printed in the United States of America

10 9 8 7 6 5 4 3 2 1

The paper used in this publication meets the minimum
requirements of the American National Standard for
Permanence of Paper for Printed Library Materials
z39.48-1984.

To the memory of my mother,
Hona Longstreet Bradley Evans,
who, had she lived to see this day,
would certainly have enjoyed it

Booth, indeed, may be said to be the only
really mysterious personage we have had in our annals,
although, perhaps, for the few years we have been an
independent republic, no nation ever made its history
so fast.

New York World, August 17, 1867

CONTENTS

ILLUSTRATIONS

———•·•⟨∞⟩•·•———

ACKNOWLEDGMENTS

This study began as a chance encounter in the Methodist Archives at Drew University, where in the course of cataloguing papers for a seminar in archival methods, I stumbled across the Booth legend in the personal files of a Methodist minister and Prohibition advocate. What followed was that incontrovertible moment of magic for all historical researchers — the encounter with the difference of the past. Faced with what at the time was the inexplicable story that Booth had escaped his pursuers, I chose to pursue the legend as a dissertation topic. While the intervening four years have rendered the legend more transparent to me, I have yet to lose my sense of wonder at how groups in American society employ the strangest stuff to order their worldviews and justify their beliefs.

The past four years have also made me realize how dependent I have been on the encouragement and assistance of others in successfully completing this project. To my dissertation adviser, Brett Gary, I owe a debt of gratitude impossible to repay. Brett's support for this project, even when its direction remained unclear, provided me with the confidence to forge ahead and spread my interpretive wings. The result, I hope, will bear tribute to his mentoring as well as to his commitment to the interdependence of intellectual and cultural studies. Likewise, to Terry Todd and Jeremy Varon, your insights and encouragement as dissertation readers, and your assistance in helping me bridge the gap between secular and religious studies, have, I hope, borne fruit. The stimulating conversation of our occasional meetings was the nourishment that kept me going across months of reading microfilm and composing chapter drafts. To Dale Patterson and the staff at the Methodist Archives, thanks for putting up with my impromptu visits and my endless questions on the intricacies of twentieth-century Methodist organization. To the staff at Rose Memorial Library, and especially Josie Cook and Lois Sechehay in the interlibrary loan office, this project truly would not have reached completion without your efforts. To my colleagues in Drew's history department, I thank you for the genuine spirit of collegiality and your support as I have wrestled with turning a dissertation into a book.

Farther afield, this project has benefited enormously from the encouragement and good advice of many supporters. I wish to thank the editors of the *Journal of Southern Religion* for granting me permission to reuse portions of my article, "Of Mummies and Methodism: Clarence True Wilson and the Legend of John Wilkes Booth," from the journal's December 2002 online edition. Other portions of the work were originally presented at conferences and seminars, including the 2003 New England Historical Association (NEHA) annual meeting, Drew University's Modern History and Literature (MHL) graduate colloquium, and a history faculty seminar at Cornell University. My thanks to the various panel participants and audience members for their comments and helpful suggestions.

Despite my best efforts to master the multitude of legend details and variants, I remain a neophyte in many respects. The topic of Lincoln's assassination (and along with it the story of Booth's escape) offers a special challenge to the historical researcher. The records bearing on the topic are not located in a single archival repository, nor even a dozen of them. There is no central source, especially when it comes to the popular production of legend texts; and the researcher must locate hundreds of newspaper, journal, and other popular texts in order to ferret the story out. The true experts on the assassination and Booth's escape have spent decades chasing down leads and the snippets of information that make up the record. I have benefited from the tutelage of several members of the Lincoln assassination studies community. Thanks especially to Steve Miller, whose knowledge of the intricacies of the Booth legend is truly astounding, and whose leads and suggestions have contributed to this study's richness and detail. Although we have not always agreed in our overall approach regarding the legend, I hope this work will do Steve's tutoring justice. I also wish to thank Michael Kauffman, broadcast technician and assassination expert extraordinary, for taking the time to meet with me — and for the cook's tour of CNN's Washington, D.C., studio.

To Su Wolfe of the American Antiquarian Society, thanks for your hospitality and for sharing with me your incredible knowledge of antebellum mummies. It opened my eyes to a facet of the project I did not originally see. My thanks as well to Scott Taylor and the staff at

Georgetown University's Special Collections, and to the staff at the Library of Congress Periodicals and Rare Books reading rooms. To Laurie Verge, former director at the Surratt Society museum, thank you for allowing me access to the society's files when this project was still in its formative stages. To Bertram Wyatt-Brown, Ed Ayers, and the other anonymous readers of the book manuscript at various stages along the way, thank you for your frank criticisms and encouraging words. To Nancy Jackson, Susan Schott, Larisa Martin, Donna Bouvier, and the rest of the editors and staff at the University Press of Kansas, I am grateful for your professionalism and diligence in shepherding this book to press. And to numerous other scholars, museum curators, legend believers, legend detractors, journalists, and librarians, I extend my thanks for your assistance in pursuing this project's many errant (yet fruitful) leads.

Finally, I wish to thank my family: my father, Clifford Evans, for his moral (and material) support over the past seven years. And my wife, Allyson, and daughters, Emily and Sarah, for living through this project with me and for putting up with their husband and father's occasional bad humor, never-ending deadlines, late hours, absence from family events, and the rest of what I have come to realize are the demands of scholarly endeavor. Now that this chapter of our common life is completed, we can hopefully look forward to enjoying the rewards of our hard work. Your presence has sustained me through the years of effort and has reminded me of what is most important in life.

INTRODUCTION

In typical midway fashion, the carnival exhibit from the 1920s presented an eclectic mix of decor. Faux Egyptian columns adorned with hieroglyphs braced each corner of the room. A decorative lintel sporting the outspread wings of a pharaonic bird spanned the back wall. At the juncture of wall and ceiling ran a banded frieze of water lilies. The whole basked in the glow of multicolored bulbs, hidden in the ceiling alcove and column capitals. In contrast, but also suggesting mystery and distant secrets, the exhibit's hand-lettered marquee proclaimed "JOHN WILKES BOOTH — HIMSELF — MURDERER OF ABRAHAM LINCOLN." On the back wall smaller boards reassured prospective customers, "Not a Picture Show," "Not a Wax Show," and most important, "An Exhibition for the Correction of American History." Portraits of Booth, Lincoln, Andrew Johnson, and Mary Surratt, and framed affidavits and copies of old reward posters provided supporting evidence for the main display in the center of the room. On a Navaho blanket, inside the canvas and wood pit, lay the preserved body of an elderly white man. Clad only in a pair of khaki shorts, his parchment skin glistened from applications of Vaseline. Once drawn in, the curious were shown the body's confirming marks. A broken thumb, the deformed leg broken in leaping from the stage, the arched right eyebrow: proof that the body was that of John Wilkes Booth. Its presence confirmed he was not killed in 1865, as history alleged (Figure 1).

While this exhibit may be the most dramatic artifact of the legend of John Wilkes Booth's escape, it is by no means the whole story. Belief that Booth evaded his pursuers has persisted from the assassination to the present. A recent court case in Booth's hometown of Baltimore once again pitted believers against the forces of historical orthodoxy. While legend adherents failed in their bid to have Booth's remains exhumed in order to determine whether they are in fact his, we should not assume this is the end of the line. The story is out there, and so is the mummy. According to recent information, "Johnny" now

Figure 1.

Booth mummy carnival exhibit, Long Beach, California, circa 1925. (E. H. Swaim Collection, Georgetown University Library Special Collections Division, Washington, D.C.)

belongs to a collector of circus paraphernalia in Silver Spring, Maryland. If so, the assassin has returned full circle after a century's absence to rest inside the Capital Beltway and, figuratively at least, in the shadow of Lincoln's gaze.

Before proceeding to explore the legend in detail, we should review the standard version of events concerning the capture and death of Lincoln's assassin. On Good Friday evening, April 14, 1865, well-known actor John Wilkes Booth shot Abraham Lincoln in the president's box at Ford's Theater in Washington (Figure 2). The president was mortally wounded and died the next morning around 7:20 a.m. After leaping to the stage, at which time he fractured a bone in his left leg, Booth escaped on horseback into lower Maryland. There, one of his accomplices, Davey Herold, joined him. Together they made their way to Bryantown, where Dr. Samuel Mudd splinted the broken leg and Booth gained a few hours' rest. The next afternoon, the fugitives continued to travel southeastward on horseback to the region of Zekiah Swamp, where they reached the plantation of Samuel Cox, a southern sympathizer. Cox ordered his overseer to hide the men in a nearby copse of pines and contacted his stepbrother, Thomas Jones, to care for them. Jones succored the two men for the next six days, and on the evening of April 21 led them to a rowboat he had secreted with the help of a black servant. They set off across the Potomac River to the Virginia shore. However, a strong flood tide and federal gunboats drove the pair back to the Maryland shore near Nanjemoy Creek, where they remained all day before trying to cross the river again the next night. This time, they succeeded in reaching Virginia and made their way to the Rappahannock River, which they crossed on a ferry accompanied by three soldiers from John Singleton Mosby's disbanded command. The three led them to the Garrett farmstead near Port Royal on April 24, where Booth assumed the guise of a Maryland veteran heading south. Herold rejoined him the next day, although news of federal patrols in the area caused the pair to spend most of the time hiding in nearby thickets. This aroused the suspicions of their hosts, and Booth asked to spend that night in the farm's tobacco shed. It was there, in the early morning of April 26, that a detachment of the Sixteenth New York Cavalry commanded by officers of the national detective police surrounded the pair. After the officials called for their surrender, Herold gave himself up. Booth refused. One of the officers set fire to the barn, and in the rising flames Sergeant Boston Corbett shot Booth with a revolver through a gap in the barn's siding. The assassin collapsed, paralyzed from the ball through his neck. Troopers dragged him from the flaming structure to the farmhouse porch, where he died a few hours later. The body was sewn up in a blanket and quickly transported back to Washington, where it was laid out on the deck of the USS *Montauk* at anchor in the navy yard. News of the capture reached the public, and the following morning hundreds of onlookers surrounded the navy yard precincts hoping to catch a glimpse of Lincoln's killer. Meanwhile, on the deck of the *Montauk*, an inquest and autopsy positively identified the body as Booth's. Army surgeons removed three vertebrae from the assassin's neck for preservation at the Army Medical Museum. Late that afternoon, the corpse was lowered from the deck of the *Montauk* to a waiting rowboat and rowed away. Unknown to the public at the time, Booth's remains were entombed that night under the floor of a nearby army storehouse.[1]

The legend, which has assumed multiple versions over the years, naturally takes issue with this version of events. A composite sketch runs as follows. Booth was not killed on the Garrett farmstead, as official history would have it. Rather, the person shot in the flaming barn was a redheaded field hand named Robey or Ruddy. Because the government agents pursuing Lincoln's assassin had a strong interest in making sure the dead man was Booth (they stood to gain the reward money and possibly were under order from high-ranking Union officials), the inquest that followed was a sham. The corpse was disposed of secretly, and Secret Service chief Lafayette Baker deliberately misled reporters by telling them he dumped the weighted body into the Potomac River. Meanwhile, Booth headed southwest under the cover of a Confederate cavalry screen. He rested awhile in Kentucky to mend his broken leg before moving westward again in the summer. On reaching the Mississippi, he crossed into Arkansas at Catfish Point. He hired on as a mule driver with a wagon train bound for Utah and eventually reached California, where he reunited with his mother and secret bride. Over the next thirty years Booth, like the biblical Cain, lived a life of exile. He traveled the world, assuming aliases and identities in an endless peregrination. In Mexico, he enlisted in Maximilian's imperial army, and escaped Suarez's firing

Figure 2.
The Assassination of President Lincoln, *Currier & Ives lithograph engraving, 1865. (Library of Congress Prints and Photographs Division, LC-USZ62 2073.)*

squads by disguising himself as an itinerant Catholic priest.[2] In China, he fought the Tai Ping rebels alongside adventurer Frederick Townsend Ward and gained the favor of the emperor for his skill and daring. When his identity was revealed in the course of an amateur theatrical production, Ward gave Booth a boat and a crew with which to make his escape. The fugitive sailed to the South Seas with his wife and unwitting companions, finding temporary refuge on the remote Pelew Islands. In a Bombay hotel, Captain Tolbert, a merchantman and ex-Confederate blockade runner, wagered he could prove Booth was alive and well in Ceylon. And in the decades following the war, residents of Hood County, Texas, suspected the mysterious saloon-keeper John St. Helen was in fact the fugitive assassin.

The journey of the legendary Booth ended in 1903 when a drifter swallowed poison in his Oklahoma hotel room. In his death throes, he admitted his true identity to those present. The news spread quickly through the Oklahoma boomtown, and a minister's wife recalled that the man had made a similar confession to her several years before. Local papers printed the story; within days it had spread throughout the Mississippi Valley. On hearing the news, a prominent Memphis attorney arrived to identify the remains of his former client, John St. Helen. Based on the confirmation of identity, the local undertaker decided to embalm the body in order to preserve it for the federal officials who were sure to arrive and claim it. They never did; and for the next several years, the mummified remains remained a local attraction. Eventually the attorney gained custody of the corpse and returned with it to Memphis. Following World War I, he rented it out to carnival entrepreneurs, launching "Booth" on his posthumous acting career. He toured the West and Midwest during the 1920s and '30s, with varying success. The settings for his display were not always as elaborate as that described earlier and shown in Figure 1. Still, it was during this time that the legend of the escaped assassin achieved its greatest exposure in American culture, in large part due to the spectacle of the mummy. The story of the mummy appeared in mass periodicals, including the *Saturday Evening Post* and *Life*. Henry Ford considered purchasing the body, and detailed the editor of his private newspaper to establish its authenticity. Clarence True Wilson, a Methodist divine and leading prohibition advocate, lectured on the legend during his cross-country speaking tours. Several popular literary works either defended or sought to debunk the story. With the coming of World War II, however, the legend and its material artifact faded from view. Both reappeared briefly in the wake of the Watergate affair, with the mummy last spotted in New Hope, Pennsylvania, in 1976. In the 1990s, a group led by a Washington-area schoolteacher sought to have Booth's presumed remains in Maryland exhumed to determine whether they were in fact his. The case generated national media attention before the group's suit was denied in Baltimore's circuit court.

⌒⌒

A fantastic story full of contradictions and imaginative leaps, the Booth legend stands resolutely opposed to mainstream historical understanding. How and why did it come to be, and how do we explain its long-running stand on America's cultural margins? We must first recognize the public's larger fascination with Lincoln's assassination. More than a million people visited Ford's Theater in 1999, and the story of his killer continues to find expression in print, movies, theaters, and popular song. A search of newspaper indexes since 1998 lists more than forty entries dealing with some aspect of the assassination or the assassin: Booth and Lincoln descendants clash on a high school football field; Booth's childhood home in Bel Air, Maryland, sells for $415,000; Dr. Richard Mudd perseveres in his half-century-long effort to clear the family name. NBC's *Unsolved Mysteries* featured the legend in 1991 and Steven Sondheim's musical *Assassins* had as its second number "The Ballad of Booth." Bluegrass artist Tony Rice and folksinger Tom Pacheco offer alternate versions of the story, with Pacheco invoking the legend in his continuing examination of a disenchanted world. The jam-band Clutch grinds out an acidic "I Have the Body of John Wilkes Booth" on its keynote album.[3] And then there are the bus tours. Each year hundreds of people participate in a twelve-hour odyssey sponsored by the Surratt Society, the local Maryland historical organization dedicated to preserving the history of the assassination. From the presidential box at Ford's Theater to the median strip of the Virginia highway where the Garrett farm once stood, travelers retrace the assassin's steps. Historian Gene Smith explains the "Booth Obsession" as the desire among participants to be in touch "with great and terrible and sad events now long passed but still possessing great power."[4]

Despite this power, most curators of the American past treat the story of Booth's escape with disdain — when they notice it at all. As historian Mark Neely Jr. observed some time ago, mainstream historians regard Lincoln's assassination largely as a footnote to the broader issues of the Civil War and Reconstruction.[5] Those who have considered the legend view it as forming part of the larger tangle of suspicion that Booth could not have acted alone. He must have been, so the argument goes, the agent of a larger, unseen organization. Given the hysteria in the North following the assassination, which interrupted the religious celebration of Easter and ongoing celebrations over Lee's surrender on April 9, suspicion that Confederate leaders were behind the killing was widespread. Equally suspected were the "treasonous" northern organizations such as the Knights of the Golden Circle (KGC) and the Sons of Liberty.[6] Over the following hundred years other suspects were taken in, including Andrew Johnson, the Catholic Church, Wall Street financiers, the Confederate Secret Service, and Lincoln's own secretary of war, Edwin Stanton.

The relationship of the escape story to these theories varies. In many the normal version of Booth's death persists; in some his escape becomes an integral part of the larger tale. The legend is implicitly a theory of conspiracy, since belief in the actor's escape automatically indicts authorities for covering up the identity of the body taken from the barn. Regardless of the legend's status, experts on the assassination are universally disdainful, categorizing stories of Booth's escape as "total nonsense" and "an old canard."[7] Testifying at the 1995 exhumation case, historian William Hanchett offered that Booth sightings were as prevalent in their time as Elvis sightings are now.[8] The late Michael Maione, formerly the National Park Service historian at Ford's Theater, admitted that visitors ask about the escape story at least once a week. He explained this phenomenon as a case of generational amnesia: younger people forget what their elders once knew and therefore revisit old tales.[9] For most of the experts, the legend's persistence reflects the workings of media-induced sensationalism, the failure of public officials and historians to present a correct account of events, and the imagination of a misinformed public. The experts' frustration with the ways in which legend proponents have played fast and loose with the historical evidence is understandable. However, the mass culture critique they invoke inevitably reduces the legend to a case of social pathology, and it fails to offer any positive explanation as to why people believed, and continue to believe, in Booth's afterlife.

The few attempts to explain the legend in a positive light have viewed it and its subject in folk-mythological terms, wherein the tendency to pathologize the story remains. Lloyd Lewis's *Myths after Lincoln* (1929) borrowed from Sir James Frazer's *Golden Bough* to explain the assassin's "immortality" as stemming from the inevitable pairing with his victim. Upon his death, Lincoln assumed the status of the dying god in northern culture, the tragic hero whose blood was shed to preserve the nation and who henceforth watched over the people from a mythic abode. According to the classical formula, Booth assumed the status of his nemesis-twin, the demon god with whom Lincoln wrestled in endless combat. As long as Lincoln remained a god, his betrayer could not die. Lewis believed that Lincoln's deification was itself a product of the particular conditions of democratic culture. Having cast off the hereditary myths of their homelands, Euro-American settlers longed for the household gods of their racial hearths. Their new country offered no suitable replacement until Lincoln. George Washington was too aristocratic; Andrew Jackson too wild. His death made Lincoln the perfect choice: he was at once larger than life, of the people, and tragic.[10] In *The Great American Myth* (1940), George S. Bryan offered a similar judgment. The product of gossip and official misinformation, the legend also reflected a universal tendency to disbelieve the deaths of notorious individuals. Historical examples, noted Bryan, included Dmitris, the murdered son of Ivan the Terrible, and Marshal Ney, the executed general of Napoleon's army. The circumstances surrounding Booth's act and capture gave rise to similar "survival tales," resulting in a myth "that for amplitude and vitality has no equal in the United States."[11] More recently, historian Constance Head has suggested that belief in Booth's survival proceeded from the tendency to regard him as a hero figure of either the romantic or the tragic type. Some people, past and present, have approved of his act. Others, while acknowledging his crime, were inclined to view the actor as a hero of the classical type, led to his downfall "by one well-intentioned but tragically misguided act." Over the years these self-described "Boothies" have kept the assassin's memory alive through the collection of relics, visits to his former haunts, and the perpetuation of legend narratives. Head concludes that the motivation behind this ardent remembering includes a fascination with notorious outlaws, devotion to the Confederate "Lost Cause," and Booth's dashing physical presence and theatrical background.[12]

These explanations, based on universal anthropological phenomena, certainly explain what the legend has stood for, at least in part. Like the experts' negative critique, however, a reliance on myth and romance tends to overlook the legend's finer features. Especially in the case of the mythical exegesis, resorting to universal structures and an undifferentiated "folk" obscures the legend's political and ideological implications, when in fact the legend clearly needed politics for its genesis.[13] This leads us to a cultural historical perspective, the leading promulgators of which over the past half-century have included E. P. Thompson and the Birmingham School, Stuart Hall, Lynn Hunt, George Lipsitz, and a host of others. The central tenet to this perspective is simply — in Lipsitz's apt paraphrase of jazz great Rahsaan Roland Kirk — that popular culture "ain't no sideshow." According to this view, popular cultural expression, even in its most marginal and eccentric forms, performs serious political, cultural, and social work. It does not represent the duping of the masses, nor is it trivial. Popular culture is the means by which ordinary human beings appropriate, contest, accept, and reject dominant economic, social, and political institutions. This perspective yields a more productive approach to understanding the legend. From this vantage point, the carnival exhibit described earlier, while a literal sideshow, is in fact replete with meanings bearing on larger cultural, political, and social issues. It presents a graphic distillation of the memory of Booth's escape that, approached carefully, promises to yield insight into the forces that have fueled it over time.

≋≋

This book attempts such a reading. Inspired by the wealth of scholarship on American collective memory, I view the legend principally as a memory of the Civil War. Belief in Booth's escape and the display of his alleged corpse functioned as commemorative activities similar to the ceremonies and reunions that characterized mainstream remembrance. Moreover, activities related to the legend served ideological and political functions in the same way mainstream activities did. The legend's carnival setting and blatant antagonism toward historical truth should not dissuade us from taking it seriously. In fact, the first benefit of this perspective is that it lets us see that if the legend is a myth (as its critics maintain), it is one among many. Historian Michael Kammen notes the public's willingness, in the case of the Civil War, "to accept mythical history that is patently unreal and verges upon the bizarre."[14] His case in point is a popular lithograph published shortly after Lincoln's death that portrayed a living Lincoln and Washington standing with Lincoln's generals. The war also gave rise to innumerable tales of the preternatural. To cite just one example: on the eve of Stonewall Jackson's death at Chancellorsville, soldiers reported that they saw him surrounded by a yellow shroud of light. None of these tales, however, has raised the ire of historians and other curators of the Civil War past the way that the legend of Booth's survival has.

Scholars have also demonstrated the extent to which the entire history of the war has been shaped by a reconciliationist and white supremacist vision deriving from another myth — that of the Lost Cause. Promulgated by southerners in the years following defeat, the idea of the Lost Cause had spread by century's end to become the dominant national interpretation of events. Its main tenets included denying that the main cause of the Civil War was slavery; rather, it was argued, the main reason for the war was a constitutional conflict over the issue of states' rights. Slavery was only the immediate "occasion" of the war. According to the Lost Cause explanation, the South had struggled valiantly against overwhelming numbers and resources to preserve its constitutional rights and way of life. Civil War expert Alan Nolan believes the Lost Cause promoted the war "as a mawkish and essentially heroic and romantic melodrama, an honorable sectional duel, a time of martial glory on both sides, and triumphant nationalism." In the course of the twentieth century it became the popular version of events, constituting a "vast mythology" whose impact on American culture includes thwarting historical understanding and progress towards racial justice.[15] Even Ken Burns's acclaimed PBS series fell victim to the Lost Cause by emphasizing the romance of the battlefield instead of providing an exploration of the deep national division the issue of slavery wrought.[16]

Viewed in these terms, the story of Booth's escape hardly qualifies as an anomaly. It is a myth among myths, a minor variant of the wholesale mainstream distortion. The question then becomes how to establish its place among the larger myth-history of America's bloodiest conflict. First, and most obviously, the Booth story would appear to abet the myth of the Lost Cause, by resuscitating the life of the white

South's "vindicator." That the legend achieved its greatest flowering in American popular culture at the same time the commemoration of his victim also underwent its greatest period of development further reinforces the relation between the legend and mainstream memory. This conjunction, however, raises more fundamental questions. Is the Booth legend merely a variant of the Lost Cause tradition? If so, how should the legend's historical contrariness be understood? Is this a case of countermemory, by virtue of its evident opposition to established historical truth? And how should countermemory be defined? Understanding the equal measure of devotion and vehement denunciation the Booth story has drawn requires some kind of explanation beyond its being part of the Lost Cause myth.

The fuller answer hinges on our recognizing that the remembrance of past events always involves present interests, and that commemoration usually includes an ideological content that serves the needs of specific groups within society. Charles Reagan Wilson's *Baptized in Blood* (1980) and Gaines Foster's *Ghosts of the Confederacy* (1987) are two seminal works that encouraged historians to consider how the mainstream commemoration of the war served contemporary ideological ends. Wilson described the statue unveilings, Memorial Day observances, and related activities as rituals of the Lost Cause, and the Lost Cause itself as a civil religion that nourished a distinctly southern way of life in the postwar South. In Foster's analysis, southerners' embracing the Lost Cause was not essentially backward-looking; rather, it was instrumental in helping the New South's middle class adjust to the dramatic transformations in its world.[17] Nina Silber's *The Romance of Reunion* (1993) considers how the literature of sectional reunion turned the South into a feminine "other" and served as a refuge for white northerners facing the pressures of their own industrializing economy. For John Bodnar, the commemoration of the Civil War dead represented the preservation of what he terms "vernacular" memory at a time when "official" memory was increasingly geared to furthering the ideologies of the nation-state and corporate liberalism. And David Blight believes that the merging of reconciliationist and white supremacist visions of Civil War memory by the end of the nineteenth century gave the country a segregated memory on southern terms.[18] This collective memory found its outlet in commemorative activities that included civil-religious observances such as Memorial Day, veterans' reunions, the dedication of monuments, and a flood of ink that has yet to subside. Fueled by the growing spirit of reconciliation between white North and South, mainstream memory of the war worked selectively to elevate the brotherhood of arms and forget the struggle for racial justice. It fostered an allegiance to the modern nation-state, an assumption of the principle of white supremacy, and an acceptance of the modern industrial economy.[19]

The Booth legend participates in this ideological thrust. Booth's escape stood for vengeance against the North; his fugitive existence into the twentieth century may be taken as a symbol of white southern unreconstructedness in the period of upheaval following the Confederates' defeat. As such, it takes its place alongside the early renditions of the Lost Cause, wherein the old southern elite attempted to revise the war's outcome by substituting the pen for the rifled musket.[20] In this connection, the phrase "for the correction of history," found amid the visual cacophony of the carnival stage, was a quintessential expression of the Lost Cause.[21] The legend stands for more, however, than southern redemption. Careful attention to its details (including the detail of a carnival mummy) and to the conditions attending their creation yields a more complicated picture. To begin with, the story's origins were more northern than southern, and as Constance Head comments, Booth's latter-day devotees are not confined to the South.[22] The legend's initial impetus came from the workings of the northern popular imagination, the northern press, and the actions of Union officials in the period immediately following the assassination. The intentions behind this imagining were quite different from those informing the southern version, and from the beginning Booth's survival was double-coded. On the one hand, it stemmed from the figuration of Booth as a romantic hero, "Our Brutus," who acted to bring down a tyrant. On the other, it was the unintended by-product of the trauma that Lincoln's assassination provoked. In their efforts to annihilate the assassin both physically and figuratively, the northern public and press created a slippery figure. His elusiveness became a means of repeating the trauma of Lincoln's death in the decades to come. Belief in Booth's afterlife also came to embody messages distinct from the memory of the war or Lincoln's assassination. In the case of the mummy especially, its display reveals other contexts, both near and far. On the near side, the construction of the embalmed remains of the supposed assassin in Enid, Oklahoma, connects the story to the southwestern tradition of the social bandit, whose exemplars included Billy the Kid and Jesse James. Like Booth, both the Kid's and James's deaths were enveloped in mysterious circumstances, giving rise to tales of survival.[23] On the far side, the carnival exhibit's Egyptian motifs drew upon the popular fascination with ancient Egypt and the display of the dead dating back to the period of the early republic.

What emerges is a variegated picture. Framed by the mainstream memory of the Civil War, the Booth legend also went its own way. Poised on the margins of the cultural mainstream, Booth's body became host to a number of dissenting impulses even as it participated in the broad sweep of Civil War commemoration. If it has served to evoke the tragedy of the assassination, it has also been appropriated for many less somber (and less honorable) projects. Thus its blatant antagonism to historical truth cannot be understood solely in terms of Civil War memory. While it may have abetted the Lost Cause interpretation of events, the remembrance of Booth's escape also evoked a moral, racial, and political past at odds with the nationalistic and modernist ideologies that characterized mainstream commemoration. Memory is never neat. As historian James Young notes, it is never shaped in a vacuum, and the motives that inform the commemoration of the past are never pure. The legend and the mummy demonstrate how the remembrance of a historical event produces competing and clashing narratives that embody distinct political and ideological messages. These narratives are often at odds with one another and with the mainstream version of events, even while they make use of common symbols and (in the case of the mummy) a single material artifact.[24]

This composite picture leads to what I believe is the Booth legend's significance as an object of study. In the first place, it offers an alternate venue for studying the workings of Civil War memory in American culture. Over the past two decades, despite a very rich interpretive effort, such study has tended to rely on a limited repertoire of sources. Commonly invoked subjects include Jubal Early, Thomas Nelson Page, Joel Chandler Harris, Millie Rutherford, the Daughters of the Confederacy, the United Confederate Veterans, *Century* magazine, and Margaret Mitchell. There is much that is admirable about the insights gained from these sources. Indeed, this volume depends on this earlier scholarship. I believe, however, that the Booth legend can provide a fresh perspective on the larger problem of the effect of Civil War memory on American culture. In the first place, its sources are both northern and southern. They cut across a range of cultural expression, including oral tradition, the popular press, official government pronouncements, political discourse, and (in the case of the mummy) a material artifact. Analysis of these sources reveals that in all cases, contemporary cultural and political issues gave the story life. Emphasizing the local conditions that attended the production of various details of the legend reveals much about the story's intentions.

Second, as a marginal cultural phenomenon — as a counterhistory with discernible political intentions — the Booth legend complicates our view of what are termed variously marginal histories, counter-memories, or vernacular memory. Over the past generation, scholars have tended — and I emphasize "tended" — to employ these terms in a uniquely honorific way. *Vernacular, counter, marginal,* and associated terms serve as keywords in a cultural critical lexicon that employs them in a positive sense to connote the struggle of marginalized groups to preserve their identities in the face of the dominant group's rendition of the past.[25] These terms often set the popular, local, and authentic nature of what are labeled *counter, vernacular,* or *marginal* in opposition to the progressive, modernizing, and homogenizing tendencies of mainstream historical discourse.[26] This has resulted in two miscalculations. The first is the assumption that memories or histories deemed marginal automatically carry morally positive valuations. Second, the by-now-familiar elaboration of oppositional cultural practices ranged against a dominant narrative is, as several critics have pointed out, often formulaic and frankly simplistic.[27] What the Booth legend forces us to recognize is, first of all, that marginality and opposition to mainstream narratives are no guarantees of moral worthiness. It would take a pretty thick rug to construe the Booth legend as expressing progressive ideologies of race, even in its northern guise. At the same time, however, there is little denying its place on the cultural margins. It reminds us that the narratives of marginalized groups can support intolerant and threatening political agendas as well as progressive ones. One need look no further than the Oklahoma City bombing for confirmation of this point. The proliferation of white militia movements in contemporary America draws upon a palette of counterhistories and countermemories, including the *Protocols of the Elders of Zion* and the *Turner Diaries*. Although the Booth legend has been less virulent in its practical effect, it incorporates related ideologies, as Henry Ford's involvement suggests. And there have been times in its history, as in the recently published conspiracy tome *Dark Union* (2003), when the legend has contributed to a harmful version of the American past. More significant, however, is the variegated nature of the Booth story, the mixing of patently racist meanings with a benign attempt to preserve local identities against nationalist onslaught. This suggests that instead of viewing marginal, vernacular, and countermemories in opposition to a monolithic and hegemonic narrative of the past, we might more accurately envision a hegemonic center around which orbit marginal narratives of varying moral qualities. This view raises the unsettling question of whether the effort made by some critics to deconstruct the dominant center will lead to the emancipation of marginal voices with dubious moral content as well as those with more positive qualities.

These notions lead to what I believe is the Booth legend's greatest lesson: how the memory of dramatic events gets confounded over time and how the original impulses that gave rise to it (in this case, the trauma of Lincoln's death) may be completely overwritten by other messages. The legend also reveals the mixing in modern America of attitudes deemed "southern" with a broader regionalism centered on small-town, native-born, Protestant America. The scholars of Civil War memory mentioned earlier have noted this crossover to varying degrees. Nina Silber's work in particular addresses the extent of northern complicity in creating the image of the Old South in an attempt to create a haven away from the anxieties of rapid industrialization. My study confirms the observation that by century's end the spirit of sectional reunion included the penetration of Lost Cause interpretation throughout white America. But it also explores to a greater degree the construction of the category "southern" in early modern America. It does so because the Booth legend is as much a northern product as a southern one. Its origins were northern; and during the period of its greatest exposure in American culture, its centers of production lay north of the Mason-Dixon line. Nevertheless, there is no denying the story's southern import and its association with the Lost Cause mythology of the war. In its complete form, however, the legend came to embody two stories, whose intentions were often confounded. The phrase "for the correction of history" stood for the rewriting of the Civil War on southern terms, but it also came to stand for a rewriting of America's larger history since the Civil War and, further, that America's destiny as God's chosen nation had been thwarted by Booth's deed and his subsequent escape.

Over the past sixty years, the confounding of messages and intentions has taken on a more sinister tone, as the legend of Booth's escape has been incorporated into a version of Lincoln conspiracy theorizing that accuses leading officials in the Union government of masterminding their commander-in-chief's murder. This version makes use of the trauma of the assassination to transmit a memory of the Civil War as pointless, and of the Union war effort as mired in corruption and without moral cause. Now the memory of Booth as a romantic, haunted fugitive has been joined to a version of the nation's past that "dis-remembers" the Civil War as an epic struggle to end slavery. As will be discussed more fully in the conclusion to this study, it is this mixing of messages — one relatively benign, the other much less so — that suggests the legend's greatest utility in understanding how counternarratives appropriate the memories of historical events to advance specious claims.

What follows is an exploration of the Booth legend's multiple layers from its origins in the antebellum period to the period of its greatest popularity, the 1920s and '30s. Given the importance of the mummy to the modern version of the legend, the book begins with a description of the mummy's construction in a turn-of-the-century Oklahoma town. My argument here is that the body of a dead drifter was inscribed with various meanings. The principal one was the story of Booth's escape. But other messages, springing from local political and cultural contexts, also contributed to the transformation of the body from cadaver to embalmed attraction. Chapter 2 moves backward in time to consider the background of the mummy's display. I distinguish between form and content and argue that the exhibition of "Booth" in Enid, Oklahoma, and later on the carnival trail drew from long-standing practices involving the exhibition of the dead. Further, this display of the dead was itself part of a broader phenomenon, which I have termed the Euro-American appropriation of the dead, dating back to the period of the Early Republic. By recognizing this cultivation of the dead in the service of racial and domestic ideologies we can understand how the mummy intoned the memory of a distant racial past at the same time it told the specific story of Booth's escape. Chapter 3 describes the legend's northern origins in the immediate aftermath of the assassination through the first years of Reconstruction. I borrow the sociological concept of "negative commemoration" to analyze how the workings of the northern popular imagination in the days following Lincoln's murder helped make the assassin a slippery figure, which in turn contributed to the idea of his escape. Also important to the legend's emergence was the symbolic potency of the corpse in the Civil War era. At the same time the war was making death banal, the national government was beginning to appropriate the dead in order to further allegiance to the nation-state. Booth's body was politically symbolic in the wrong way, so government officials sought to impose secrecy on the proceedings of Booth's capture and burial. (Their efforts, needless to say, backfired.) Chapter 4 considers southern postwar narratives, including oral traditions, Booth impersonators, and retrospective accounts at the end of the century that helped reawaken doubts regarding the assassin's true fate. My focus here is on the figure of Booth as outstanding individual, the honorable southern gentleman who stands above the crowd. In Chapter 5 we return to Enid to consider the career of Finis Langdon Bates, the Booth legend's premier modern promulgator and the man legend critics love to hate. His role in promoting the Booth mummy is most often dismissed as the efforts of a charlatan attempting to profit from the body. Bates, however, synthesized strands of the legend, significantly transforming its meaning. From evoking the trauma of Lincoln's death on the one hand, and serving as a symbolic means of vindication for southerners on the other, Booth's presumed escape and the conspiracy that abetted it were based on a growing mistrust of government. Bates's account stands as one of the first theories in the modern era implicating the federal government in crimes against the nation.

Chapter 6 describes the legend's rise from regional folktale to national phenomenon, largely due to the transformation wrought by Bates. Here I focus on the relationship during the interwar period (1919–1940) between the legend of Booth and the mainstream commemoration of Abraham Lincoln. Lloyd Lewis's mythological account helps elucidate how belief in Booth's escape opposed the mainstream commemoration of Lincoln at the same time it shared in the revisionist interpretation of the war. I also examine several of the popular works of the period, including Izola Forrester's *This One Mad Act* (1937), Bernie Babcock's *Booth and the Spirit of Lincoln* (1925), and Otto Eisenschiml's *Why Was Lincoln Murdered?* (1937). Chapter 7 concludes the study of the Booth legend in its heyday by considering Clarence True Wilson, a Methodist minister and prohibition advocate. Based on Wilson's personal papers (housed in the Methodist Archives at Drew University), my analysis focuses on the coincidence in time between his activities regarding the Booth legend and his leading role during the 1920s in support of the national prohibition amendment. This coincidence, and Wilson's interpretation of the Booth story, suggests that, for Wilson and like-minded conservatives, Booth's escape served as an explanation for the erosion of traditional evangelical optimism in the face of increasing criticism from the modernist mainstream. Wilson's own fervent belief in America as God's providential nation, and in the direct inheritance of this status from the Israelites to Anglo-Americans, also ties in to the preceding discussion of the mummy as a racial icon.

Finally, Chapter 8 considers the legend in contemporary America. After fading from view during World War II, the story of Booth's escape reappeared in the late 1950s and has remained alive ever since. Recent years have found it closely joined to the conspiracy theories surrounding Lincoln's death. A few versions of the old legend still appear, and the exhumation trial in 1995 was notable for not pushing a theory about who killed Lincoln. Other than these, the major appearances of the Booth story in mainstream culture associate it with latter-day adaptations of the Eisenschiml thesis, which has grown more vindictive with time. Understanding the Booth legend and its allied conspiracy theories in contemporary America requires placing it in the context of what scholars view to be the larger American conspiracy mind-set and the professionalization of Lincoln studies in the past forty years. As a result of these developments, historians have actively opposed the story and have taken steps to discredit it.

Over the course of my research I have become aware of how crucial the issue of narrative is to my own effort at conveying an interpretation of the Booth story's place in American culture. On the one hand, standards of scholarship and logical clarity require fidelity to analytical discourse. On the other, adopting too scientific a tone risks obscuring the legend's idiosyncrasies — the myriad elements that make it such a rich source for plumbing the formation of popular historical discourse. A restricted and overly rigorous analytical approach risks returning the story to where it has lain for so long, to the realms of the absurd and folk mythology. The middle approach, which recognizes its valid, contemporary purposes, requires a certain narrative richness. Communicating this richness, I have come to realize, means adopting what Edward Ayers terms "open narratives." In contrast to "fixed narratives," which hew to the conventional logical apparatus of scholarly discourse, open narratives "let the reader in on the way the argument is being constructed." In contrast to the traditional approach, in an open narrative the historian may visibly grapple with problematic sources and their presentation. The point is not to construct some esoteric poststructuralist elixir, but instead (following William James), to insist on "the multiplicity and complexity of everyday experience, [a] focus on the individual, and [a] tone of empathy and respect for beliefs" the historian may not share. This attention to the multiplicity and wonder of ordinary experience has its philosophical roots in James's notion of a "pluriverse" as well as in the phenomenologist's attention to the details of the lifeworld. Open narratives allow more space for the verbatim record. Primary sources take precedence over fully enclosed argument. Again, quoting Ayers, "open histories ask storytelling and language to do more work. Instead of using the narrative as a means to an analytical end outside the story, these histories attempt to fold the analysis into the story itself."[28] Ambiguities may remain unresolved, as human experience is neither continuous nor always logical, and the inclusion of detail is bound to disrupt neat categorizations.[29] I have therefore attempted to craft a narrative in which the individual voices of the Booth legend receive more due than they might in a more rigorously theoretical treatment. I am aware of a certain tension here, as the study's basic assumption of the legend as an example of collective memory vouchsafes ideological outcomes. This approach, however, allows for the irony, pathos, and idiosyncrasies of the story to stand forth. In the final analysis, this book explores how the legend of John Wilkes Booth has taken shape over the course of its 140–year history. My hope is that readers will come away with a sense of the legend's playfulness, irony, and pathos as well as an understanding of the ideological purposes it has served.

1

MAKING THE MUMMY

————— •‹∞›• —————

Everyone is the other, and no one is himself.
(Martin Heidegger)

It started as a lonely death. David George, a drifter without known family or friends, lived in neighboring El Reno before following the Rock Island Railroad northward to Enid, Oklahoma, in late 1902. He arrived shortly before Christmas and settled in, with his single trunk, at the Grand Avenue Hotel. Descriptions depict a southerner in his sixties, unremarkable except for an aura of former respectability hanging about his clothing and manners. He claimed to be a house-painter but did not act the part of a workingman. He frequented saloons and spent his days in the hotel's reading room. His quarters at the hotel consisted of a second-floor cubicle, set off from the other hotel rooms by partition walls that did not reach the ceiling. From the perspective of Enid's middle-class citizenry, George was a respectable indigent. He remained a cut above the hobos who roosted at the Rock Island depot, whose knife fights and larcenies occasionally threatened the town's order. Nor did he frequent the mixed-race cantinas of Enid's African American ghetto in Boggy Hollow.

Because he had been in town so short a time, no one could attest to George's state of mind. We know only that on the morning of January 13, 1903, he purchased fifteen grains of strychnine from the Watrous-Harley Drugstore — enough, he is reported to have said, "to kill a d —— d hound with."[1] Following a solitary breakfast at a local café, he returned to the hotel near midmorning. Some time later cries were heard from the second floor. The hotel clerk and several guests ran upstairs and found that the cries were coming from George's cubicle. His door was locked, so one of the more agile present climbed over the transom and opened the door from the inside. The aging drifter lay writhing on his bed, convulsing, muscles spasmodically contracting in the agony of strychnine poisoning. Doctor Champion was sent for, but the case was hopeless: George expired around 11:30 a.m. Following a brief examination (the vial of poison lying nearby satisfied most of the witnesses on the cause of death), his body was removed to the city morgue, located in W. B. Penniman's furniture store and funeral parlor. A coroner's jury impaneled that afternoon considered the evidence in order to certify the cause of death.[2]

Enid's newspapers reported his death matter-of-factly. Judging from their pages, suicide was no stranger to the land. The week following George's demise witnessed the much more sensational suicide of a distraught laborer who shot his wife in the stomach before turning the gun on himself. In George's case, the *Enid Daily Wave*, the town's Democratic party organ, printed a detailed account the afternoon he died. The headlines announced it as a case of "despondency," brought on perhaps by the suicide's financial straits. Letters found among his effects suggested that he had been receiving financial support from one George E. Smith of Colfax, Iowa; about the letters the *Daily Wave* reported, "The latest one found concludes, 'Go to First National Bank of Enid and get $25.' This money, those who know him say he spent at saloons." George had claimed to have considerable wealth, and several weeks before taking poison he had dictated a will bequeathing property and a life insurance policy. But he later renounced the will; and at the time of his death, according to the paper, "it is not believed he had anything of value."[3] In the absence of any known kin or local acquaintances, town officials telegraphed Smith in the hopes he would identify the body and arrange for proper burial.

The coroner's jury announced the next morning that George had died "by the cause of heart trouble, superinduced by alcoholic poison and some other poison unknown to this jury, which was administered by his own hand."[4] This verdict foreclosed the need for an autopsy. Later that morning, the county attorney ordered Penniman to preserve the corpse pending Smith's arrival. This was standard practice in cases such as George's. Without Smith's intervention, the penniless drifter was bound for a quick burial in a pauper's grave. But when the chance of locating distant kin or acquaintances appeared probable, partial embalming preserved the corpse for viewing and possible shipping. The undertakers anticipated being reimbursed by the arriving relatives.

The first stage of David George's posthumous career thus sprang from the circumstances of a solitary death and contemporary funerary practices. At this point, however, the legend of Booth's escape intervened. Jessica Harper, the wife of Enid's Methodist minister, read of George's death on the afternoon of January 13. She remembered him from three years earlier in El Reno, where she lived before marrying, and where she counted among her friends the daughter of the family in whose house George boarded. During the time that George was a boarder at her friend's house he fell seriously ill, possibly from an overdose of morphine, and the two young women ministered to him.[5] On what the man thought was his deathbed, he unburdened himself to Jessica, saying, as she recalled: "I have something of value to tell you. I am going to die in a few minutes, and I must tell some one. I believe you are a friend and I don't believe you would do anything to injure me." After securing Jessica's promise not to reveal the secret until after his death, he continued: "Did it ever occur to you that I was anything other than an ordinary painter: I told you once before and you laughed at me. Now I am going to tell you — I killed one of the best men that ever lived." Jessica asked him who it was, and he replied with Lincoln's name. He also revealed, according to Mrs. Harper, the existence of a conspiracy among "men in high official life" who desired Lincoln and Seward dead. When he leaped to the stage at Ford's Theater, breaking his right [sic] leg, Mrs. Harper continued, there were men there, southern friends, who helped him reach a hiding place. He was disguised and taken to a waiting vessel in Chesapeake Bay, and from thence to Europe. Mary Surratt, the widow who was hanged as a co-conspirator for her role in aiding the plot, was innocent, according to George/Booth. He therefore was responsible for her death and that of the others who were executed as co-conspirators.[6]

The Reverend Harper visited Penniman's on the afternoon of January 14 as the body was being prepared for embalming. According to the retrospective account of embalmer W. H. Ryan, Harper walked in to where Ryan was working and exclaimed, "Do you know who that is?" When Ryan calmly replied "George," Harper retorted, "No, sir, it isn't. That is the body of John Wilkes Booth, the man who killed Abraham Lincoln."[7] Penniman, in his account, described the minister entering as fluid was being injected into the body, and "as the operator had not taken the customary precautions to keep things neat and sightly," Harper quailed as he delivered his wife's message.[8] According to both Ryan and Penniman it was at this time that the decision was made to fully embalm the remains.

The body of David George now entered the second phase of its construction, undergoing a transformation both physical and imaginative. From our perspective it may seem incredible that the oral testimony of a single woman, mediated — in accordance with the gender norms of the times — through her clergyman-husband, was deemed sufficient evidence to pickle the drifter under the pretense he was Booth. Two points should be kept in mind here. First, the post–Civil War South and West saw many cases of individuals who either attempted to impersonate Booth or were assumed by others to be him. George's deathbed "confession" could easily have been the statement of an impersonator. Second, we should not assume that Harper's story was taken seriously, at least not at first. Penniman may have used the revelation as a pretext for doing what he intended to do anyway. Undertakers occasionally took liberties with unclaimed corpses, especially if the dead man had achieved notoriety. Instead of granting the deceased a pauper's burial, they might sell the body to a carnival operator, or hold on to it for display as a local attraction. Outlaws were favorite subjects for this treatment, both because they were notorious and their bodies frequently went unclaimed. By virtue of his newfound identity, George shared these attributes.[9] Penniman may also have used the body simply to practice embalming techniques. In his own words, "the operation was being done for the purpose of research and education," a euphemistic way of saying perhaps that the corpse, because it lacked standing in the community, became a practice dummy for the embalmers. The body underwent three or four procedures before preservation was complete. At one point, the undertaker allowed a traveling salesman of funeral chemicals to perform an injection so that he could say he had a hand in the work.[10]

Apart from the macabre goings-on at the morgue, there was still the matter of George Smith. If Smith arrived and claimed the body as that of David George, the whole affair would have fizzled out. However, his arrival on the evening of January 15 did nothing to discourage the growing rumors. He identified the remains as those of George but acknowledged having known him only about a year and a half. Their acquaintance had quickly ripened into a close friendship despite a disparity in age. George had made the younger man the beneficiary of his life insurance policy, and it was against this that Smith had loaned him money. The old man had always paid him back, except for the last two loans. Smith described George as highly educated and a Shakespeare scholar. George, said Smith, had traveled widely, in the Holy Land, Assyria, Europe, and Africa. Smith was ignorant of his friend's supposed identity as Booth; as for the details of George's past life, he could only relate what the old man had told him: he was from Mississippi and had killed a man in Texas.[11] Smith left the next day for El Reno in order to track down the properties listed in the will. What happened to Smith afterward remains uncertain. Some reports state that he returned to Enid empty-handed, others that he never returned. In any event, Smith never committed the remains of his friend to the earth, and the corpse remained unclaimed.

By reinforcing the mystery surrounding the body, Smith's testimony contributed to the process that had already begun to transform the identity of the dead drifter. Now began the imaginative portion of the mummy's construction. The Harpers' story was quickly reported in the local papers, and they may also have been called to testify at a reconvened coroner's jury. E. C. Moore, editor of the *Garfield County Democrat*, a weekly Bryanite paper, dredged up an old reward poster to compare with the body on the slab.[12] Local notables were asked to comment on the similarities between the faded portrait and the corpse. Men who had known Booth on the stage testified to the striking likeness, "allowing, of course, for the lapse of time since that great tragedy."[13] In its afternoon edition of January 15, the *Wave* reported a striking resemblance. (The absence of reliable graphic evidence probably facilitated these assertions.) Other physical similarities, including a broken right leg, were also noted. (It was actually Booth's left leg that was broken in his leap from Lincoln's box.)

The *Wave*'s editor, J. L. Isenberg, also raised the issue of uncertainty regarding Booth's fate. It was a "well-known" fact that the government never confirmed Booth's death, he wrote, and the rewards for his capture were never paid. The *Atlanta Constitution* some ten years earlier had stated that Booth was alive and living in Mississippi.[14] The allegation of historical uncertainty introduced a third element into the corpse's transformation. It drew on long-standing beliefs that Booth had escaped and that the federal government had never properly established the fact of his demise.

Those promoting the story also resorted to quasi-science. Two Enid physicians produced an issue of the *Medical Monthly Journal* devoted to the physiognomies of famous regicides. The descriptions relied on the nineteenth-century practice of phrenology, which held that a person's moral character could be determined from the shape of the head and facial features. Booth, killer of the nation's greatest president, was, according to the *Journal,* "kephalonard. The ear excessive and abnormally developed; inclined to the so called satanic type. The eyes were small, sunken, and unequally placed." With another local doctor in tow, Isenberg compared this account with the body on the slab. They concluded that the "general description is almost perfect in the corpse . . . We must acknowledge that the dead man shows all the marks credited to Booth in almost every particular." The *Wave*'s editor also compared George's handwriting to an example of Booth's found in *Harper's Magazine.* The writing, he reported, matched perfectly. The next day a man who claimed to have known Booth but who had not viewed the corpse declared that it could be identified as the assassin's by certain marks below the right knee and on the right side of the face under the eyebrow. "The scars," the *Wave* reported breathlessly, "were found before [he] was allowed to view the body."[15]

The rumors also encouraged a spate of biographical elaboration. From the drab, despondent loner of initial reports, David George assumed a mysterious past and captivating personality. No longer a simple painter who spent his money in saloons, "he was a man of great intelligence and of fine appearance . . . He seems to have had considerable knowledge of Shakespeare and the poets and at times [f]reely quoted from them . . . He always dressed well, had sufficient money for his needs and was gentlemanly in his bearing . . . From random remarks it was learned that he had traveled extensively . . . His lonely way of life and a palpable sense of mystery surrounding his past years and antecedents give color to the fact that, whether the present rumor is true or not, he has had some good reason to hide his identity."[16] Even as the Harper story emerged, "there have been rumors, mysterious and dark, as to the dead man's identity." He was scarcely ever short of money. When in his cups he "would entertain a crowd by both repeating and acting portions of Shakespeare and the poets . . . His diction and facial action was that of the old school, but polished and dramatic."[17] This commentary quickly obscured the realities of George's penniless existence. In a matter of days, the faceless drifter gained a respectability he never had in life. He assumed qualities marking him as an exceptional individual. He stood out from the ordinary run of mankind (the masculine inflection is intentional here): his financial resources placed him beyond the exigencies of the market economy; his oratorical prowess evidenced his power in the public sphere. His bearing and presentation being "that of the old school" hearkened back to a previous age when gentlemanly accomplishments mattered. With this blend of attributes, only recourse to a mysterious and tragic past could explain George's final act.

Buttressed by this sort of embellishment, Jessica Harper's story took hold. Her narrative also drew strength from the doubt regarding the assassin's true fate and the ambient level of historical knowledge regarding Lincoln's assassination. Detailed accounts of the murder and Booth's flight had only begun to appear in the 1880s. Moreover, the reminiscences of participants (or alleged participants) that had been published in *Century* magazine and elsewhere often differed on significant details, including the location of Booth's burial. From the start, historical knowledge — or the lack of it — was involved in the mummy's construction. Indeed, over the entire course of the legend's development, the relation of historical discourse to popular culture is crucial.

Believability was also enhanced for reasons having little to do with the actual evidence and more to do with the identity of those engaged in the telling of the story. Although the *Garfield County Democrat* might allude to the "credulity of the people," the initial round of mummy making was largely the work of Enid's opinion leaders, including newspaper editors, businessmen, medical doctors, and local officials. With the exception of Mrs. Harper, these participants were all white male entrepreneurs from Enid proper. Their efforts in support of the story — providing newspaper coverage, lending medical authority in the examination of the corpse and in the act of embalming — even while sometimes undertaken from a posture of skepticism helped establish the authority of the emerging narrative. In unraveling the meanings attached to this narrative, the motivations of the major players are an important factor.

The larger public, too, was not slow to weigh in. The growing sensation got a boost from the speaking appearance of William Jennings Bryan in Enid on the same evening as the Harpers' and Smith's revelations became known. The Great Commoner's speech at the Opera House drew a thousand listeners, and their congregation in town undoubtedly helped disseminate the growing rumors over the body in the morgue.[18] Over the next few days, people began demanding to see the body, and Penniman obliged. He later related that for almost two weeks "excitement ran high, and in that time it is safe to say that ten thousand people saw the body of the alleged assassin." Country folk drove for miles to see the corpse, and children came with their teachers at the end of the school day, history books in hand, "that they might pursue intelligent investigation of the case."[19] The *Garfield County Democrat* noted on January 29, "The cadaver of what is claimed to have once been the clayey casket of the immortal part of the sensational assassin, John Wilkes Booth, lay in state here for nearly ten days." The Republican *Eagle* corroborated Penniman's figure of 10,000 viewers, pointing out that many hailed from the regions outlying Enid. It is difficult to gauge the accuracy of this number. Data from the 1900 census show a total population for Enid of around 3,400 and for Garfield County, of which Enid was the seat, of 22,076. The claimed 10,000 therefore represented around 45 percent of the total county population — a very high level of participation even for an event of this magnitude. But adding in the population for the adjoining counties of Grant, Kingfisher, Woods, Noble, Kay, and Logan drops the percentage to less than 10 percent of the aggregate, a more believable figure. We can safely conclude only that a sizable number of people came to view the body.[20] There were also reports of relic gathering: Penniman's morgue was being carried away piece by piece and the buttons on the suit of clothes George had been dressed in kept disappearing. Other rumors began flying about. A young woman recently placed in custody in order to testify against her father in a case of incest was thought by "the credulous" to be Mary Surratt, Booth's executed co-conspirator.[21]

The sole dissenters, apparently, during the height of the local mania were the area's Union veterans. They scoffed at the idea that George might be Booth. Their historical sense was more certain. Booth had been killed by Boston Corbett "and buried so deep that the buzzards and wolves could never reach him."[22] Additionally, some among their number resented the story's imputation that the government had not succeeded in punishing the killer of their beloved commander. They were sensitive to the implications of Jessica Harper's story, with its suggestion of high-ranking conspirators. Here are the first indications that the corpse, in the midst of the sensational and ghoulish fabrications so far predominating, was also assuming political meanings. The opposition of the Union veterans to the tale indicates that feelings of bitterness about the war remained intact. This political shaping was reflected in the differing coverage provided by the town's three major newspapers. The Democratic party's *Wave* took the lead in promoting the truth of the story; the *Eagle* and *Democrat,* while devoting equal amounts of ink to the sensation, did so from an attitude of skepticism, and their skepticism increased as time went on. The identification of George with Booth raised up memories of the Civil War, and despite the growing reconciliation between white North and South by the turn of the century, the claim that Booth escaped hit a nerve among the northern veterans.

Despite the local clamor and the continuing air of mystery, by the beginning of the week following Bryan's speech the story reached a halt. Despite suggestions that they do so, territorial officials declined to become involved. Nor did they offer their opinion on events. On January 21 Penniman suspended public viewing, and the corpse, it was reported, was placed in "cold storage" outside the morgue. On the same day, the *Wave* announced it hoped to reveal startling news the following day, "as a gentleman has billed himself to arrive in the city tonight who writes that he knew Booth to be alive one year ago." But the next day the paper acknowledged that its and the undertaker's interest in the case had ended, at least for the present: the "gentleman," who was supposed to be coming from Memphis, Tennessee, had failed to materialize. George's will had been probated, and as suspected his legitimate estate consisted of the contents of his traveling trunk, deflating somewhat the tales of his mysterious wealth.[23] According to the *Eagle* many "intelligent and well-posted people" remained convinced the corpse was Booth's, but without further confirmation there was little point in pursuing matters further.[24] The body of the drifter entered a state of limbo, removed from the public gaze, either placed in cold storage (according to some reports) or buried in a pauper's grave (according to others). And here the affair might have ended.

At the same time the story wound down around Enid, however, it began to travel farther afield. The role of the press in creating the sensation reached a new stage, as newspapers far from Oklahoma generated an echo that rebounded back to Enid and gave the story renewed vigor. By the weekend of January 17, the news of the suicide's possible identity had migrated via local editions and the wire services to the major cities of the Mississippi valley. The *Memphis Commercial-Appeal* featured George on the front page of its Sunday, January 18, edition alongside other lurid tales of escape and self-destruction. Over the next two weeks, the *Kansas City Journal* and *St. Louis Globe-Democrat* ran pieces that were then clipped by other papers throughout the country. This rebroadcast of the story to a wider, distant audience eliminated local detail and highlighted a few salient points: George was portrayed as a wealthy man and the confession came from his own lips. The role of the Harpers and the drifter's lonely, smoky past dropped from view.

Most important to the mummy's construction was the production of further commentary that tended to validate its claims. A St. Louis paper printed the testimony of a retired showman who maintained that he once knew Booth. When the actor visited St. Louis, they had often dined "at a restaurant kept by Martinis, a Spaniard, once famous as a juggler."[25] The showman offered his opinion that Booth had never been killed and that Edwin Booth's deathbed request to see his brother was proof that J. Wilkes had lived. From Illinois, one of the alleged survivors from the party that buried Booth was shown George's "confession" and said, "The whole affair of Booth's capture and the disposition of his body was a peculiar circumstance and shrouded in mystery."[26] This veteran believed it possible the authorities had substituted another man's body for Booth's in order to quiet the country. Again the issue of historical uncertainty helped to drive the story, and the disquiet over the killer's fate did not always issue from southern sources.

The story also attracted those seeking to benefit personally from the turn of events. In early February, Mrs. Charles Levine of New York

City wrote the mayor of El Reno claiming she was Booth's daughter. Her maiden name was Laura Ida Booth, and she claimed her mother had married the fugitive assassin in Tennessee. She was born of the union but had never set eyes on her father, who had deserted the family in the 1870s. Could the mayor possibly furnish her with the details of the estate and where exactly her father lay?[27] She estimated the estate's value at $30,000 and retained a New York attorney to advance her case. Other claimants sought to benefit from the body either via the publicity it offered or by appropriating the cadaver directly. Some of these interlopers were harmless enough. Bentley Sage, an "eminent palmist," came to read George's hand. It was, he reported, of "the spatulate type, from which I learn that the subject was emotional, erratic and governed almost entirely by inspiration." Its owner acted under impulse and, though gifted, never achieved his promise in life. He failed to join his poetic vision with practical results, and this in turn produced moodiness. His thumb revealed an unbending nature.[28]

These outside interventions marked the third stage in the mummy's construction, clearly distinguished from the first two by the fact that people outside of Enid now shaped the story. There were lines of convergence between the outside response and the initial local construction, foremost among these being the issue of historical uncertainty. But there were differences as well. In fact, Penniman and those around him began to chafe at the outside competition. Having launched the story, Enid's own cultural entrepreneurs now witnessed its return, but not always on their terms. These developments also affected the corpse's physical disposition. Once removed from public view, the undertaker had neither placed it in storage nor buried it. These stories were intended to mislead the public. Why the ruse? The *Eagle* published the first photo of the body on February 19, and noted incidentally that Penniman was holding the body "by order of those who would be supposed to have authority."[29] The weekly *Democrat* offered a more sanguine interpretation. Large offers had been made for the corpse, the paper reported, and several enterprising showmen had seen it and believed it to be Booth's. Now thoroughly embalmed, the body "looks lifelike and as white and firm as marble. The remains will doubtless soon be exhibited all over the union."[30] The New York woman was probably part of a plan, similar to an earlier scheme involving a petrified man in southwest Missouri, to authenticate and capitalize on the corpse. The endgame in this case, the *Democrat*'s editor believed, entailed exhibiting the body at the upcoming St. Louis Exposition, where it was sure to clear $200,000.[31]

Once the body was removed from the public gaze, Penniman moved it to the casket room in the back of his funeral parlor. George/Booth was propped in a chair and a newspaper was placed in his hands. In this pose he was photographed (Figure 3) and shortly thereafter appeared in a full-page advertisement for a manufacturer of embalming fluids.[32] Here matters rested for the next several months. Whatever enticements the showmen may have offered, George/Booth remained where he sat. Visits apparently continued, albeit on a more limited basis, and interest waned as Enid's residents moved on to other matters. But it would return.

Why, we may ask, did events in Enid develop as they did? To begin with, place was paramount. Though the bulk of legend accounts pay scant attention to the Oklahoma town where George chose to end his days, Enid was significant in its own right, and the sociocultural forces at work there had important consequences for this story. The construction of George's mummy was a borderlands phenomenon, and his body came to express some of the social, political, and cultural dichotomies marking this turn-of-the-century frontier boomtown. Enid and the surrounding region of the Cherokee Strip hosted an incredibly mixed population. Euro-American settlers mixed with African American and Native American populations. Among the whites, a sizable German immigrant community was juxtaposed with the native born. Rural pioneers rubbed elbows with commercial townsmen, producing a clash of material and spiritual cultures. Garfield County, named for the assassinated president and former Union general, sat close to the Oklahoma Territory's regional dividing line. The southeastern half received the bulk of its settlers from the states of the Old South, whereas the northwestern portion favored settlers from the Midwest.[33] Politically, the beginning of the twentieth century saw the emergence in the Oklahoma Territory of a "politics of race" and the erosion of Republican control, which would culminate in a Democratic takeover at the time of Oklahoma's statehood in 1907.[34] Overwriting these social, political, and cultural developments, Enid's entrepreneurs engaged in incessant boosterism to increase the town's commercial fortunes. Newspaper editors, who were

Figure 3.
Embalmed remains of David E. George in Penniman's funeral parlor,
Enid, O.T., February 1903. (E. H. Swaim Collection, Georgetown University
Library Special Collections Division, Washington, D.C.)

the main producers of booster rhetoric, often made use of symbolic appeals, including the myth of the frontier, to project their message.

Enid was a new place, and everything (or so it seemed) was up for grabs. In September 1893, six months after Frederick Jackson Turner proclaimed the closing of the frontier, 100,000 eager claimants entered the Cherokee Strip in north central Oklahoma in an all-out dash to claim a piece of virgin prairie. The opening of the Strip (or Outlet, as some referred to it) was the culmination of a fifteen-year effort by whites to settle the "surplus" holdings of the Five Civilized Tribes. Chief promoter of the Oklahoma settlements in the early days was David L. Payne, a Kansan who led settlement expeditions from 1879 to 1883 into what were then unassigned Indian territories. These "boomers" were removed by federal troops for their incursions into land the government was committed to protecting for the tribes. But Payne and his followers resorted to other methods, including rhetorical persuasion. Beginning in the early 1880s, editorialists began describing the Indian Territory as the Land of Promise, blessed with abundant resources and a gentle climate. In the course of the campaign noted Kansas journalist William J. Reynolds, writing under the nom de plume "Kicking Bird," dubbed the unassigned territories the "Land of the Fair God," an appellation evoking the perennial Euro-American fantasy of agrarian bliss.[35] Endowed with fertile soil and caressing winds, the untrod prairies needed only the civilizing mastery of the white race to spring forth in bounteous plenitude. Preventing settlement of the free lands, whose current Indian residents lacked either the skill or the desire to bring forth their bounty while white settlers remained without land, was, according to the boomers, a travesty of democracy and white racial destiny.[36]

Congress initially resisted this pressure, but eventually relented and opened the unassigned lands to settlement. Beginning in 1889 and ending in 1901, five public land runs were held. The opening of the Cherokee Strip in 1893 was the largest, in terms of land area and number of participants. It came to be known simply as "the Run," an event that captured the popular imagination then and continues to do so today.[37]

The fervor at the time also stemmed from the mechanics involved. In principle, the Run was a democratic affair, and a person's chances of gaining a quarter section (165 acres) theoretically rested entirely on his or her determination and a dash of luck. It was a mass event of unprecedented scope. The quintessential image is that of a rider on horseback, galloping inland to reach a surveyed section of land. Once there, he or she would hastily "stake" a claim before spending the rest of the day either fending off claim jumpers or heading to the land office to file their claim. Many of Enid's first settlers did in fact reach the town on horseback in the fifteen-mile race from the eastern starting line. Many more arrived by train, as the Rock Island Railroad had established a line through the territory prior to the opening. Despite the efforts of federal officials to ensure fairness, however, and despite the appeals to agrarian virtue contained in the boomer literature, the Run was rife with the manipulations of speculators and dishonest practices. Members of the Cherokee nation were granted allotments before the opening, which led to intense speculation and affected the selection of town sites. Some whites, dubbed "sooners," hid out in the Strip prior to the starting time and grabbed claims before the honest entrants had a chance to reach them. During the Run itself claim jumping was endemic. Those who played by the rules were sometimes bitterly disappointed when an interloper filed on their claim.[38] In assessing the 1889 opening, Stan Hoig wrote, "At the worst the run can be viewed as an act of conglomerated human greed . . . At the best it can be seen as a fulfillment of God-fearing citizens who wished to build homes for themselves."[39]

As land agents prepared the Strip for settlement, it was surveyed and divided into counties, each receiving a temporary alphabetic designator. Enid, named by a Rock Island official after the heroine in Tennyson's *Idylls of the King,* was platted as the seat for County O. It lay astride the old Chisolm Trail and along the line of the Rock Island Railroad. The federal government also selected it as the site for a land and postal office. Blessed with this conjunction of transportation and governmental assets, Enid became one of the Strip's most desired destinations. The day before the Run its sole residents were the occupants of the two federal offices. By day's end on September 16, a forest of tents and covered wagons stretched across the empty lots — the temporary abode for an estimated 10,000 people. Overnight, Enid had become a boomtown, one whose future survival depended entirely on rising land values, agricultural production, its status as a county seat, and its potential as a transportation center on the southern Great Plains.[40]

This instant city suffered reverses in its first years of life. The Run unfortunately coincided with the onset of the worst economic depression up to that time in American history. Agricultural prices declined through the 1890s and, adding to the settlers' woes, drought struck the Plains. Many failed and quit their claims. The imperious Rock Island line threatened Enid's existence by refusing to stop there. It established a competing community and depot, dubbed North Enid, on the railroad's land allotments some three miles to the north. Enid's residents were initially forced to haul persons and material by wagon to the station. Lesser towns succumbed to such tactics and relocated. In fact, the Rock Island argued that Enid was so insignificant it could be moved in a day. But the town's citizens did not suffer the indignity lightly. They initiated a "railroad war," with the town's first newspapers, the *Wave* and the *Eagle,* leading the assault. The *Wave*'s intemperate editorials directed against North Enid's citizens kept them in a state of constant furor, even leading to an assault on the paper's editor. Matters reached a boil in July 1894, when intrepid citizens from Enid sawed through the trestle leading into town, plunging the northbound train into the chasm of Skeleton Creek. A congressional investigation resulted in a visit from Senator Henry Teller of Colorado, who, the story goes, saw a three-story faux-brick building from a distance and deemed Enid properly located. After the passage of federal legislation requiring railroads to stop at all county seats, the Rock Island finally opened a depot in Enid on the first anniversary of the Run.[41] Enid had survived its most perilous moment.

By 1900, with a population of 3,400, Enid was the third largest center in the territories after Guthrie and Oklahoma City. Following the difficult years of the 1890s, the town entered a period of sustained growth, transforming itself from settlement boomtown to a regional wholesale and manufacturing center (Figures 4 and 5). The keys to this economic good fortune included the assets Enid was born with — fortuitous location, a bountiful agricultural hinterland, and the gift of county government.[42] In addition, Enid undoubtedly benefited from the larger western expansion, which in turn depended on the return of plentiful rains and a global rise in agricultural prices. The first decade of the twentieth century was, Robert Athearn noted, the golden age of western agriculture. It was also a period of great change. The rusticity of the mining camps and homestead settlements gave way to a more "progressive" society centered on towns and modern industry. Interest in developing the West shifted from the agriculturists to the townspeople, many of whom were recent arrivals to the region. Even while the members of this "instant city gentry" helped refashion the myth of virtuous western yeomanry, they were eager to undertake commercial expansion and civic improvements. It was the age of the civic boosters — close relatives no doubt to the settlement boomers who preceded them, but devoted to aggressive, modern commercialism.[43] Though perched on the eastern side of the line demarcating the arid, "short-grass" country, Enid shared in this social and economic movement. Although Enid's entrepreneurs had displayed a commercial temper from the town's founding day, the fervor for land values had shifted toward the idea of securing the town's future through "improvements." By the first years of the twentieth century, Enid boasted rudimentary electrical and telephone service, a public high school, a university, and a business school. The old Opera House, built in the months following the Run and long the town's main social center, would shortly be replaced by the modern Loewen Theater. Brick buildings replaced flammable wooden structures. According to the *Eagle,* by late 1902 Enid boasted eighteen manufacturing plants and sixteen wholesale distributors. Boasted the *Eagle:* "The Car of Progress Is Advancing and Enid Has a Reserved Seat."[44]

In short, David George did not spend his last days in a sparsely settled, frontier town. In leaving El Reno, the drifter was migrating toward modernity and commercialism, a move seemingly at odds with the description of him as a denizen of the "old school." In fact, his arrival coincided with Enid's greatest commercial triumph, the wooing of the Frisco, a major railroad and the Rock Island's main rival in the region, to extend its trunk lines through the town and establish a depot. The deal involved granting a sizable right-of-way to the road on the town's south side and, as was typical for the era, paying the line a bonus. According to a neighboring town's newspaper, Enid invested $100,000 dollars in this campaign. It was money well spent for those with commercial interests, since the deal included granting "jobbers' rates" — discounts on carload freight charges — on the Frisco's lines into and out of Enid. The town's manufacturing and wholesale concerns gained an indelible edge over their regional competitors in Wichita and Oklahoma City. The new line not only lowered their own costs; it also virtually guaranteed a trade monopoly to all towns along the Frisco's lines within a sixty-mile radius of the city.[45] Despite some months of trepidation before actual construction of the trunk lines

Figure 4.
Enid, O.T., in the early 1900s, showing the Watrous Drug Store and White
House Saloon on the east side of the town square.

Figure 5.
Enid, O.T., in the early 1900s: Labor Day celebration in town center.

began, by January 1903 the *Enid Eagle* could report, "There is now no doubt as to the intention of the Frisco people to fulfill their every promise to Enid." Nine years after the railroad war threatened to leave Enid without a depot at all, the town was ready to become central Oklahoma's most important railroad entrepôt, with lines reaching to St. Louis, Wichita, Oklahoma City, Texas, Denver, and the Louisiana Gulf. A Frisco official allayed townspeople's fears the same week that Penniman ended viewing of the corpse: "You Enid people have no cause to be alarmed," he was quoted as saying. "Don't get nervous but take things easy . . . The Frisco is going to do more for Enid than the most sanguine of you ever dreamed of."[46]

The optimism of the town's boosters needed little prodding from the Frisco man. Paralleling the material achievements at hand, Enid's "progressives" maintained a barrage of hype, including bands, civic events, and a continuous stream of print. Early-twentieth-century America was the heyday of small-town boosterism, before the literary onslaught of the modernists brought it into disrepute. Edward Ayers believes it replaced valor on the battlefield for the younger generation deprived of that chance; and in its southern context, at least, the ideology of boosterism "served as a gospel, an article of faith, a banisher of doubt."[47] Boosting was an expected editorial function and Enid's various publications, despite their vociferous differences over political matters, joined in promoting their town. Their reporting of the George affair in the midst of this effort makes clear that it was from the beginning a publicity stunt. The German weekly *Die Enid Post,* somewhat removed from the mainstream of Anglo commercial culture, noted as much by the end of the first week. Whatever the outcome of George's identity, "Eins ist sicher . . . Enid's Name ist während dieser Tage im Munde von Millionen Menschen" (rough translation: "One thing is certain . . . Enid's name is today on the lips of a million people").[48] That was the point — to emphasize Enid's place on the map. George's body was put to work as soon as the Harpers' revelations became known and, coincidentally, when the Frisco deal was certain. It served to promote Enid's presence throughout the Mississippi valley. The story's function as a publicity stunt also explains why after a certain time local editors killed the story, or declared it a hoax. Once outside interests appropriated the story for other purposes, Enid's promoters lost interest in keeping it alive.

As a publicity stunt, the corpse took its place alongside other manifestations of hyperbole exercised by Enid's press. In the fall of 1902 the *Wave* began running a half-page spread headlined "Garfield County! An Edenic Spot in the Land of the Fair God — Where Prosperity Rewards the Frugal and Industrious." Farming was easy, the labor involved "trifling" compared to that east of the Mississippi River, since "no surface rock disturbs the smooth gliding of the plow; no stump puller is necessary here." As for the weather: "Outside of the almost continuous soaring of the Gulf current of winds, the climate of Garfield County is very pleasing indeed. The winters are almost always mild and the summers a little warm, yet quite pleasant, nights quite cool and invigorating." Oklahoma, middle earth, happy medium between the antipodes, was never troubled by scarlet or yellow fever. Its population was 98 percent white, of a hardworking class "tempered by misfortunes in other parts of the country. Many who came here in destitute circumstances find themselves in possession of valuable lands." Real estate values had soared in four years, with land costing from $15 to $100 an acre. The central trading point for an estimated 36,000 people, Enid had a population of 3,830 people, all — we are told — doing well. In the past year "new brick blocks have sprung up like magic." There were opportunities in manufacturing, and the city "has become a leading candidate for the permanent state capital."[49] A more graphic effort entailed the map appearing as a regular feature in both the *Wave* and the *Eagle* at the time of George's suicide. It was circular, in the venerable tradition of medieval *mappo mundi,* with Middle Earth — in this case Enid — centered in its compass (Figure 6). Radiating outward to the hinterland ran lines of steel. The surrounding lesser towns of Drummond, Dover, Kingfisher, and El Reno — towns fated to a one-track or at best two-track existence — dotted the lines sweeping outward. Enid's tributary counties were listed along with their principal crops. Beneath the map, statistics record the hinterland's agricultural plenty. On the edge of this orbit, given no great emphasis, were the established regional centers of Wichita and Oklahoma City.

These appeals invoked the myth of agrarian bliss to boost Enid; like the George story, they were directed at an outside audience, the regional readership of the Mississippi valley, whose capital and people the boosters hoped to attract. In addition to its obvious quality as a publicity stunt, however, George's body also conveyed local meanings,

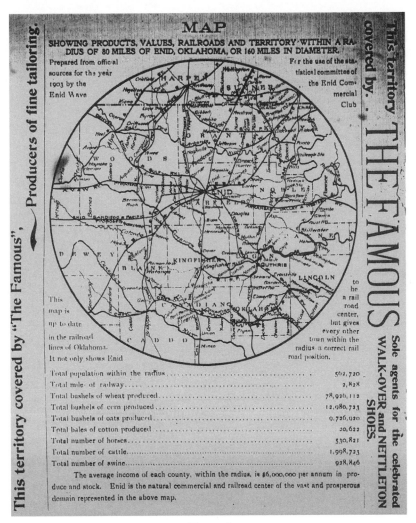

Figure 6.
Map of Enid from the Daily Wave, *Jan. 13, 1903.*
(Author's collection.)

and it is here that the actions of the boosters become more complex. Culturally, while the boosting community used George for its own purposes, he also represented the older frontier type. And politically, although Garfield County remained Republican throughout this period, in his identity as John Wilkes Booth George represented the southern Democrats, as well as the racial implications this suggested. To understand this part of the story requires taking another look at Enid's development with a view to the diversity that marked its opening decade.

From the beginning, Enid displayed a cacophony of rude frontier living and civilized accoutrements. Photos from the early days show tents pitched alongside frame structures with sash windows and hardware on the doors. Surreys congregated with heavier wagons better suited for unbroken country. While homesteaders built sod houses or dugouts, the town's early entrepreneurs shipped precut lumber to erect storefronts. Before the end of its first year, Enid boasted a three-story building with a tin facade painted to look like brick. (It was this faux urban demeanor that convinced Senator Teller of the town's permanence.) Newspapers began publishing from tents only days after the opening of the town. Lawyers specializing in land transactions set up shop in the open air. Storekeepers carried China tea, while horse races and occasionally bullfights were held in the five-acre town square. Inside Jim Utsler's saloon, ceiling fans ran off belts powered by a steam engine, while across the bar hung the quintessential late-century saloon mural, *Custer's Last Stand*.[50]

The clash of material cultures complemented the Strip's population. This borderlands settlement, as noted earlier, was marked, in its first years especially, by ethnic and racial diversity. The Indian Territories had served as the promised refuge of the eastern Indian tribes since the 1840s. They had maintained a tradition of successful self-government for decades and resisted the incursions of the Euro-Americans. Historian Murray Wickett argues that the white population's efforts to dominate education, politics, and law were successfully challenged by Native and African American groups during the Oklahoma Territory's opening decade. The collision of these groups forced a measure of adaptation and acceptance on everyone's part, at least in the early days. In the case of black Americans, the special conditions of settlement in the Oklahoma Territory afforded political and social freedom long after the states of the Old South had instituted Jim Crow. Oklahoma became a new Promised Land, and black enclaves were established at Langston, Guthrie, and in Logan and Kingfisher counties — both adjacent to Garfield. Among whites, settlement patterns also resulted in what Douglas Hale refers to as a cultural dichotomy, between the southern-dominated southeastern half and the northern-influenced northwest.[51]

These settlement patterns helped establish the Republicans as the dominant party, aided by the role federally appointed officials played in administering Oklahoma during its territorial phase.[52] The influx also prompted the unfortunate but seemingly inevitable white racist backlash. By the opening years of the twentieth century, the period with which we are concerned, relative racial tolerance began to break down as white supremacy, traveling under the banner of the regular Democratic party, began its ascent to power. The "politics of race" came to dominate territorial politics in the years preceding statehood in 1907, and the practical result was the withering of Republican power in favor of the Democrats. Despite, or perhaps because of, African American support, the Republicans found themselves unable to repel the attacks accusing them of fomenting racial miscegenation and "nigger government." They divided between "lily whites" who advocated whites-only government and those who remained committed to a policy of racial equality in government. This split further weakened the Republicans' political fortunes.[53]

Determining the precise position of Enid and Garfield County in this political transition is difficult. The county name and political results suggest that a Republican majority held sway through 1903. Patterns of settlement also placed Garfield County in the northern-dominated section of the future state, although its position on the eastern border of the Cherokee Strip placed it close to the more southern-oriented counties of "Old Oklahoma." Despite these northern, commercial, and Republican leanings, however, dissenting political forces did exist in Enid. There was, for example, a cultural cleavage between the railroad-centered entrepreneurs of the commercial centers and the rural farmers. Worth Robert Miller's analysis of this town-hinterland dichotomy established that rural voters were more likely to vote the Populist ticket than were the inhabitants of the commercial centers. This voting pattern cut across the North-South split and added to the complexity of the territory's voting patterns. After 1896, when the People's Party won 17 of 39 territorial legislative seats, third-party strength faded and the populists opted increasingly for "fusion" tickets with either of the two principal parties. The populist threat was serious enough for the Republicans to gerrymander the districts in 1895. In Garfield County they created two voting districts out of Enid and North Enid on the assumption that the urbanites would outpoll hinterland voters in both.[54]

Republican dominance was also challenged by Enid's two Democratic and one Populist newspaper. Of these, J. L. Isenberg's *Wave* partook of a heritage of unreconstructed Democratic journalism, whose practitioners included Wilbur Storey of the *Chicago Times* and Morrison Munford of the *Kansas City Times*. Of Munford, Frank Luther Mott once remarked that he belonged "to that species of western journalism which occasionally indulged in picturesque abuse of its opponents and backed its statements by gunplay when necessary."[55] The same could be said of Isenberg except that when once shot at, he ran away. Political invective flowed freely from his editorial pen. It reached a pitch during the Fall 1902 contest for territorial governor, the results of which were so close that the Democrats contested the results. Republican incumbent Bird McGuire received a serious challenge from Democratic hopeful Bill Cross, with the Populists crossing over to the Democrats. The *Wave,* avowedly standing for "democracy" and white supremacy, lampooned black opposition to "lily-white" officeholders in nearby Kingfisher: "Cash Register Cade [the Republican party boss] has concluded to send two Guthrie spell binding negroes to Skinfisher to hotatrelize [?] the negroes into line."[56] These racial slurs were only part of Isenberg's repertoire of political balderdash. When the election turned out too close to call, the *Wave* was quick to raise charges of ballot tampering and unseemly deeds in the dark of night. The Democrats demanded recounts, and Cross forces filed election contest papers. Hundreds of ballots were apparently disqualified as mutilated when voters stamped Cross's name twice, once under the Democratic column and again under the Populist column. Democrats also alleged that their opponents had imported railroad gangs and black voters to swell the Republican count. In Garfield County, the Republican majority stood at 57 percent, but elsewhere in the Strip their prior advantage evaporated in the face of the Democratic surge.[57]

The fact that the construction of David George as John Wilkes Booth took place just after the closely fought election suggests that the body may have served a politically symbolic purpose for both the

Democrats and the marginalized populists. This possibility is supported by the Union veterans' displeasure over the publicity over the George/Booth affair. Isenberg's role in promoting the fortunes of ascendant southern Democracy and his advocacy of the Booth hypothesis two months following the election also suggest a linkage. The *Wave* took the lead in promoting the story in the days following George's suicide. It was Isenberg who arranged for the comparison of the body's features with the description of Booth in the *Medical Monthly Journal*. And his paper was alone in alleging that government officials had never properly certified the assassin's death. The presence of a sizable Democratic minority by late 1902 makes it probable there were others in Enid willing to promote the body as a political icon. Booth stood for southern vindication and white racial supremacy in the minds of many southerners, and in the opinion of some northerners as well. The resuscitation of the stories of his escape and their inscription on the body of the dead drifter owed as much to the political climate as to Mrs. Harper's testimony. Arguably, her story might never have taken hold if it had not been for the volatile political transition then in progress. George died at an opportune time for Democratic dissenters in the Enid community. The biographical elaboration of him as Booth, and Booth's bearing as a southern gentleman, politicized his body and contributed symbolically to the politics of race.

The Strip's diversity, however, encompassed more than ethnic or racial difference, giving the corpse other symbolic dimensions. Like other borderland settlements, Enid had fewer social controls than did more settled regions; and this fact coupled with the Strip's speculative opportunities attracted a wide spectrum of humanity. Enid native and journalist Marquis James recalled Enid as a place of transience and hidden pasts. It was a temporary stopover for many who, once the Run ended and settlement took over, found adapting to civilization impossible. James estimated that by 1903 half of the initial 100,000 settlers had moved on: "The far field was ever greener. Cowboys, barbers, telegraphers, bill posters, and railroad men were accepted as drifters as a matter of course. Carpenters, painters, and brick masons built one boom town and scattered to build another." James observed the Strip was settled by those "who for one reason or another had lost out, been run out or weren't doing well enough to suit themselves in the places they came from. It often helps such persons to brag of what they used to have and be."[58] In such a world, people frequently claimed distinguished ancestries and lost (or misplaced) fortunes. Under the circumstances, it was best not to inquire too diligently into a person's past. Hence, the figuration of George as endowed with a mysterious past occurred in a ready context. He was a familiar character type in the early years of settlement. The region was also infested with more dangerous birds of passage, outlaw bands such as the Doolin and Dalton gangs. Despite settlement, the vastness of the country still afforded ample hideouts for such lawbreakers. Violence was a chronic feature of the numerous "whiskey towns" that sprang up on the borders of the new settlements, capitalizing on their proximity to the Indian reservations, where liquor was forbidden.[59]

Beginning in the 1880s, the Oklahoma Territory gained a reputation for harboring bandits that would last through the Great Depression. The outlaws enjoyed a measure of popular support, especially among poorer rural residents, and when gunned down by the marshal's posses their bodies were frequently displayed. The intrepid Dick Yeager, alias Zip Wyatt, crossed the line when he killed a settler, but when he was shot and jailed in Enid in the summer of 1895, he became a celebrity and entertained visitors from his cell. On dying from his wounds some months later, the body was photographed in its casket.[60] In Richard Maxwell Brown's analysis, the outlaw gangs of the region comprised a type of "social banditry," a feature of the broader "Western Civil War of Incorporation," which pitted the forces of progress and capital against those seeking to preserve traditional ways of life or the independence of small landowners. The division between the progressives and the outlaws also tended to reflect political orientations born of the Civil War: those on the incorporating side tended to be Republican and supporters of the Union, while the bandits often hailed from a Confederate background.[61] Hence, the transient population and its criminal element reflected a major social division within the territory between modernizing groups and those belonging to a world that was rapidly disappearing.

The recourse to the myth of the frontier, with its allied vision of agrarian bliss, in the midst of Enid's commercial success was, as Robert Athearn noted, a typical approach. It also helps explain how Enid's boosters could use the dead David George as a publicity stunt, and provide him with a biography that emphasized his connection to an imagined world of gentility, poetry, and noncommercial exploits. The construction of George/Booth was also the result of contemporary social forces, and Enid's cultural entrepreneurs drew upon his dual identity as both a denizen of the Strip's early years as well as his supposed identity as Booth. He stood for the passing world of the Run, a world rapidly disappearing in the face of commercial "progress." Thus even as George/Booth served the purposes of the new commercial order, he also represented what it was not. His lifestyle befitted the early years, when the undeveloped territory accommodated persons who for varying reasons could not adapt to the conditions of settled existence. As claims were proved and towns grew, the footloose "man of mystery," whether outlaw or housepainter, had less room to roam. The irruption of the New West resulted in the marginalization of such semi-indigent personalities. As Athearn remarked, they lost their romantic status and came to be viewed instead "as transients, homeless people who were unable to find the West of their choice, drifters who were unsure of themselves. Chambers of Commerce shunned them, for they that did not join the crowd were not apt to be taxpayers."[62] And there were other evocations of an imagined Old West. The rise of the Wild West show and other fin-de-siècle permutations — in which the *display* of the frontier "hero" was the conspicuous motive — occurred in the midst of the borderlands' actual incorporation into the commercial mainstream. George certainly did not qualify as a hero, but the drifter was as much a part of the passing order as the more adventuresome cowboys and gunslingers. The appropriation of his body to promote Enid's commercial fortunes drew on the same nonexistent world as that contained in the narrative paean to the Land of the Fair God.

Thus, at the same time the body of George/Booth served as a remembrance of an imagined past it also became a symbol for the politics of white supremacy. Enid's commercial society, despite its northern-Unionist orientation, chose to confound the body's political and nostalgic messages. The reunion of white North and South had as an essential part of its formula the acceptance of racial intolerance as a condition of commercial success. But Booth's body, or the body presumed to be his, also drew upon a longer tradition of racial identification, one that invested the corpse with religious significance. It is to this further context that we must turn in order to understand how the mummy functioned regardless of its assumed identity.

FAR CONTEXTS

2

*And Joseph commanded his servants the physicians to
embalm his father: and the physicians embalmed Israel.*
(*Genesis 50:2*)

At the same time Enid's promoters pushed the body to serve their boosting ends, and even as it came to assume political meanings, the exhibition of George's remains also partook of long-standing practices involving the display of the dead. Making sense of George's progress as a posthumous attraction requires that we distinguish between his function as a medium for the meanings discussed in the previous chapter and his quality as a material artifact in its own right. The distinction here is akin to that of content and form, with the form in this case being the body and its exhibition, regardless of the particular stories that became inscribed upon it. The distinction is, of course, not absolute. Nonetheless, it is clear that George's display, in Enid and later on the carnival circuit, expressed cultural developments independent of the legend and Enid's near contexts.

In exploring this farther context — the popular display of the dead in American culture — and the place of George's mummy in it, the touchstone throughout is the figure of the carnival exhibit. In its visual components — the cacophony of Egyptianism, Lincoln iconography, Navajo blanket, and historical documents — reside the clues to the mummy's ties to earlier forms of exhibition. Although George's display drew from the southwestern tradition of dead-outlaw viewings, the mummy's genealogy also encompassed a more "venerable" genre. More than carnival enticements, the motifs of the Booth mummy exhibition were remnants of real events in the cultural past — events that, taken together, constituted the Euro-American appropriation of the dead. This appropriation in turn contributed to the construction of Euro-American identity in the antebellum period by endowing mummies with racial identities and linking them to the inhabitants of biblical Israel. This combination of racial and religious assimilation helped Euro-Americans forge an imagined physical link to the ancient Israelites, a link that in turn solidified white Americans' prior claim on the New World. In short, the ancient mummies displayed in antebellum America functioned as racial-religious icons for the Euro-Americans who viewed them. Although chronologically removed from the original death displays, the Booth mummy likely served a similar function. The result was a conjunction of intentions between the politics of race in Enid and the longer-term vision of racial identity embedded in the carnival display. This syncretism between form and content no doubt contributed to the legend's longevity in the American popular imagination.

≈≈

To start, it is important to recognize that the people who viewed George's corpse at Penniman's were familiar with the exhibition of dead human beings. Their familiarity sprang from intimate knowledge — the burial of friends and family. In frontier Oklahoma, Angie Debo noted, "the hitchracks were deserted during a funeral; the whole countryside gathered in sympathy at the home of the bereaved, where the body was laid away in a grave on the claim."[1] It was part of the ceremony to gaze on the corpse — the ubiquitous "viewing" still practiced in Protestant and Catholic cultures — before it was buried. In addition, the Euro-American settlers were familiar with more public displays of the dead, and it is from this tradition that George's exhibition drew. As mentioned earlier, dead criminals were often exhibited in George's day, and Penniman's initiative in displaying the corpse of Booth/George had ample precedent. The public display of the dead dated back to the period of the early republic. It ranged from the lying in state of famous public figures, to the exhibition of criminals and lynching victims, to the work of scientific institutes, and finally, to popular entertainment, including dime museums and carnival sideshows.

In other words, what happened to George's body was not unique. While the political and sociocultural messages his body came to express marked him off from the ordinary run of sideshow fare, as an embalmed attraction he was one among many. Mummies were a common feature of traveling carnival "museum" shows in the early twentieth century, where they shared space with pickled fetuses, wax figures, and stuffed animals.[2] His near contemporaries included Hazel the Mummy — the remains of a young Kentucky woman who chose suicide over arrest for the murder of her husband and four deputies — and George's fellow Oklahoman, petty outlaw Elmer McCurdy. All three experienced similar journeys: a combination of notoriety and no (or uncaring) kin led to their preservation and local display. The bodies of all three were eventually sold to carnival entrepreneurs and became attractions on the sideshow circuit. McCurdy's travels ended only in 1976, when he was discovered on the set of the television show *The Six Million-Dollar Man* and returned to Oklahoma for burial.[3] There was, however, one important distinction between George's exhibition and that arranged for the other two: in his guise as Booth, the drifter was accorded dignified surroundings, while Hazel and Elmer were marketed purely as crime sensations.

The still exhibits of the carnival midway, known in the trade as "mummies and dummies," were the poorer siblings of the live freak shows that featured human oddities such as fat men, sword swallowers, dwarves, and the like. Both were common at county fairs and amusement parks until the mid-twentieth century. Their golden age coincided with that of the railroad circuses, from the 1880s through the 1930s, when the combination of national rail infrastructure and the proliferation of county fairs made traveling sideshows staples of American culture. The exhibits traced their origins to antebellum dime museums, which in turn developed out of the natural history cabinets of the eighteenth century. The colonial-era cabinets featured geological specimens, Indian artifacts, and animal remains. Exceptional items were referred to as "curiosities," and their display formed a part of Enlightenment erudition. Post-Revolutionary America witnessed the transformation of the semiprivate cabinets into public museums. Artist Charles Willson Peale receives credit for launching the most famous enterprise of this type when he added natural history specimens to his Philadelphia portrait gallery in an effort to attract visitors.[4]

The Booth mummy's earliest predecessors dated to the era of the natural history museums and included Native American as well as Egyptian remains. Exploration and saltpeter mining in Kentucky's Mammoth Cave complex beginning around the War of 1812 led to the discovery of several preserved bodies, most of which were removed for display elsewhere. Scientist/politician Samuel L. Mitchill described one such body, and the details he provided supply important clues to how Euro-Americans viewed the remains. The body had been carefully wrapped inside layers of woven cloth and deer hides. The cloth was of an unusual warp and woof, similar to the textiles of the Pacific Northwest and the Hawaiian Islands. The innermost covering, noted Mitchill, "is a mantle of cloth like the preceding but furnished with large brown feathers, arranged and fastened with great art, so as to be capable of guarding the living wearer from wet and cold." The body was that of a young male who had sustained a fatal blow to the skull: "The skin has sustained little injury; it is of a dusky color, but the natural hue cannot be decided with exactness from its present appearance. The scalp, with small exceptions, is covered with sorrel or fox hair. The teeth are white and sound. The hands and feet in their shrivelled state are slender and delicate."[5]

Black miners digging saltpeter discovered a female mummy in a limestone sepulcher beneath the floor of Short Cave (near Mammoth) in 1813. Known to posterity as "Fawn-hoof" for the circlet of fawns' hooves found about her neck, she became America's best-known antebellum mummy — "Kentucky's posthumous belle," in the words of travel writer Nathaniel Parker Willis. The literary outpouring she inspired included Chateaubriand's *Atala* and the musings of Mammoth Cave's mulatto slave explorer and guide, Stephen Bishop. Her posthumous wanderings were orchestrated by Yankee impresario Nahum Ward, who purchased the mummy from the cave's owners in October 1815. He placed it on exhibition first in Lexington, Kentucky, and later in Philadelphia, where it was supposedly destined for Peale's Museum. Peale, however, never obtained the mummy, and Ward continued up the eastern seaboard and either sold or presented the mummy to the American Antiquarian Society in Worcester, Massachusetts, in 1817.[6]

Fawn-hoof attracted the attention of naturalists, who provided detailed descriptions of her person and accoutrements and in the process helped clarify her mysterious origins. John Hay Farnham, a member of the American Antiquarian Society, found Fawn-hoof remarkable, for the art of embalming, he wrote, "in its ancient perfection, was, I believe, confined to the Egyptians, with perhaps the exception of their Asiatick neighbors."[7] Ebenezer Meriam, who engaged in saltpeter manufacturing at Mammoth Cave during the War of 1812, penned a retrospective account in his New York *Municipal Gazette* in 1844. In her limestone sepulcher, Fawn-hoof sat "in solemn silence." The deer skins covering her body "appeared to have been dressed in some mode different from what is now practiced by any people." Meriam also found the cloth unusual, believing it resembled that produced in the South Sea Islands. As for the mummy itself, the hair was red and the teeth white and perfect. The features were "regular"; and, calculating from the length of an arm bone, Meriam "judged the figure to be that of a very tall female, say five feet ten inches in height." He concluded, "Of the race of people to whom she belonged when living, we know nothing." Nonetheless, the quantity of headdresses, beads, and necklaces found with her offered some clue, for "with the present inhabitants of this section of the globe, but few articles of ornament are deposited with the body. The features of this ancient member of the human family much resembled those of a tall, handsome American woman. The forehead was high, and the head well formed."[8]

The display of Egyptian remains followed soon after that of Native Americans. The first Egyptian mummy reached the United States as early as 1800, although public exhibition did not begin until after the War of 1812.[9] In 1818, an Egyptian mummy arrived in Boston, although there is no evidence it was ever displayed. That honor fell to Padihershef, a stonecutter from the catacombs of Thebes, who reached Boston in April 1823. The mummy was the gift of a Dutch merchant who hoped the curiosity would benefit some civic purpose. Installed at Doggett's Repository of the Arts, it enjoyed instant acclaim, attracting the "best" people, and Doggett extended the display through the summer. In the fall, it was decided to send the treasure on an extended tour of the eastern seaboard. As the first Egyptian mummy displayed in the United States, Padihershef, it was anticipated, would reap rich rewards on being exhibited. The show received good notices in New York and Baltimore, and while in the latter city spent six weeks at Peale's Museum. Unexpectedly, however, the sensation waned, owing to an influx of Theban corpses in the months following Padihershef's arrival. There was, one commentator noted at the time, a glut on the market; and by 1824, Egyptian mummies had become "as cheap as candidates for the Presidency."[10]

As with the Native American remains, naturalists provided detailed accounts of the imported bodies. John Collins Warren, a Harvard anatomist, was among those who examined Padihershef before the mummy's public exhibition. Like Ebenezer Meriam, who had examined Fawn-hoof, Warren paid close attention to the mummy's hair coloration and condition of the teeth. He found that much of the body's hair had been removed; "just enough of it [was] remaining, however, to show that it was not black, nor crisped, nor woolly, but of a brown or reddish brown colour. The teeth are perfect, so far as they can be seen; quite white, and shaped like those of the European, contrary to the opinion of some learned men, that the Egyptians had the incisor teeth pointed like the canine or dog teeth."[11]

Egyptian mummies were big business, much bigger than the exhibition of Indian remains. Su Wolfe of the American Antiquarian Society has catalogued nearly 700 whole bodies and body parts reaching the United States in the first half of the nineteenth century. Not all were slated for public exhibition. Presbyterian colleges acquired the bodies for their biblical associations, and Mormon leader Joseph Smith purchased four mummies from a traveling exhibit while he resided in Kirtland, Ohio. Paper manufacturers also imported large numbers of Egyptian cadavers for their linen wrappings, which were stripped off and boiled down to make paper. Although marked by these local practices, the American "mummy mania" was part of a transatlantic craze that emerged in the wake of the Napoleonic conquest of Egypt. Exhibition broadsides and newspaper accounts printed in the United States often combined local and overseas commentaries, providing insight into how the mummies were received in Euro-American culture.

An exhibition pamphlet published in Ithaca, New York, around 1827 opened with an extract from Adam Clarke's *Commentary on the Holy Bible,* in which the renowned biblical interpreter asserted that there was a "strong probability" that the body of the patriarch Isaac still existed, as Joseph had taken great care to have his father's remains embalmed and securely entombed. The brochure followed with

"A Few Reflections" of the pseudonymous "Brotos," who contemplated the inevitability of bodily decay, the immortality of the spirit, and the mummy's familial past. On gazing upon "this ancient relick of mortality," his thoughts "involuntarily reverted" back to the time when it was the abode of an immortal spirit: "this now disgusting mass of deformity, animated by a living principle, [once] played her part in the theater of life." He mused, "She may have been the idol of her parents and delight of friends — She may have been beautiful, accomplished, and, among the proud daughters of Thebes, the proudest. But, what is she now?" For Brotos, the mummy in its bodily deformity evoked the "solemn question" regarding the nature of the immortal soul: "Where now is the spirit that fled this ruined tenement, three thousand years ago? What is its mode of existence? Does it retain all its faculties, of thought, and consciousness? Does it increase in knowledge and power?" Brotos advises his readers to look upon this ancient remnant of mortality and learn the lesson it speaks.[12]

Other writers eschewed the emphasis on the inevitable corruption of the flesh and found in the mummies "perfect preservation" a less dismal message. "A Gardner" wrote the *Painesville (Ohio) Telegraph* in early 1835 to offer his reflections on the ancient relics and provide detailed information on four mummies then exhibiting in Cleveland (and soon to be purchased by Joseph Smith):

> History, indeed, calls to mind spirits which have long since been traversing the golden works of the celestial world: but, how much more are we neared to them, when we can commingle with bodies *spiritless,* who traversed this earth thousands of years ago, as we do now, possessing passions and wants, ambition, avarice and superstition likes [*sic*] ourselves.

The writer went on to say that many "conjectured that the doctrine of the resurrection was embodied in the Egyptian religious faith, and others again suppose that the practice of embalming their dead originated in their abhorrence of decay." For this writer, to view the remains "and to realize that I was viewing one of my own species who had lived like myself and been a member of a community th[r]ee or four thousand years ago, produced a sensation like that of associating with people of another world."[13]

Egyptian mummies were almost always represented as familial beings, hailing from biblical times and of regal lineage. The subscription proposal for George R. Gliddon's mummy unwrapping at Boston's Tremont Temple in 1850 promised *"two highest-class Egyptian mummies"*: ANCH-ph*****, daughter of a high priest of Thebes, who lived about the time of Moses; and Got-mut-as-anch, daughter of a priest and scribe, who dated to the time of Solomon. Gliddon planned to unwrap the first before his Boston audience, saving the other for a similar exhibition in Philadelphia. His list of subscribers, published in the proposal, indicates that despite the deluge of bodies in the wake of Padihershef's arrival two decades earlier, ancient Egyptian remains continued to attract the "best" people.[14] An 1824 broadside advertising the exhibition of Captain Turner's mummy in Connecticut stressed the proprietor's financial exertions in obtaining the most perfect mummy ever imported into the United States. The mummy, the reader is assured, "undoubtedly is the mortal remains of a Lady of very high rank, as none but the very rich were embalmed in this style" (Figure 7).

The representation of the ancient dead as horrors did not take place until the twentieth century, when the supposed curse of the tomb of Tutankhamen and a fascination with the undead in the wake of World War I transformed the innocuous mysteries of an earlier age into threatening wraiths.[15] The modern popular depiction got its start with the horror film classic *The Mummy* in 1932, and continues to the present with the 1999 remake, starring Brendan Fraser and Rachel Weisz. At the same time, the early twentieth century saw the venues for the display of ancient mummies shift from popular outlets to the high-culture precincts of universities and museums. Popular displays tended to feature the recently dead (and preserved), usually outlaws or other individuals invested with a sensational past.[16] The exhibition of George's remains fits the popular pattern, as George was recently deceased and, in his role as Booth, certainly possessed a notorious past. However, the Booth exhibit also borrowed from the earlier tradition, in which mummies were represented in dignified terms and as unthreatening artifacts.[17] It is also worth noting that during that earlier, antebellum period, ancient mummies were not the only

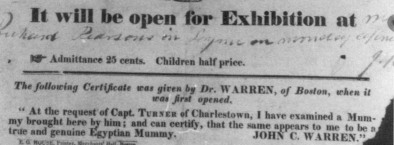

Figure 7.
Broadside for an antebellum mummy display, circa 1824. (Broadside BDSE 182-E32e, Connecticut Historical Society, Hartford, Connecticut.)

popular death displays. Anatomical museums also displayed skeletons and body parts, including the remains of criminals, thus mixing scientific uplift with lurid sensationalism and providing an entirely different representation of death and the body from the display of the ancient dead.[18]

⁓⁓

But what ideological purpose did the antebellum mummies serve? The answer is at once obvious and startling: obvious in that the bodies took on racial meanings; startling because rather than representing the ancient remains as racially "other," Euro-Americans appropriated them into the fold of their own identity. Scholars have paid a great deal of attention to the ways in which white, middle-class viewers objectified display objects, both living and inanimate, as the "other" in order to establish difference and construct their own identities.[19] Less attention has been paid to how viewers identified with the object of their gaze and the role of this identification/appropriation in identity construction. In fact, Euro-Americans often identified the mummies as racially white. They did so as part of a larger goal: to establish a suitable prehistory, one that would emphasize white Americans' tangible connection to ancient Israel and their prior claim on the New World.

Euro-Americans, like their European counterparts, energetically appropriated the bodies of the ancient dead to establish their own identity. In the case of the Egyptian mummies, the dozen or so perambulating Jacksonian America were just a fraction of the deluge of ancient bodies that were shipped to Europe and America in the century following Napoleon's Egyptian campaign (1798–99).[20] The Napoleonic conquest stands as the watershed event in the modern occidental occupation of the Middle East, and the excavation of Egyptian antiquities ranks among the conquest's more serious consequences.[21] The explorations by Napoleon's savants stimulated public curiosity in Europe and America and resulted in a burgeoning Egyptomania that found expression in the gathering of artifacts as well as in architecture, the visual arts, and opera. The British takeover of Egypt in 1801 marked the beginning of outright commerce in mummies. The growing demand for bodies, many destined for private collections, fueled the beginning of organized excavations and plundering. Over the course of the nineteenth century, thousands of ancient cadavers from the catacombs at Thebes were shipped to Europe and America. Occidental tourists to Egypt could participate in staged "discoveries" of wrapped remains while visiting the tombs (although some of the corpses were of very recent vintage). The western fascination with Egypt's ancient dead also went beyond simple collection and viewing. A popular Victorian parlor entertainment involved the unwrapping of mummies before invited guests.[22] Mummies were even used in manufacturing. At the same time the Egyptian dead were venerated as objects of mystery and antiquity, they were ground, burned, and shredded for "useful" applications. (This dualism prompts one to ponder to what extent ritual activities in modern occidental societies, including the staged viewing of human remains, include the simultaneous debasement of the ritual object.) In the United States, the principal industrial use of the bodies was in paper manufacturing.[23]

The gathering of Indian remains in America dates from the same period, and in both Europe and North America, the appropriation of the dead occurred in the midst of European territorial aggrandizement.[24] In America, the collection of Indian mummies also reflected (and contributed to) Euro-Americans' fascination with the origins of the continent's native populations. Stimulated by the discovery of ancient mounds throughout the Mississippi valley, this fascination gave rise to the so-called Myth of the Mound Builders, the central component of which was the non-Indian origin of those who built them.[25] Proposed candidates included Toltecs, Israelites, Celts, Hindus, Malays, Danes, and Welshmen — the last-named supposedly having sailed to America with Prince Madoc ap Owen Gwynnedd in the twelfth century. Allied with the assumption that they were the New World's original inhabitants, the Mound Builders' Indo-European identity served useful ideological purposes in the young republic. Robert Silverberg's thorough study of the myth and reality of the mounds underscores two motives for belief in ancient, non-Indian inhabitants of America. The first was the Euro-Americans' desire for a grand and heroic past, on the order of that evident in the Old World and to the south in the kingdoms of the Aztecs and Incas. Discouraged at not initially finding monumental remnants equal in grandeur to the pyramids, nor any Indian civilization equal to the gold-encrusted kingdoms of Central

America, colonial settlers longed to establish a usable past based on the traces of "awesome antiquity on which romantic myths could be founded."[26] The discovery of the mounds in the 1770s provided the basis for a prolonged literary and scholarly outpouring that took many forms. Josiah Priest's *American Antiquities and Discoveries in the West* (1833) and William Pidgeon's *Traditions of Dee-Coo-Dah* (1853, 1858) were two best-selling works of this genre. Both authors offered a pretense of archeological fact (often quite extensive) culminating in theories explaining the origins of the Mound Builders. Priest's account featured a stirring vision of ancient armies massing on the plains, in numbers and vigor equal to the hosts of Alexander, Cyrus, and Tamerlame. He believed America was the landfall of Noah's ark and attributed some of the mounds to antediluvian inhabitants.[27] Pidgeon asserted, "Ancient Egypt . . . has also left her impress here." The first travelers in Kentucky had discovered in the caves "a number of mummies, preserved by the art of embalming in as great a state of perfection as was known by the ancient Egyptians."[28]

Pidgeon mobilized a theory of cultural diffusion to buttress his assertion of the ancient presence of the Egyptians on New World soil. Since the peculiar custom of embalming practiced by the Egyptians was found here "in a state of perfection, not exceeded by the mother-country, most evidently leads to the conclusion, that a colony from Egypt, or some nation of Africa, . . . at some time inhabited that region of the country."[29]

The romance of the mounds was graphically captured in painter John Egan's rendering of an excavation conducted around 1850 (Figure 8). His work also expressed the racial hierarchies in antebellum America. Black laborers dig in the foreground, while at the center front two white figures (presumably Dr. Dickinson and an associate) study a diagram. Off to the side, a group of Indians sit near their tepees, apparently uninvolved in the nearby proceedings. In the cutaway of the mound itself lie rows of neatly recumbent skeletons of the Mound Builders, seemingly suspended in air.[30]

The myth contributed to America's antebellum religious ferment by abetting the persistent belief, dating back to the sixteenth century, that America's native inhabitants were descended from the Lost Tribes of Israel.[31] The sacred text of the Mormon Church, the Book of Mormon, made use of the myth in establishing Mormonism's genealogical link to ancient peoples. In the Mormon account, the New

Figure 8.

John Egan, Panorama of the Monumental Grandeur of the Mississippi Valley, *detail:* Dr. Dickerson Excavating a Mound, *circa 1850. (The St. Louis Art Museum, Eliza McMillen Fund.)*

World was populated around 600 BC by the sons of Lehi, an Israelite, who crossed over the Great Sea from Israel at the time of the Babylonian captivity. Over succeeding centuries, the descendants of Nephi, the godly son, and Laman, the lawbreaker, were at war until the Nephites were exterminated at the Battle of Cummorah (ca. AD 400), near present-day Palmyra, New York. Nephi had prophesied this occurrence, also foreseeing that God would punish the Lamanites for their transgressions: their skin took on a coppery hue and they lived as savages. Nephi also foretold the subsequent arrival of the Gentiles in the land of promise, and said that they would scatter the "dark and loathsome" inhabitants of the land. Of these newcomers, Nephi said, "I beheld that they were white and exceeding fair and beautiful, like unto my people before they were slain" (1 Nephi 13:15).

This evocation of white racial beauty points to the mound builder myth's second usage (certainly not restricted to the Mormons) in justifying Euro-American conquest. If the living Indians were not the autochthonous population, as lost tribe advocates argued, but instead were descended from the destroyers of this ancient civilization, their own subsequent destruction involved no moral error. Indeed, it might even be taken as divinely ordained retribution. The myth thereby served the clear ideological purpose of justifying the takeover of Native American lands. As Silverberg reminds us, the controversy over the origin of the mounds may have entailed a romantic impulse, but it was no harmless academic debate: "it had its roots in the great nineteenth-century campaign of extermination waged against the American Indian."[32]

The identification of the ancient Thebans as racially white served similar ideological ends. The assertion of their whiteness, however, did not go unchallenged: a prolonged debate took place in the antebellum period, with white abolitionists and free blacks asserting the ancient Egyptians' African lineage. In his recent study of antebellum race theory, Bruce Dain analyzes the debate's sources and permutations. Black American interest in ancient Egypt emerged in the late 1820s, inspired in part by the new vogue for ancient Egypt.[33] African Americans found a usable past in the biblical account of the human exodus after the Flood, as well as in historical accounts by Herodotus. These classical accounts had stressed the blackness of the Egyptians, either through their assumed ancestry or on the basis of physical features. The biblical narrative in particular posed a challenge to those asserting a Euro-Egyptian lineage and the innate inferiority of Africans as a separate race. The Old Testament scriptures stressed the unity of humankind and the idea that the world's population (following the Flood, and later after the fall of the Tower of Babel) sprang from a single source. Genesis related that Noah's sons (Shem, Japhet, and Ham) each inherited a portion of the earth, and that Ham's lot was Africa. Unfortunately, Ham's progeny were cursed by Noah when Ham discovered his father lying naked in a drunken stupor: "Cursed be Canaan; a servant of servants shall he be unto his brethren" (Genesis 9:25). As early as the sixth century AD Talmudic commentators used the curse to explain the blackness and features of contemporary Africans, including the Egyptians. The Hamitic hypothesis, as this explanation came to be known, was used to assert the "degradation" of Ham's descendants.[34] But black writers responded by pointing out that the curse applied specifically to Ham's son Canaan, and that Ham's other sons, Cush and Mizraim, were the ones who had founded Ethiopia and Egypt. The grandeur of these ancient civilizations, evident in the monuments and artifacts they had left behind, proved the rationality and expertise of African civilization.[35]

The ancient mummies became tokens in this ideological struggle. The anonymous author of "Mutability of Human Affairs," an article published in *Freedom's Journal,* visited the mummy exhibit at Peale's New York museum in 1827 and was stunned into somber reflection by the power of what he saw there. Whites exhibited the remains of his ancestors, much as they controlled the bodies of latter-day blacks. Had not Egypt's kings, for whom the pyramids were raised in order to prevent their desecration, "been torn from their 'vaunted sepulchers' and exhibited to a gazing world? *Have not they too been bought and sold?*"[36] The representation of the mummies as white, grand, and mysterious was a usurpation of Africa's grand past, but one that affirmed the "mutability" of human affairs and the black race's fallen condition.

The Euro-American effort to represent the ancient Egyptians as racially white reached its apogee in the scientific researches of Samuel Morton (1799–1851), the Philadelphia anatomist considered the founder of the American school of ethnology. The late Stephen J. Gould demonstrated how Morton fudged his data in order to conclude that Caucasian crania — including skulls found in the catacombs of Thebes — had a larger capacity, thus "proving" the mental superiority of whites, the separate creation of humankind's "races," and their fixity over time.[37] Morton's identification of the ancient Egyptians as racially white, though charged with scientific pretense, was no different from the assumptions of the mound mythifiers. His supporters included George Gliddon, an English-born Egyptologist and United States consul in Cairo, who supplied Morton with hundreds of skulls from the catacombs.

Gliddon also unwrapped mummies before American audiences, and the ties between the mummies' identities and those of their viewers may be gleaned from the report of a lecture he gave in New York City in 1847. Gliddon set forth "a wonderful scene before the eyes of his audience" of an ancient people uprooted from their ancestral homes on the banks of the Nile, who traveled the world and reached its four corners. They left their imprint — in monuments, the arts, and the preservation of the human body — on all the world's civilizations:

> Who can tell how much we owe to this ancient race — to this very priest of Osiris whose form lies before us as it was placed in the sepulcher more than 4,000 years ago? True, if he could live and speak to us and claim to have taught our ancestors civilization, we might perhaps reply truly that we had not been inapt pupils in the school.[38]

The emphasis on straight or red hair, white teeth, slender digits, and well-formed foreheads found in antebellum accounts was not incidental. Even before Morton undertook his quest to establish the "scientific" basis for white superiority, these were among the markers in the emerging physiognomic language of race. That these features indicated white, or at least nonblack, features, is corroborated in other texts. An anonymous writer in the *New England Monthly* in October 1833 attacked the notion of ancient Egyptian blackness by appealing to Champollion the Younger's interpretation of the hieroglyphs at the tombs of Boban el Malluk, in which the famous Egyptologists interpreted a group of twelve men, led by Horus, shepherd of the people, as representing the four distinct races of humankind. In the anonymous writer's retelling, the four groups of three were distinguished by facial features, skin color, and hair. The last group, though clothed in the skins of oxen and painted like savages, "are of a delicate white complexion. Their noses are straight or slightly arched; their eyes are blue, their beards are of a light or red color, and they are tall in figure."[39]

This argument received perhaps its most extreme treatment in a post–Civil War pamphlet by "Ariel," published in 1867. It denied monogenesis and the Hamitic hypothesis altogether to argue that blacks were a pre-Adamic or beastly race, and were not among Noah's descendants. God had foreseen the future attempts to discredit Ham's descendants as black, and so instructed Mizraim in the arts of bodily preservation. The preserved corpses would "be *forever* a testimony of God for Ham, and they, like his descendants, were like the children of the older brothers, their equal, in all the lineaments that stamp the race of Adam with the image and likeness of the Almighty, and belonging to the white race." These "mummied witnesses of Ham" would protest "by their long, straight hair, by their high foreheads, by their high noses, and by their thin lips, now hushed in silence forever, that the slander, that their father was the progenitor of the negro, was a *slander most foul* — a slander most *infamous*." This slander might so arouse their indignant bodies that the long-deceased children of Ham would be "so electrified by these foul aspersions, as to burst their sarcophagi, and tear the cerements of the grave." God, Ariel concluded, intended through the mummies to teach a lesson, that "there was an *importance*, in being of the white race, *to be attached to it.* . . . Millions of these mummied bodies have been exhumed this century, but *not one* negro has been found among them."[40]

From a present-day perspective, it is difficult to comprehend the author's frantic, racist frothing, although his reference to the mummies bursting their coffins resonates eerily with their depiction in contemporary popular culture. It is the appeal to *attachment*, moreover, that is most compelling. The grandeur of classical Egyptian civilization, touted by antebellum blacks and whites alike, explains why Euro-Americans insisted so strenuously on identifying the land of the pharaohs as racially white. It does not, however, provide the full explanation. For this we need to turn to Euro-American, and more specifically Anglo-American, religious history and a complex of terms, including Anglo-Saxonism, Anglo-Israelism, and the corollary Lost Tribes thesis.

Anglo-Saxonism, the belief in the special political and religious destiny of the Anglo-Saxon people, had its roots in the English

Reformation. Dissenting churchmen sought to justify the break with Rome by arguing for the older origin of the English church. John Foxe's *Actes and Monuments* (1563), better known as the "Book of Martyrs," related that after laying Christ in his tomb, Joseph of Arimethea journeyed to England, where he established a branch of the true church.[41]

In the next century, the Puritans intensified the concept, assuming for themselves the mantle of God's people. Shortly after the founding of Massachusetts Bay Colony, some began to assert the Puritans' literal descent from the Israelite host. Anglo-Israelism, as this doctrine came to be known, originated in the writings of the Ibero-Dutch rabbi Menasseh ben Israel. His account of Marrano traveler Antonio de Montezinos's claim to have encountered members of the Lost Tribes in South America was first published in 1650 and translated shortly afterward into English as *The Hope of Israel* at the urging of Menasseh's English correspondents. Not only were they fascinated with the rabbi's relating of Montezinos's "discoveries"; their Puritan imaginations were also enticed by his biblical exegesis. Drawing from the Book of Daniel (12:7) and Deuteronomy (28:64), he argued that the dispersal of the Jews was nearly complete, and would be complete when they were readmitted into England.[42] Once this occurred, the messianic deliverance would take place, and Israel's redemption would be assured. The resettlement of the Jews in England therefore took on cosmic significance: it was the culmination of sacred history for Jews and Christians alike.[43] Ben Israel's writings confirmed the Puritans' own millennial convictions, especially those of the "Fifth Monarchists," who believed that the Puritan revolution had ushered in the fifth and final era in human history. It was at this point as well that the thesis of the Lost Tribes joined with English ideas of special providence. As J. F. Maclear has noted, New England's early leadership "sought to accommodate Indians in the total scheme of human history, the church's triumph, and the final judgment."[44]

In his published correspondence to Thomas Thorowgood, author of *Jewes in America, or Probabilities that those Indians are Judaical* (1650), Puritan missionary John Eliot argued that although the Lord had scattered the Ten Tribes of Israel to the corners of the world "and made their rememberance [*sic*] to cease among men, as he threatened . . . ; yet the Lord hath promised to bind them up again, and to gather together those dry and scattered bones, and bring them to know the

Lord."[45] Thus Eliot wished to establish the importance of fostering the conversion of the Algonquin tribes. The belief in contemporary Indians' Jewish identity continued through the eighteenth and into the early part of the nineteenth century. Writers who advocated the Indians' conversion often pled for their humane treatment. Biblical prophecies, evangelist Charles Crawford argued in 1801, "should induce the whole people of America to treat the Indians with as much lenity and forbearance as possible." The "sure word of prophecy," in Crawford's reading, also meant that once converted, "all the descendants of the house of Israel, among which are many Indians, will be restored to the land of their forefathers." In what amounted to a millennial colonization scheme, the evangelical missionary argued that Native Americans would return to Jerusalem "somewhere near the year 1900. Many of the Indians will then relinquish their land to the white people."[46] Fifteen years later, Indian agent and missionary Elias Boudinot (whose name the better-known Cherokee chieftain later adopted) continued the defense of Native Americans based on their ties to the people of Israel:

> Blessed be God, that there is yet hope that the day of their visitation is near — that the day-star from on high, begins to appear, giving joyful hopes that the sun of righteousness will soon arise upon them, with healing under his wings. — There is a possibility, that these unhappy children of misfortune, may yet be proved to be the descendants of Jacob and the long lost tribes of Israel.[47]

Yet Boudinot's appeal, like Crawford's, mixed what was by then a centuries-old eschatological tradition with a secular desire for land: "Who knows but God has raised up these United States in these latter days, for the very purpose of accomplishing his will in bringing his beloved people to their own land."[48] In doing so, these latter-day Fifth Monarchists signaled the shift from a concern with accomplishing biblical prophecy to the rapacious political Anglo-Saxonism of manifest destiny and the white man's burden. Reginald Horsman has noted the culmination of this transformation by 1850, when Anglo-Saxonism and allied tenets assumed a racist cast. Rather than expressing the triumph of democratic republicanism (or of God's special mission for the American people), American expansionism came to be seen as "evidence of the innate superiority of the American Anglo-Saxon branch of the Caucasian race."[49] The display of ancient bodies in America thus began at an opportune moment, when this ideological transformation was under way. In their ancient whiteness, the bodies served as a kind of symbolic bridge between a past age of unified human origins and millennial concentration on the one side, and a present age of racial differentiation and expansionist discourse on the other.

Lying on its Navajo blanket, under a canopy of Egyptian motifs, the mummy of David George was far removed from the circumstances that shaped the representation of antebellum mummies. And yet there was something dimly familiar about the discourse that surrounded him. While impossible to determine precisely, the later exhibition of the dead drifter carried many of the marks that had earlier served to evoke a linkage to biblical places and ancestors. And some of those who viewed the body — as will be noted later in this study — did resort to the language of whiteness in describing "Booth's" remains.

NORTHERN ORIGINS

I am a northern man.

(*J. Wilkes Booth*)

George Bryan's book *The Great American Myth* (1940) remains the most detailed study of the Booth legend's beginnings. In Bryan's view, the story that Booth escaped his pursuers owed its creation to three factors. The first is a universal human tendency to be skeptical regarding the death of notorious individuals, especially when they meet untimely ends. This skepticism leads to the propagation of "survival tales," products of the popular imagination that often endure for years as oral tradition. In nineteenth-century America, the lost royalty of Europe were favorite subjects for this sort of imaginative play. Napoleon's Marshal Ney, executed in 1815, reappeared in the Carolinas in the person of a mysterious schoolteacher. Archduke Johann Salvator of Austria, who disappeared on a sailing ship, was spotted in Texas, Ohio, and New York. Ahasuerus, the Persian ruler mentioned in the Book of Esther, encountered a Mormon near Salt Lake City as late as 1868. In the post–Civil War era, Bryan wrote, the South and Southwest were especially fertile ground for stories of this kind. In addition to lost royalty, the popular imagination fixed on a different type of liminal personality. Along with Booth, the region spawned speculations regarding the fate of William Quantrell, Jesse James, and Billy the Kid.[1]

In the case of Lincoln's assassination, this "natural" human tendency received critical support from the operations of the popular press and government officials. Bryan implied that these two factors transformed what would have remained a vague, if enduring, oral tradition into a flagrant slap in the face of historical truth. Newspapers repeated the stories of Booth sightings in the days preceding his actual capture, thus lending the authority of print to the rumors of his escape. They also helped sow disinformation, as in the famous cover of *Frank Leslie's Illustrated Newspaper* showing the assassin's corpse being dumped into the Potomac River (Figure 9) when in fact it had been secreted under the floor of an army storehouse. Unfortunately, public authorities, who should have concerned themselves with making sure that the northern public was kept fully informed, paid no heed to the "quidnuncs and the newspapers." Had it chosen to, the federal government could have issued a comprehensive account on the assassination and Booth's capture. But it did not, with the result that the whole subject became mired "in a tangle of disorder and error, . . . from which it has not yet been set free."[2]

Bryan thus asserted government's responsibility in shaping historical narrative, and further implied that the authorities were opposed in this effort by unruly elements including the press and popular gossip. At heart, his criticism entailed a mass society critique, since he viewed the dissemination of information as imperiled by forces of popular disorder. This position reflected developments in Bryan's own time, including the rise of federal involvement in historical interpretation beginning in the 1920s and the ongoing debate over the problem of public discourse in a mass society. The issue of information control became particularly acute as America prepared to enter World War II, and *The Great American Myth* may have been intended in part as an object lesson for a new generation of public officials engaged in the then-emerging propaganda war.[3] My viewpoint is obviously opposed to Bryan's: it considers these "unruly" elements as prime sources for uncovering meaning in American culture. But Bryan's basic framework can help us make sense of the Booth legend's appearance on the American cultural stage. Shorn of its cultural judgment, his enumeration of the intersection of popular imagination, mass media, and efforts of the state to control information accurately describes the triangular dynamic that prompted the legend's birth. The way these three factors interacted was influenced by broader cultural and political contexts, including northern political dissent, the symbolic potency of the corpse in the Civil War era, and the trauma of Lincoln's death.

This formula also qualifies the legend — understood as the product of this interaction — as a northern production. In the days following

FRANK LESLIE'S
ILLUSTRATED
NEWSPAPER

Entered according to the Act of Congress in the year 1864, by Frank Leslie, in the Clerk's Office of the District Court for the Southern District of New York.

No. 503—Vol. XX.]   NEW YORK, MAY 20, 1865.   [Price 10 Cents. $4 00 Yearly. 11 Weeks $1 00.

The sketch below was furnished by one of the two officers employed in the duty of sinking the body of Booth in the middle o the Potomac. Although not authorised to divulge his name, I am able to vouch for the truth of the representation.

NEW YORK, May 10th, 1865.   F. LESLIE.

Figure 9
Cover illustration, Frank Leslie's Illustrated Newspaper, *May 20, 1865.*
(Library of Congress Prints and Photographs Division, LC-USZ62 6939.)

Lincoln's murder, the white South was incapable of producing the story, since it lacked two of the three necessary ingredients. Portions of the southern populace may well have envisioned Booth's escape, and doubtless this idea gave rise to verbal speculation. However, such rumors received no confirmation, no authorization, and no mediation from either popular print or the Confederate state. Southern government had ceased functioning by April 1865, and the southern journalistic enterprise, to the extent it remained in existence, operated under the watchful eyes of federal authorities. Reports of the assassination appeared belatedly in the southern press, and the news was withheld in some areas by authorities who feared that rejoicing by Confederates would lead to bloody reprisals by Union soldiers.[4] With the exception of Texas, where the federal occupation had yet to impose itself, southern journals confined their coverage to reporting the facts and editorial expressions of pious regret.[5] Further, the collapse of southern public culture resulted in an information vacuum in which rumor ran amok. At the same time news of Lincoln's shooting reached them, southerners heard that an armistice was being signed, that the European powers had recognized their cause, and that French military intervention was imminent. Confederate nurse Kate Cummings observed, "None of our people believe any of the rumors, thinking them as mythical as the surrender of General Lee's army. They look upon it as a plot to deceive the people."[6] In this atmosphere, allegations that Booth escaped carried no bite, as they were only so many more drops in an ocean of suspect tidings.

In the North, it was a different matter. Although censored on occasion during the conflict, northern journalists enjoyed a relatively free hand, and Lincoln suffered the bitter lampoons of Democratic editors. The northern public also benefited from an objective sense of events, provided by regular dispatches issued by the Union government and reprinted verbatim in the major dailies. It is in this context that the Booth legend first appeared. However, instead of its being part of the universal tendency to disbelieve the deaths of notorious figures, survival tales regarding Booth are more usefully seen as part of the larger social-psychological reaction to the trauma that the assassin's act provoked. Lincoln's assassination triggered a massive outpouring of emotion among the northern public, manifested in public grieving, celebrations by northern dissidents and their arrest and/or mobbing by infuriated loyalists, sermons, speeches, the decoration of buildings in black bunting, the closing of saloons and billiard halls, and civic proclamations. From the heights of jubilation over Lee's surrender a week earlier, the North plunged into despair.[7] When Secret Service chief Lafayette Baker arrived in Washington to aid in the search for the killers, he found the mood there "fearfully intense." The public's attention was focused solely on grieving and apprehending the murderers. "Every face which did not bear the affected anxiety or indifference of Southern sympathy, had the gloomy, mournful aspect of inexpressible, bewildering horror and grief."[8] That Booth murdered Lincoln on Good Friday only added to the pathos, and northern churches were filled to overflowing on what was dubbed "Black Easter."[9] The culmination of this unprecedented event saw the procession of Lincoln's funeral train from Washington to Springfield, Illinois, as it retraced the path of the president's first inaugural voyage. The extended obsequies lasted twelve days and extended over 1,600 miles. Over the objections of his distraught widow, Lincoln's embalmed remains were detrained at major points along the route and viewed by over a million people.[10] In the midst of this national mourning, uncertainty regarding the assassin's fate provoked rumors concerning his whereabouts, the arrest of people who resembled the dapper actor, and other cases of mistaken identity. As events in our own time testify, malefic tragedy produces an overwhelming desire to locate and punish the perpetrators of the crime. Finding Booth became northern society's prime concern, and the uncertainty over his whereabouts increased the level of anxiety among the populace. The traumatized imaginations of northerners worked to resolve it by "finding" the assassin, but the result was the opposite of that desired. Uncertainty increased with each false arrest, each mistaken assertion regarding his fate. The New York Times noted the rush to judgment on April 17, commenting, "Rumor has arrested Booth a dozen times already, and many persons will retire to-night in the confident belief that he is confined on a gunboat in the Navy-yard." A day later, the World testified to the public apprehension in an editorial headed "Has the Assassin Escaped?"[11] As he made his way up the Potomac on Sunday afternoon, journalist George Alfred Townsend noted, "Uncertainty and mystery increases the general awe and confusion." Five days later, with Booth's position still unknown, curiosity over the actor surpassed the attention paid to Lincoln's remains. Newsboys hawking their papers were stopped from crying the false news of the assassin's arrest.[12]

The newspapers fostered anxiety by reporting Booth sightings and the arrest of Booth look-alikes. The impact of stories appearing in one journal was leveraged through the practice of "clipping," whereby newspapers frequently excerpted each other's copy. On April 19, the day of Lincoln's state funeral in Washington, Booth was reported to be traveling with a band of thirty heavily armed horsemen in St. Mary's County, Maryland. After a brush with the federals, which they easily repulsed, one of their number was captured, but Booth had escaped. Tellingly, the military message traffic reporting the event contained no mention of Booth and spoke simply of the cavalry action. An officer aboard a federal gunboat apparently supplied the crucial embellishment.[13] Diverging assumptions regarding Booth's avenue of escape also promoted uncertainty. On Easter Sunday, the papers printed an official dispatch warning authorities along the border with Canada to be on the lookout, as the conspirators were likely headed their way. At the same time other sources pointed eastward, toward the Chesapeake coast, where Booth and his "confrères" were sure to head.[14] Secretary of War Edwin Stanton, convinced early on of Confederate complicity in the plot, believed that Confederate guerrilla John Singleton Mosby knew of Booth's plan and may have been effecting a rendezvous with the conspirators along the upper reaches of the Potomac. Others believed the assassin remained concealed in Washington, even in the catacombs of Ford's Theater, waiting for the excitement to abate before slipping away.[15]

Cases of mistaken identity began to be reported, as zealous citizens apprehended those whose appearance or behavior raised suspicion. The publication of reward notices beginning on April 17 probably contributed to their fervor.[16] In Chicago, the leading man at McVicker's Theater was decoyed from his eatery to the central police station and arrested for resembling Booth. When the mistake was discovered, the chagrined flatfoots brought the actor back to his beer, "when a general good time was enjoyed by all parties."[17] Another actor was apprehended by a crowd in Eastport, Maine, and the group refused to disperse until the man delivered a speech from the veranda of his hotel.[18]

Between April 20 and 22 — at the same time Lincoln's funeral train made its way to Baltimore, thence to Harrisburg and Philadelphia — the major dailies reported that a traveler aboard the Philadelphia & Reading Railroad was followed for three days, "on suspicion." Contributing to the suspicion was the line of the P&RR, which led from Philadelphia to the hard coal country in northern Pennsylvania and afforded one of the most direct routes from Washington to Canada. The chase began when a traveler noticed "Booth" on the regular evening train between Reading and Pottsville on April 19. The gentleman approached the suspect, spoke to him, and shook his hand. During the conversation, "Booth colored up several times, and appeared annoyed and desirous of avoiding observation. The gentleman is positive it is Booth, having known him for several years." The alert citizen detrained at Pottsville but did not inform the station master of his encounter until just before the train pulled away. Federal detectives posted at the depot tried telegraphing to the next station, but the operator was not on duty. The railroad then fired up a spare locomotive and the detectives, with their informant in tow, sped up the line to overtake the train. When they finally caught it, the suspect was gone. Whether he had transferred to another train or taken off on foot, no one could tell. More messages flashed up the line and the conductor at Tamaqua tapped back, "The man is on the train." Orders were sent for his detention, but again he evaded his pursuers. By now the entire railroad was alerted, and the traveler's suspicious behavior kindled suspicions that he was in fact Booth.[19]

The mystery was solved the following day, when the P&RR's superintendent reported how the traveler, aware of his pursuers, left the train and walked back along the line in the dark, hopping a coal train before being arrested. In the meantime the informant, required to make a deposition before the justice of the peace, had a change of memory. He really did not know Booth, he now said, and was not on familiar terms with him. He had seen him once in a Baltimore theater seven years earlier. As for the traveler, the informant had seen him the evening prior to their encounter in a saloon, "drinking freely."[20]

The Keystone Cops atmosphere of this incident does not diminish the fact that the trauma and anxiety resulting from the assassination raised the ambient level of suspicion in northern society, which was already heightened by the political divisions of the war. Not only physical similarity, but inappropriate behavior — such as imbibing in the midst of national mourning — invited the scrutiny of zealous citizens. In Pennsylvania alone, a half-dozen men were apprehended for looking like Booth, or acting like Booth was thought to act. Stories like the train chase also suggest that suspicions tended to reflect middle-class morality. After the rage passed, a Washington editorial noted that the scrutiny northerners brought to bear on their fellow citizens, while it originated in patriotic motives, "in some cases" were "unwise and unjust manifestations of the popular feeling."[21]

The range this popular feeling took, and how the idea of escape figured in the larger traumatic reaction, may be gauged in letters received by the Bureau of Military Justice. Designated by Stanton to manage the assassination investigation and prosecute the conspirators, the Bureau coordinated the gathering and dissemination of information bearing on the plot.[22] Among the hundreds of pieces of correspondence logged by the Bureau's clerks are several dozen letters from private citizens informing the authorities of suspicious behavior or Booth's suspected whereabouts. A naval architect from Brooklyn advised that he had been informed "by a lady of this city" of a suspicious person living on Clermont Avenue, who had denounced Lincoln and his Cabinet after the President's reelection: "The lady told me she heard him say, the President and the Cabinet will not live out their time."[23] A Washington bureau clerk conveyed his suspicions regarding a visitor to his home on the basis of the man's being in the city on a drunken spree while the nation was in mourning, his acknowledged rebel sympathies, and "the general tenor of his conversation, & the remark 'I believe John Booth is not a mile from here.'" A Philadelphia clerk wrote of his interview with John Lyons, who called at his office to report the behavior of one Pearson, a southern refugee who had made himself conspicuous by his conduct. The man's wife and children expressed disloyal statements, going so far as to wish for the president's death. His wife was among the first to hear of the assassination and circulated the information "with joy." Pearson himself was often away from home; he explained his absence by claiming he was a detective on Colonel Baker's force. Shortly before the assassination, Pearson gave his wife $5,000, "just at a time when they were sorely pressed for means." He had not been seen since the death of the president.[24] Countering the suspicions of loyal citizens were malicious letters sent by those delighting in the murder. One note purported to be from the assassin himself and announced his safe arrival in Canada: "I crossed at Buffalo I dressed myself up in

Woman's Clothes & painted my cheeks." Another, reprinted in Secret Service chief Baker's memoirs and one of the very few with a southern provenance, was a cipher letter reportedly found by a loyal Unionist floating near the wharf in Moorhead City, North Carolina. Decrypted, it read, "Dear John — I am happy to inform you that Pet. has done his work well. He is safe and Old Abe is in hell. Now, sir, all eyes are on you — you must bring in Sherman. Grant is in the hands of Old Gray ere this."[25]

Clearly, political allegiances determined the content of this correspondence, with loyalists finding conspirators in their midst and dissidents asserting Booth's escape as part of their glee at Lincoln's death. It is important to remember that at the time of his murder, Lincoln remained a controversial figure in the North, adored by some and reviled by others. Many northerners hated him for the war's slaughter and the Emancipation Proclamation. This political component colored the public's imaginings even in the midst of the nation's collective trauma.[26] There was a third kind of letter, however, devoid of obvious political intentions, in which the writer alleged either to have seen Booth or to know where he was. Among this group were communications from mediums and spiritualists who, as Baker put it, "offered the government the benefit of their prophetic gifts."[27] While useless from an investigator's standpoint (although whether the accusations of the patriotic citizens were any more useful is doubtful), these notes provide more hints on just where the northern public imagined the assassin might be. Booth was "seen" in specific locales, and he adopted specific disguises. To begin with, he was almost always situated in interior spaces, usually those frequented by the urban middle class. Among these letters was the poignant note of a Methodist minister, writing on behalf of "an intelligent lady" from Elk Neck, Maryland, who had worshipped at a local Baptist church on Black Easter. As the preacher ended his sermon, the woman turned in her pew and noticed four men entering the church. One of them resembled Booth, whose likeness she had seen in the *Philadelphia Inquirer* and *Harper's Weekly*. The man's hair "was dark wavy dark eyes his forehead high complexion fair & exceedingly good looking, his hair parted on same side, she watched his countenance during the last prayer, his countenance was sad she said."[28] Another person wrote that Booth lay concealed in a house near Middleburg, Virginia. The setting was decidedly bucolic: a one-story cottage with a steep roof set against hills in the background, with a garden laid out in squares in the front. Others found him in more urban settings. One writer alleged he lay concealed in the house of Boston's mayor, "probably in some subterranean room." A devout woman from Ohio dreamed the assassin was in Reading, Pennsylvania, in the house of a person named Cromwell. One informant wrote from Chicago that Booth was seen entering a well-known brothel, disguised in women's clothing.[29] In a few instances, the locations were precise. A gentleman from Newark, New Jersey, wrote apologetically concerning his lady friend, a clairvoyant, who was convinced that while entranced she espied the assassin's hideout; he could be found in the recess of a second-floor clothes closet in a house at No. 11 J Street in Washington. Another writer from Boston also said Booth was in the Capital, at No. 61 Massachusetts and Eighth Avenues, where he "goes out in the disguise of a negro, and also did before the assassination. He hides upstairs in a concealed closet."[30]

None of the correspondents imagined Booth where he actually was, lying in a swamp; nor did any of them entertain the possibility that Booth would lose himself among society's lower strata. Booth's "escape" was decidedly middle class. Aside from the brothel in Chicago, the imagined destinations in the days following his heinous act included a railroad car, a Baptist church, a country cottage, a restaurant, a saloon, and the upstairs closets of single-family dwellings or boarding houses. No one imagined him in the wild, on a forlorn trek across the Appalachians toward Canada, or beating through the thickets of northern Virginia. Those who "saw" him placed him close to themselves — culturally and socially — in middle-class public and domestic spaces. That many of the correspondents were women (though they all, like Mrs. Harper, conveyed their information through a male intermediary) may have encouraged the domestic details. The larger impulse at work here, however, was the notion of the perpetrator in one's midst — the enemy within or, more properly, the "other" within. Even as northerners imagined Booth in their midst, they also imagined him dressing as a woman or disguised as an African American. These conflicting feelings over Booth's act and person would find further expression in popular publications. These Booth sightings reveal the feelings of guilt many of the writers may have harbored — a typical response, according to psychologists, among survivors following a traumatic death. The escape stories also reflected the deep divisions in the North regarding Lincoln. He was hated and loved, deified and demonized, as caricatures in major northern journals illustrate. Much of the northern debate over Lincoln ended abruptly with his murder, but much of it was driven underground.

Traumatic responses can embody their own content, assuming shapes unrelated to the trauma. So it was with northerners' thoughts of Booth. People began to give these inchoate tales of survival meanings independent of the immediate cause. These meanings sprang from the political divisions running through northern society, and from Lincoln's divided reputation. These political ambiguities and uncertainties worked to render the assassin's location and figure also indeterminate. Thus it was that the northern public began the process of despatializing Booth by placing him both inside and outside their own society, contributing to the idea of his elusiveness.

In addition to straight news coverage, northern papers immediately began to explore the assassin's person in an effort to explain his crime. Biographies, comparisons to past regicides, and editorial commentary on Booth's state of mind proliferated. Dime novels and pamphlets also appeared in the weeks and months following the assassination, helping to define how the assassin was viewed in the North. This popular literary effort was the second factor that gave birth to the legend. The effusion in print was matched by equally intense oral performance as ministers, politicians, and civic leaders held forth from pulpits and rostrums.[31] In much of the speechifying, Booth received only summary treatment; preachers hardly uttered his name, probably in keeping with the precept that the damned receive no recognition. The prevailing public viewpoint asserted that he was only the tool of a larger conspiracy fomented by the Confederate leadership.[32] In contrast to the sermons and public pronouncements, newspapers devoted considerable space to explicating the assassin and his act. The allegations of a grand conspiracy remained, but there also emerged the image of Booth as a lone madman, driven to perfidy by his inordinate desire for fame. The portrait, however, was complex and, in places, ambiguous. Alongside condemnations of Booth's act and descriptions of his villainy were analogies to classical antecedents and paeans to the actor's beauty. The result was the creation of a mixed figure, one that bred more uncertainty and reinforced his growing elusiveness.

Sociologist Gary Fine has coined the term "negative commemoration" to describe how society frames the reputations of persons deemed villainous. According to Fine, negative commemoration entails a twofold process. *Demonization* results when the ambiguities of a person's moral character become erased to preserve only the evil core. Similarly, the construction of *nonpersonhood* involves the erasure of the person's identity, including any virtuous moments he or she may have enjoyed, to focus solely on the single, highly condemnable act.[33] In practice this process entails the production of cultural texts by "reputational entrepreneurs" (journalists, politicians, historians, artists, and others engaged in public discourse) in newspapers, journals, biographies, statuary, paintings, and even popular demonstrations. Written narratives often reconstruct the offender's biography in order to find evidence for the present transgression in the person's past life. Insignificant events dredged up (or invented) from childhood may be reinterpreted as foretelling the deviant act. Physical description of the individual may place him or her racially or ethnically outside the group. The construction of this "core deviant" identity is capped by attributing base motives to the villain's act.[34]

The building of Booth's reputation began only days after the shooting, even as the assassin waited for the opportunity to cross over the Potomac from his hideout in the southern Maryland pinelands. Thomas Jones, the Confederate sympathizer who hid Booth and Herold, brought them newspapers; Booth thus could read of his damnation as it was published. We know from his diary that the coverage dismayed him: "I am here in despair. And why; For doing what Brutus was honored for, what made [William] Tell a Hero. And yet I for striking down a greater tyrant than they ever knew am looked upon as a common cutthroat."[35] Most galling must have been the attitude of prosouthern papers like Washington's *National Intelligencer,* a paper he undoubtedly requested, since it was to this publication that he addressed his statement (never published) on the eve of the assassination. The *Intelligencer* referred, in describing Booth's probable escape by boat, to "demon passengers."[36] Booth may even have read the commentary on his private "To Whom It May Concern" letter, which was found in a packet left with his sister and published in the *Philadelphia*

Inquirer on April 19. The *Intelligencer* clipped the article the next day, noting that the letter was meant to vindicate "some desperate act." The disclosure in it that Booth had attended John Brown's execution in 1859 suggested the assassin had absorbed from Virginia governor Henry Wise "those detestable sentiments of cruelty which have culminated in an infamous crime." The *Intelligencer* concluded that the letter established its writer's insanity.[37] Nor would Booth have found relief outside Washington. In attempting to alleviate public apprehension over Booth's escape, the antiadministration *New York World* asserted that the assassin could nowhere gain sanctuary, as the "moral sense of Christendom" would see to justice. Even in the rebellious southern states, "no nook or corner of this continent will be found . . . which shall not be too small to be the hiding place of this miscreant, whose sacrilegious hand has struck so foul a blow."[38]

As Booth had hoped for, comparisons were made to the crime of Brutus. Also mentioned were Cain, Charlotte Corday, Ravaillac, and Judas. But the northern press failed to grant him the political justification these historical analogies, at least in the case of Brutus and Corday, suggested. Instead, the emphasis was placed on their — and, by analogy, his — depravity. It was alleged that among the assassin's favorite verses was the couplet by the English dramatist Colley Cibber: "The aspiring youth that fired the Ephesian dome,/outlives in fame the pious fool who raised it." The burning of the Temple of Artemis at Ephesus in the fourth century BC by Erostratus constituted an act of ultimate sacrilege. Booth's association with the Greek youth was intended to illustrate how vanity and an inordinate lust for fame impelled his crime.

Classical analogies were matched by biographical elaboration. Following Booth's death, *World* correspondent George Alfred Townsend told the murderer's life tale and the passage of his last days. Townsend's construction of Booth's villainous reputation is noteworthy for its content as well as for the exposure it received. A prolific and popular columnist, his assassination articles were reissued in pamphlet form and later reworked into the accounts of other writers.[39] He began by noting that Booth was the "hero" of a single deed, "and the delineation of him may begin and be exhausted in a single article." This delineation begins with the killer's ancestry. Wilkes's father, popular Shakespearean actor Junius Brutus Booth, "in every land was a sojourner as his fathers were." He was of Jewish descent and exhibited "that strong Jewish physiognomy which, in its nobler phases, makes all that is dark and beautiful."[40] Events from Booth's past also foreshadowed his nefarious act. He was a flighty youth who grew into a frivolous and dissipated young man. To his mother he was affectionate without being obedient, and of all her sons, "he was the most headstrong in-doors and the most contented away from home." As a boy, he shot cats.[41] As an actor, he failed initially and gained the reputation of having no promise, lacking enterprise, and being careless in his craft. He was booed in Philadelphia. His success, when it did come, came first in Richmond, owing in part to the fact "that the hospitable, lounging, buzzing character of the southerner is entirely consonant with the cosmopolitanism of the stage." In the South, an actor's social status is nine times what it is in the North: "We place actors outside of society and execrate them because they are there. The South took them into affable fellowship, and was not ruined by it, but beloved by the fraternity." Booth's southern success made him resolve to become a "star," a term implying little merit in Townsend's eyes: "A stock actor is a good actor, and a poor fool. A star is an advertisement in tights who grows rich and corrupts the public taste."[42]

The negative image of Booth in the popular press complemented the public's imagining of him as being outside decent society. His real identity as an actor facilitated the effort since, as Townsend remarked, actors stood outside northern society. Not only the wandering Jew, Booth, in his thespian guise, meant he would be likely to adopt "detection defying" disguises, "including dressing as a woman or a negro."[43] Both his profession and his supposed ethnic identity helped construct his otherness. His attributed moral character served the same ends by emphasizing his dissipation and his inability to perform as a serious actor, with the origin of these flaws being a childhood refusal of domestic discipline. The result was a person who knew moral right only in "scintillations," a failing that led to numerous illicit affairs with women and ultimately to despicable murder.[44] Other commentators pushed Booth's character assassination further, finding the ultimate explanation for his outrage in insanity.

To understand how such popular literary efforts contributed to the idea of Booth's escape requires that we return to the work of Gary Fine. Fine links the concept of negative commemoration to Durkheimian social theory and argues that this process, like the more frequent commemoration of society's heroes, helps reinforce social cohesion by delimiting moral boundaries and the consequences of stepping outside them.[45] The process of pushing out, of excluding the malefactor through the building of his or her villainous reputation, abets the idea of the villain's escape (and survival) by emphasizing his or her physical, occupational, and moral displacement outside the limits of decent society. In their efforts to exclude him, Booth's reputational entrepreneurs helped create his elusiveness, thus complementing the uncertainty over his physical location. Political factors also played a role in creating this elusiveness. Fostering social cohesion, especially in stressful times, often involves the scapegoating of one individual in order to draw attention away from members in the society whose own actions may appear less than virtuous.

Here we should recognize what historian Robert McGlone describes as the "politics of insanity." Booth's demonization, particularly the emphasis on his actions as being those of a madman, requires careful examination. As was the case in the construction of the Enid mummy, newspapers' political allegiances influenced their coverage. If the *New York Times* may be taken as representative of pro-administration coverage, very little ink was devoted to the assassin's person. Northern loyalists focused instead on the existence of a greater conspiracy; it was the prosouthern, antiadministration papers that devoted the most space to the assassin's excoriation. Their scapegoating may have been an honest expression of repugnance at the deed, but it also embodied an important political content. McGlone's examination of the portrayal of John Brown as insane following his capture at Harpers Ferry reveals that in addition to its being prompted by his attorneys in an attempt to secure a lesser sentence for their client, it was also promoted by the Republican party in order to distance itself from Brown's act.[46] Booth's demonization was part of an effort to depoliticize his act, as northern papers with Democratic or southern leanings sought to distance themselves from him in the fury that followed Lincoln's assassination. The *World* and the *Intelligencer,* known for their antiadministration and prosouthern views, forcefully denied the assassination's political dimension at the same time they constructed Booth's villainous reputation. Booth's crime, asserted the *New York World,* "is no political offense, but a most flat and absolute murder." Had Lincoln been struck down earlier in the conflict, then it would be possible to assign his killing some political purpose. But at this late date, with northern victory assured, "it plays a part, not of policy, but of despair; it represents not the temper and the habits of a people, nor even of a section of a people, but the frenzy of a faction or an individual."[47] In an editorial published on April 21, the *Intelligencer* appealed to the common sense of the American people, and counseled "a more calm consideration of the *political facts and exigencies of the case*." What this consideration would bring to light remained to be determined, and those proven guilty of aiding Booth in his great crime should be punished. Whatever the determination, however, it did not follow, "either as a wise or logical deduction, that we shall *be unjust to the loyal sentiment of the South*." The facts to date indicated that the assassination was at most the adventure of a few "wicked, perverted, and desperate spirits, not uncommon to such times as these."[48]

In contrast to the spoken record, which downplayed the figure of Booth to concentrate on the perceived greater evil, the opposition press attempted to neutralize its own past disloyal statements by portraying Booth as demonic. In what would become an enduring and tragic tradition in American history, the theory of the mad, lone gunman originated in part from an effort to neutralize the political significance of the act. Booth's figurative exile served to mask the dissent of the northern opposition press and to reflect attention away from the sizable community of northern political dissenters.[49] This effort was not completely successful, as there were numerous reports of loyalists exacting retribution on dissenters when the latter proclaimed their glee at Lincoln's death too loudly.[50] As far as the popular press was concerned, however, an odd balance was struck: as the northern populace imagined the enemy within, reputational entrepreneurs worked to focus attention outward, onto the deplorable character of John Wilkes Booth.

However, at the same time he was portrayed as insane, or as driven by an inordinate desire for fame, Booth also began to be figured in romantic terms. Townsend's description of Booth's ancestral links was followed, in the same biography, with an evocation of his classic beauty, "in the Medician sense." He was, the journalist rhapsodized, among the finest exponents of vital beauty ever seen. From the waist up he was a perfect man, "his arms as white as alabaster but hard as marble. Over these, upon a neck which was its own proper column, rose the cornice of a fine Doric face, spare at the jaws, and not anywhere over-ripe, but seamed with a nose of Roman model, the only relic of his half-Jewish parentage."[51] This description had its basis in fact, as Booth's *cartes de visite* do show a handsome man with fair skin and dark features. The emphasis on the actor's attractiveness may have been a journalistic ploy intended to enhance readership. It also marked Booth as an uncommon criminal. Physical and mental exceptionality are the marks of the favorite, and the betrayal of the favorite is a perennial trope in mythic villainy. Lucifer was God's favored archangel who rebelled against him, and Brutus was favored by Caesar. Booth's portrayal served to further blur the assassin's image by mixing demonic attributes with features that, in the lexicon of nineteenth-century American culture, evoked high-mindedness. Townsend capped his description with the all-important description of Booth's forehead as "lofty" and "square." As the descriptions of the antebellum mummies attest, in the phrenological language of the period the shape of the forehead indicated a person's moral and racial status. (In contrast to Booth, the forehead of his fellow conspirator George Atzerodt, a German, was described as "low, and the general contour of his features stamp him as a man of low character, who would stoop to any action, no matter how vile, for money."[52]) Notwithstanding Townsend's desire to demonize the actor, Booth was endowed with moral enlightenment and favored with the physical attributes of white racial perfection.

Likewise, analogies to past malefactors served to blur the line between hero and villain. The references to Judas and Ravaillac (the murderer of France's Henry IV) were straightforward enough, as the reputations of both men carried no redeeming trait. But comparisons of Booth to such figures as Brutus, Cain, and Charlotte Corday (who murdered the French revolutionary leader Marat in his bathtub), were covertly honorific, even if the northern papers denied it. Southern papers, in the few accounts that did surface, clearly eulogized the assassin as a latter-day Brutus or Corday.[53] Cain, though guilty of humankind's first murder and banished to wander, carried God's mark as protection and became the founder of cities. Even as dissident northern papers attempted to distance themselves from the murder by demonizing its principal antagonist, their portrayals suggested continued resistance to Unionist political discourse. Forced on the defensive by the calamitous turn of events, opposition editors deployed an array of figures to protect themselves from northern outrage while still communicating their sympathy with the southern cause. Even as they pushed Booth outside the boundaries of the northern moral community, northern opposition papers also subtly honored him. These publications fostered Booth's elusiveness, in a figurative sense at least. Combined with the continued uncertainty over his physical whereabouts, the slippery portrait presented in print helped support the idea that Booth would successfully elude his pursuers. Rather than completing his demonization, these descriptions of Booth, with their hidden classical illusions and the emphasis on his exceptionality, began a process of romanticization. Booth began to appear as a romantic villain — not a hero, exactly, but someone whose horrific actions were balanced by attractive personal traits of physical beauty, sexual attractiveness, and honor (Figures 10 and 11).[54]

The figure of the romantic villain achieved its clearest expression in two fictional works that appeared in the months after the assassination. Ned Buntline's *The Parricides; or, The Doom of the Assassins* (1865) and Dion Haco's *J. Wilkes Booth, the Assassinator of the President* (1865) were both published in New York City. Buntline, pseudonym for Edward Z. C. Judson, was a prolific writer who went on after the war to discover and fictionalize Buffalo Bill Cody. Haco (also a pseudonym) was a lesser-known scribe, but he too had other titles to his credit, including *Perdita, The Demon Refugee's Daughter* and *Larry, the Army Dog Robber*. Both authors wrote dime novels, popular adventure stories featuring standard plots and stereotypical characterizations. Buntline's forte before the war included sea stories, Mexican war tales, temperance tracts, and nativist attacks on foreign immigrants.[55]

The appearance of both works in 1865 suggests that treatment of the assassination was not confined to the realm of civil-religious ritual and somber public discourse. Fictionalization (as the current spate of movies and novels depicting terrorist attacks on civilians also indicates) became another means of interpreting the tragedy. Both authors constructed plotlines in which Booth's crime resulted from his membership in the Knights of the Golden Circle (KGC).[56] They played on the suspicions, voiced by the *New York Times* in an editorial earlier in the year, that treasonous northern societies were responsible for the president's murder.[57] Haco and Buntline devoted considerable attention to the elaborate initiation rites of the secret society. The title page of Buntline's *Parricides* depicted Booth in a cloak, face averted, surrounded by hooded figures on their knees,

Figure 10.
J. L. Magee, Satan Tempting Booth to the Murder of the
President, *Philadelphia, 1865. (Library of Congress, Prints and
Photographs Division, LC-USZ62 8933.)*

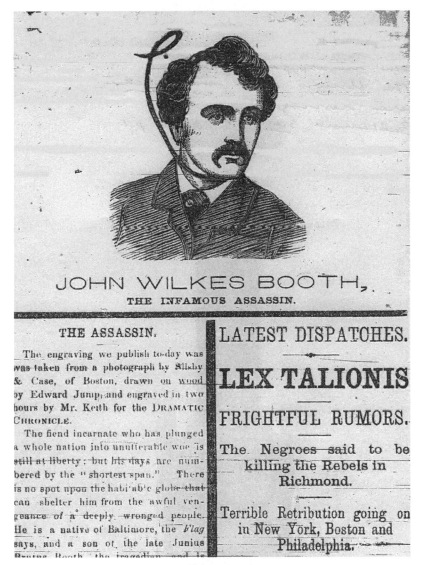

JOHN WILKES BOOTH,
THE INFAMOUS ASSASSIN.

THE ASSASSIN.

The engraving we publish to-day was was taken from a photograph by Silsby & Case, of Boston, drawn on wood by Edward Jump, and engraved in two hours by Mr. Keith for the DRAMATIC CHRONICLE.

The fiend incarnate who has plunged a whole nation into unutterable woe is still at liberty; but his days are numbered by the "shortest span." There is no spot upon the habitable globe that can shelter him from the awful vengeance of a deeply wronged people. He is a native of Baltimore, the *Flag* says, and a son of the late Junius Brutus Booth, the tragedian, and is

LATEST DISPATCHES.

LEX TALIONIS

FRIGHTFUL RUMORS.

The Negroes said to be killing the Rebels in Richmond.

Terrible Retribution going on in New York, Boston and Philadelphia.

Figure 11.
"John Wilkes Booth, the Infamous Assassin," San Francisco Chronicle, *April 17, 1865. (Author's collection.)*

with the foremost pointing a sword at his heart. Haco's account featured an initiation of several stages, beginning in a room with thirty doors, and followed by the swearing of an oath, a test of fidelity, and the proclamation of the society's president that henceforth Booth would be known among his brothers as Sir Hector of the Golden Sock and Buskin.

The actor as portrayed in both works is notable for his punctilious sense of honor; in fact, it is this commitment to honor combined with his oath to the society that leads to Booth's committing the murder. In Buntline's account, a distasteful Italian named Orsini manipulated the vain thespian to murder, thus suggesting immigrant threat combined with northern treason. For Haco, it was female intrigue: Booth is induced to strike the president by a suggestion whispered by a lady in his ear during a Richmond soiree before Lincoln's inauguration: "See what popularity such a hero would gain among us. . . . It would conduce to his immortal fame and make him equal to Brutus of old."[58] Both authors revile the assassin's deed and, like earlier portrayals, insist that his motivation was vanity and an inordinate quest for fame. However, the two authors also provide Booth with an explanation located in outside agencies, the murky working of the KGC and behind-the-scenes influence of dirty foreigners and intriguing women. Booth stands apart from much of the unsavoriness that surrounds him, being depicted as gallant, handsome, sociable, and committed to honorable behavior. This mixed figure of his villainy on the one hand and his romance on the other comes through clearly in the confidence of Ella, a character in Haco's book who was based on Booth's real-life mistress, to her sister: "He has the most brilliant eyes and fine curly locks as dark as the raven's wings, and were it not for his overhanging brows would certainly be considered by every one as the handsome man he really is."[59] The reader is left to wonder, among this amalgam of brilliant eyes, overhanging brows, honorable decorum, and violent murder, where Booth really stood.

In addition to the imagination of an overwrought populace and the efforts of the popular press, we must also consider a third factor in the creation of the Booth legend: the role of the Union government in fomenting mistruth and thereby contributing to the idea of Booth's escape. Experts from George Bryan on agree that government actions fostered rumors of escape by shrouding the details of the assassin's death in secrecy. Secretary of War Edwin Stanton here takes center stage, as it was his War Department that pursued the conspirators, and Stanton issued explicit instructions for handling the prisoners and the body. At least one deliberate piece of misinformation was publicized, when Lafayette Baker, acting under Stanton's orders, misled the public into believing that Booth's corpse had been dumped in the Potomac.

In contrast to the imaginative and literary expressions that fostered uncertainty over Booth's fate, the government's contribution to the mystery rested in its handling of the material evidence. Like the Kennedy assassination a century later, the actions of those who oversaw the apprehension of the assassin and his conspirators were unfortunately not as complete, nor as precise, as history would like. The self-serving statements of Baker in particular distorted the record. The mining of the discrepancies in the evidence by legend advocates, however, did not begin until the end of the century. It was then that the retrospective accounts of ex-soldiers claiming to have witnessed the capture and burial cast doubt on the official version of events. This dissection of the details regarding the "body in the barn" continues to the present day, fueling the endless debate between "Boothies" and the custodians of historical order.[60]

At the time of the actual events, what propelled the rumors was the government's unwillingness to expose Booth to public gaze. After his capture and death on the Garrett farmstead, members of the capture party sewed the emaciated actor up in an army blanket and placed him on a military steamboat for transport back to Washington. Stanton ordered the boat to the Washington navy yard. In the dead of night, sailors transferred the body to the deck of the monitor *Montauk*, in whose steel hull Booth's manacled and hooded co-conspirators were also being held. News of the arrival spread quickly through the capital, and the next morning thousands of people visited the yard hoping to glimpse the assassin's remains. Only those connected with the proceedings gained entry, although Baker's account alleges that at least one southern sympathizer reached the corpse and snipped a locket of hair from its head. Hundreds stood watching from the yard's perimeter until late afternoon, when the body was lowered into a rowboat and gradually disappeared beyond a spit of land.[61] This gave rise to the belief that Booth had been buried in the river, and it is worth noting the coincidence between symbolic expectations and practical results: the body's apparent watery grave accorded with public admonishments that Booth be denied Christian burial, to expel him even from the community of the dead: "accursed of men and doomed of God, the very arch-fiend's mock." He would go to his reward "unhousel'd, unanel'd, no reckoning made."[62] Journalist Townsend asked Baker where the body had gone, but the wily detective demurred. "Never," Baker replied, "till the great trumpeter comes shall the grave of Booth be discovered."[63] The journalist's imagination needed no further prompting:

> They carried the body off into the darkness, and out of that darkness it will never return. In the darkness, like his great crime, may it remain forever, impalpable, invisible, nondescript, condemned to that worse than damnation, annihilation. The river bottom may ooze about it laden with great shot and drowning manacles. The earth may have opened to give it that silence and forgiveness which man will never give its memory. The fishes may swim around it, or the daisies grow white above it; but we shall never know. Mysterious, incomprehensible, unattainable, like the dim times through which we live and think upon as if we only dreamed them in perturbed sleep, the assassin of a nation's head rests somewhere in the elements and that is all.[64]

On a symbolic level, the effort to annihilate Booth's remains was an attempt to expel any remnant of his existence from the northern body politic. Attempts to impose oblivion, however, can, ironically, produce its opposite. So it was with Booth. Efforts to annihilate his presence, both symbolically and actually, in fact worked to promote the idea of his escape. Like Erostratus, Booth's classical antecedent, prohibition became an act of instatement, and the attempt at erasure served only to more firmly entrench the dissident figure in memory.[65] But why did Stanton and the officials under him act the way they did? Were they acting out a predetermined symbolic language of their own (consciously or not), or were they simply following routine procedures in handling the corpse of an infamous Confederate? For the conspiratorially minded, the secrecy masked sinister motives. By their calculus the body hauled back to the Washington was not the actor's. Subterfuge was therefore necessary in order to prevent the public from discovering the real identity of the dead man. Legendeers have made much of the statement of Dr. May, the local surgeon called to the inquest (apparently under some duress), who had removed a tumor from Booth's neck the year before. May noted that the body was "much changed and altered," appearing older and more freckled than he remembered Booth being.[66] The allegations of willful misinformation hiding evil intentions would crest with Otto Eisenchiml's book *Why Was Lincoln Murdered?* (1937), which accused Stanton of masterminding Lincoln's murder to guarantee the radical Republican program for reconstruction. At the other end of the spectrum lay Bryan's accusation of neglect, in which misinformation arose because of the government's failure to properly manage the story.

Neither extreme provides a reasonable, *positive* explanation of why government authorities acted as they did. One proceeds from circumstantial evidence to dubious conclusions. The other views the War Department under Stanton as indifferent or incompetent in managing information, itself a dubious assessment. The traditional view of government news management was voiced in 1918 by future Lincoln luminary James Randall, who rued the debilitating effect on military operations of "a period of keen journalistic enterprise [coinciding] with a time of laxity in the matter of press control."[67] Whether the government failed to guarantee the security of military information was only part of the story. Recent scholarship has established that Lincoln and his cabinet had a public communications strategy in place. Stanton effectively controlled the dissemination of information to the northern press to favor desired political outcomes. In fact, his official dispatch relating Lincoln's assassination was the first use of the "inverted pyramid" style of reporting, a watershed event in journalism history.[68]

The answer to why Stanton imposed strict secrecy on the disposal of the killer's remains surfaced two years after the fact, in the course of a congressional committee intent on ferreting out the misdeeds of President Andrew Johnson. Called to testify before the committee, Lincoln's former minister of war provided a straightforward answer: it was done merely to prevent any recognition of Booth's body by southern sympathizers.[69] But this simple reply glossed over profound motivations. It was the corpse's symbolic power that worried Stanton, and his concern had its foundation in fact. Clippings of hair had been gathered from the assassin's head, first on the Garrett porch and later aboard the *Montauk*.[70] Stanton's concerns, however, went beyond the gathering of simple physical artifacts. He was well aware of the body's symbolic potential, a potential borne of antebellum attitudes toward the corpse, Civil War politics, and the transformation of the dead in the service of the state brought on by the conflict. Stanton's awareness may also have stemmed from his own morbid predilections: he reportedly kept the remains of an infant daughter in a metal urn for several years.[71] In any case, his official actions at the time prove that his appreciation of the significance of the body extended to the public, political sphere. His critics recognized it as late as February 1869, when Booth's remains were turned over to his family for reburial in the family plot (this being one of Andrew Johnson's last official acts as president). The *New York World* held Stanton responsible for fomenting "a factitious mystery . . . around the burial of the poor lifeless remains." It condemned the "malignant imbecility" of "this Pennsylvania lawyer, turned high priest of Moloch," who performed "mummeries" over Booth's corpse.[72]

It was Stanton who oversaw the ritual exhibition of Lincoln's corpse through northern communities, while he worked to efface the symbolism of the assassin's body. It was surely not Stanton's decision alone to prolong Lincoln's obsequies in this fashion; political leaders prior to Lincoln had undergone similar treatment. In Lincoln's case the interests of state overrode the wishes of the family, and Mary Todd Lincoln did not accompany the funeral train. It was, as contemporaries noted, a political display, the value of which depended on where one stood. Stanton's opponents recognized the purposes Lincoln's exhibition served, and accused Stanton of drawing out the ceremonies in order to gain political advantage for the Radical wing of the Republican Party. Others, such as Congressman Shelby Cullom, saw the political-ritual aspect of the display as a means of consolidating northern political sentiment by arousing northerners' patriotism.[73]

The transportation of Lincoln's corpse offered a supreme opportunity to reestablish social order and allegiance to the Union cause, following four years of divisive struggle. The passage of the body through New York City, as elsewhere, involved the closing of businesses, the decoration of city streets, processions, speeches, and the gazing upon the departed president's corpse. Events were minutely organized and reflected the civic organization of the time and place. When the funeral train reached Jersey City on the afternoon of April 24,

German singing societies offered dirges as the body was ferried across the Hudson to New York. Once over the river, a military procession guided the elaborate horse-drawn catafalque to City Hall, where Lincoln lay in state — with the casket open — overnight. On the stroke of midnight, in the candlelight of City Hall's shrouded dome, the singing societies struck up a funeral requiem. Viewing continued into the morning. An estimated 120,000 people viewed the president's remains, and in the end some had to be turned away.[74]

At noon the following day, a massive procession escorted the funeral cortege to the Hudson River Railroad depot for embarkation to Albany. The Grand Marshal led off, followed by the cortege and military units. Next came civil officials, trailed by the clergy and the chamber of commerce. After that were featured the Masonic Order and other fraternal groups, who were succeeded by temperance societies, trade groups, social clubs, and civic societies from Brooklyn. Last — and nearly excluded from the line of march save for the intervention of Secretary Stanton — were associations of the city's African American populace, carrying banners that read "Abraham Lincoln, Our Emancipator" and "Two Millions of Bondmen He Liberty Gave." The procession took four hours to pass by, and by the time the last of it reached the depot, Lincoln's train was several hours gone. Most eerily perhaps, all proceeded quietly, the silence broken only by the sound of dirges, tolling bells, and booming minute guns. The whole was marked by somber order: "Never before," one recorder noted, "had our citizen soldiers appeared with fuller ranks or in better order, or had our civic and other societies appeared to better advantage."[75] Indeed, for New Yorkers this was a moment of supreme atonement, as the city had erupted in July 1863 in antiadministration riots that had claimed over a hundred victims.[76] Now, as the president's bier passed by, "every head was uncovered in that vast crowd, and all bowed in reverence."[77]

That Lincoln's body should be used to this purpose — to solidify political allegiance and civic order — had precedent in American history. Washington's death in 1799 also led to funeral processions throughout the new nation. The Father of His Country, however, was not corporeally present. Communities paraded empty coffins as Washington's remains stayed safely within the precincts of Mount Vernon, cared for by his family.[78] In Lincoln's case, advances in the chemical embalming of the body brought on by the necessities of the war meant that Lincoln could be physically present for hundreds of thousands of American citizens. Funerary technology thus helped further the interests of the nation-state. Lincoln was, if not the first, among the first leaders of modern nation-states whose remains were forced to endure sustained exhibition in the service of the nation. Stanton's partisan political purposes aside, Lincoln's posthumous display across the nation's northern quadrant served as an icon of national immortality. Viewed in civil-religious terms, the preservation of the national dead — their immortality, so to speak — ensures that of the nation.[79] Control over the domain of the dead confirmed the indivisibility of the Union and the republic's indestructibility. Lincoln effected in death what he had been unable to achieve in life — the unification of northern political sentiment. As Herbert Mitgang noted, while Lincoln lived, "his enemies were alive."[80] But in death, he united the country so that even many Copperheads were forced to repent. The first lesson taught by Lincoln's death, and reinforced by the exhibition of his remains, was of the heroic sacrifice needed to sanctify the Union.[81] Though Lincoln was the outstanding exemplar in the American veneration of the dead in the service of the nation, the exhibition of his body also marked a general development across the western polities. In John Gillis's opinion, by the end of the eighteenth century "the living came to haunt the dead."[82] Governments and individual members of nation-states began venerating their fallen patriots through a variety of commemorative acts, including civic rituals, statuary, and historical narrative. In the context of this study, using the dead in the service of the nation is another example of Euro-American appropriation of the dead. In the opinion of some scholars, it also marked a turning away from the fulfillment of the democratic experiment in favor of a nationalistic death cult.[83]

Booth and Lincoln were among several volatile bodies from the period, beginning with that of the martyred John Brown in 1859 and ending with Booth's six years later. When Brown was executed following the Harper's Ferry raid, northern abolitionists hoped to exhibit his corpse to rouse antislavery sentiment. One abolitionist suggested procuring the body and placing it in an iced coffin so that it could be taken to all the North's principal cities, where the people could see Brown's face and, presumably, the mark of the rope around his neck.[84] Unfortunately for these plans, Brown's widow proved more resolute than Mary Todd Lincoln (or the forces arrayed against her were less insistent), and his remains were shipped directly back to his farm in upstate New York. Nonetheless, his corpse was put to use in the most popular song of the Civil War North — "John Brown's Body Lies a-Mouldering in the Grave."

The Civil War brought about a sea change in attitudes about death and the body, as a result of the war's murderousness, technical advances in preserving corpses, and a newly aroused sense of nation. At the same time the war's slaughter (in terms of deaths, the Civil War remains America's costliest war) made death banal, the corpse entered more fully into the service of the nation. Matthew Brady's posed battlefield scenes brought the image of martial carnage before thousands of northern viewers. This imaging of death mimicked antebellum funerary portraiture but mocked death's intimacy. The intimacy and domestication of the corpse that had marked antebellum attitudes toward death were not entirely forsaken, but death became an increasingly public affair, and was commodified and made banal as soldiers and civilians became anaesthetized to its presence.[85] Commemoration of the dead was enlisted in the service of the nation. The principal vehicle for this would become Memorial Day, a civil-religious ritual that originated with the decorating of graves of fallen soldiers with flowers during the war.[86] In the North, formal observances on a national scale began in 1868 under the auspices of the Union veterans' group, the Grand Army of the Republic (GAR). Southerners soon developed their own version of the holiday of remembrance. Ideology took hold early on, and the northern dominant interpretation combined religion and nationalism in what David Blight describes as a victory cult that provided northerners with a narrative by which to understand the loss of family and friends. Memorial Day provided a means for spiritual recovery and historical understanding, and it redefined the nineteenth-century ideal of manly heroism by consecrating the Union dead as founders of a new social order. It became a legitimizing ritual of the new sense of nationalism that emerged out of the war.[87]

What Booth experienced, even as he lived out his final days, was the flip side of this massive memorialization. Instead of transcending death, he experienced annihilation, figuratively as well as literally. The calls for the dispersal of his remains were rooted in traditional responses toward those deemed to have transgressed commonly understood boundaries. But the reaction to Booth's act was compounded by civil-religious and political motivations. Thus Booth, who craved a political definition for his act, found his wish denied by those he had presumed to be his supporters as well as by the government, from whom he expected little mercy. Stanton's decision to annihilate the assassin's presence was the reverse to Lincoln's elaborate exhibition. Practical political reasoning may have dictated the secretary's course, but his actions also grew from his appreciation of the new symbolic power of the corpse. Stanton, however, neglected to consider what may be called the Erostratus effect. Combined with the popular imagining of Booth's whereabouts preceding his capture, and the ambiguous figuration the assassin received in the press, the secret annihilation of his remains worked to guarantee his survival. Uncertainty, ambiguity, and annihilation, all borne of politics and death's new symbolism, created the conditions for Booth's survival.

Eventually, the idea of Booth's escape might have passed from the popular imagination, as the trauma waned and the northern press moved on to other subjects. The theory resurfaced a year after the assassination, however, in very different circumstances. What had been a serious response to the political and cultural exigencies of the moment now came to be appropriated in seriocomic fashion by political actors intent on more prosaic ends. Booth's escape moved from the realm of the civil-religious to that of political theater, and along the way provided some of the best grist for future generations of legend believers. In 1866, in the course of debating the apportionment of reward money for the capture of the assassin and his co-conspirators, Senator Garrett Davis of Kentucky voiced concern in the chamber regarding the assassin's true fate. He wanted proof of the assassin's demise, saying, "I have never seen myself any satisfactory evidence that Booth was killed." Why wasn't his body brought before the public gaze? Why the secrecy? And why was he shot when he was surrounded in the barn with no means of escape?[88] Beginning with the fictional *Bloody Junto*, published in 1869, Davis's comments became a staple of legend lore. They were recalled most recently at the 1995 exhumation trial by the plaintiff's attorney, when he confronted William Hanchett on the witness stand with them.[89] But, as Hanchett rightly noted, Davis's comments were senseless unless taken in context, and the context shows that the senator was engaging in light-hearted banter on the last day of the congressional session and that the real object of his attack was not the credibility of Booth's demise, but the reputation of Lafayette Baker. Identify Booth, the transcript of his remarks continues, "and these men ought to have their reward, but I doubt whether this man Baker ought to have anything. I believe he was a much bigger villain than any man he was pursuing. I do not doubt that at all; and I believe he is such a man as to get up now a story of the capture of Booth when Booth had not been overtaken at all. [*Laughter.*]"[90]

Baker's reputation was a complicating factor, and the senator's re-marks would be followed, in early 1867, by the chief detective's reve-lation that he had misled the public on the disposal of the body.[91] It had become apparent by this time that his version of the capture was largely self-serving, aimed at securing a lion's share of the reward money rather than serving as an accurate account of what transpired. Baker's actions show that the responsibility for distorting the histori-cal narrative fell squarely on the shoulders of the public officials en-trusted with executing the capture. Rather than any plot or conspir-acy, the motives for this distortion were pecuniary. The chief detective sought to place himself and his two subordinates, Lieutenant Luther B. Baker (a cousin) and Colonel Everton Conger, at the center of events. The two subordinates rode with the cavalry force and partici-pated in the capture. Baker remained in Washington, and in order to vouchsafe his own contribution concocted a strategy meeting at which he correctly divined the assassin's route into Virginia. He fabricated the testimony of a fictitious Virginia freedman, who provided the eye-witness testimony needed to authenticate Baker's brilliant guess at Booth's whereabouts. The press swallowed this story whole, although Townsend hinted at possible subterfuge in the opening line of his capture report: "A hard and grizzly face overlooks me as I write. Its in-considerable forehead is crowned with burning sandy hair, and the deep concave of its long insatiate jaws is almost hidden by a dense red beard. . . . This is the face of Lafayette Baker."[92] The story he was about to relate, Townsend carefully noted, was told to him by Baker. The Se-cret Service head may have also added romantic flourishes to his ac-count of Booth's end. He had the assassin utter various clichés, in-cluding "Tell Mother I died for my country" and "I did what I thought was for the best," as his life ebbed away. In his expiring moment he asked to have his paralyzed hands raised before his eyes and muttered, "Useless, useless."[93] A recent review of the medical evidence suggests that the bullet's path through his neck may have traumatized Booth's voice box, making speech difficult or impossible.[94] What became obvious in retrospect is that Baker and his minions filched the intelligence of Major James R. O'Beirne, a provost marshal commanding a detachment scouring southern Maryland, who struck the assassin's trail near Bryantown. This news was telegraphed back to the War Department when O'Beirne requested permission to cross over the Potomac in pursuit. His request was denied as Baker set his own forces in motion.[95]

Senator Davis's humorous slights at Baker's reputation fed off the general suspicions regarding the events of Booth's capture. Baker cast further doubt on the already suspect story by testifying before the House Committee of the Judiciary in February 1867 that he had witnessed treasonous correspondence between Andrew Johnson and Jefferson Davis while Johnson was military governor of Tennessee. He also revealed the existence of Booth's diary, which had lain forgotten among the evidence collected by the Bureau of Military Justice two years earlier. In the case of the treasonous correspondence, Baker's allegations proved to be false, leading two members of the committee to conclude it was unlikely that the former chief of detectives had told the truth about anything.[96] About the diary, however, what Baker related was the truth, and the revelation of its existence caused quite a stir. Subpoenaed by the committee, the diary was examined by Baker, who asserted that pages had been removed since he had turned it over to Edwin Stanton following Booth's capture. The issue of the missing pages, like Davis's utterances, has served as a source text for legend believers. The producers of *The Lincoln Conspiracy*, a movie and accompanying book released in 1977, alleged that they obtained copies of the missing pages through an appraiser of Americana who had found them among papers in the possession of Stanton's heirs.[97]

At the time, the diary's usefulness was clearly tied to the political contest then going on between Andrew Johnson and the Radical-controlled Congress. In fact, the committee before which both Baker and Stanton testified on the events of the assassination convened to inquire into Johnson's conduct. It welcomed Baker's allegations of

Johnson's misdoing, although the detective's reasons for casting suspicions on his former chief stemmed from a personal grievance. Johnson had dismissed Baker in 1866 for his conduct in the Lucy Cobb affair. Mrs. Cobb, a Washington socialite, served as a pardon broker between southerners and government officials. Securing pardons for a fee was illegal, and Lucy Cobb's behavior, in Baker's opinion, was disreputable. She had "an understanding with the President, and that he dare not refuse her requests."[98] Outraged at this behavior, Baker mounted a sting operation and caught Mrs. Cobb with marked notes taken as payment for a pardon that she received from Johnson. In the hullabaloo that followed, Baker came out on the losing end and retired to Philadelphia to compose his memoirs. For the Radicals, however, the idea of tampered evidence served their purposes well. From belief in a conspiracy theory directed from Richmond, political actors in Washington now turned their suspicions on Andrew Johnson. Leading the charge was former political general and recently elected congressman Benjamin Butler, who declaimed from the House floor: "Who spoliated that book? Who suppressed that evidence?" Butler asserted, as have others since, that the diary would have led to Mrs. Surratt's exoneration, since in it Booth clearly indicated that up until the last days, the plan had been to capture Lincoln, not murder him. The question then became who had changed Booth's mind and "who it was that could profit by assassination who could not profit by capture and abduction of the President."[99] The insinuation was clearly directed toward the current occupant of the White House, although Mary Lincoln had voiced her suspicions regarding Johnson only weeks after her husband's murder.[100] Butler's attacks on Johnson were politically useful, as Radical congressmen marshaled support to vote the articles of impeachment against Johnson. In July, Butler offered a resolution establishing an assassination committee, vested with the power of subpoena and pardon, to consider more fully the conspiracy that had felled Lincoln. The proposed preamble established that the crime "is believed to have included in its plan and perpetration many persons holding high positions of power and authority, . . . who were acting through inferior persons as their tools and instruments."[101] The resolution passed, 100 to 28, with 40 abstaining. Among those supporting the measure were Thaddeus Stevens, James Garfield, and Ignatius Donnelly. The first was the

Radical leader in Congress; the second, also elected president, would also fall to an assassin's bullet; the third, a future populist, would later author his own conspiracy text — *Caesar's Column*.

The committee found nothing, and the insinuations of Johnson's complicity in Lincoln's murder faded once the impeachment furor died. But the impact on the Booth legend's formation was substantial, not only in perpetuating the idea of Johnson's involvement, but also by providing the critical kernel of the modern legend: the allegations of government malfeasance by those inside government. Building on the triad of popular imagination, literary embellishment, and the desire to annhilate the assassin's remains, the political theater of Washington insiders added a fourth component to the legend's beginnings and further added to its northern character. It also marked the first instance of an interaction between the sacred and the banal or, perhaps better put, between civil-religious ritual and the carnivalesque. In the future, the distinction between the two would become increasingly confounded. By the end of 1867, and well before the variant of the legend deemed southern had time to form, the commemoration of Booth's death had run the gamut from the politically sacred to political farce.

THE SOUTHERN LEGEND

They pass thee by, though loyal heart,
To others pay their reverence.
Fear not—some future day will bring
Thy sacrifice its recompense.
Some day a people proud and free
Will their former wrongs deplore
And flock in living tribute to
A nameless grave in Baltimore.
(Emily Lee Bradt)

At the same time the North elaborated its uncertain image of the assassin, it is reasonable to assume that for southerners, Booth's escape served as a form of vindication, even revenge. Belief in the assassin's survival undoubtedly assuaged the distraught feelings of many southern whites following Appomattox, and the legend grew in response to their reaction to the assassin's act. As a result, the way it developed differed markedly from the way it did in the North, both in form and content. Whereas the northern version was contemporaneous with events and relied on ample written as well as spoken testimony, the southern variant was more retrospective and oral in form. These qualities reflected differences in how the legend was produced in the two regions. And while the legend in the North emerged out of ambiguity, annihilation, the politics of insanity, and the symbolic potency of the corpse, the Southern version was from the beginning more positive. Booth appeared as a romantic hero, whose act retained its political character. Even when not seen as a political act, the murder was viewed as an affair of honor. From the start, the southern version of the legend stood as an affirmation both political and personal.

Nonetheless, the southern version of the legend is not without its own ambiguities. Although much of what follows may seem to be obvious, a closer look at the rebel version's genesis in the decades following defeat reveals how this story, too, came to embody messages distinct from the subject at hand.

Although its public expression was suppressed, the record of private letters, personal reminiscences, and newspapers shows that the southern reaction to Lincoln's assassination ran the gamut from horror, through guarded approval, to unguarded glee.[1] Clearly, Booth's act uncorked the pent-up hatred of Confederate citizens who considered Lincoln the agent of their misfortunes. When the news reached the Johnson Island prison barracks on Lake Erie, rebel prisoners cheered. Their enthusiasm diminished only slightly when the soldier-guards fixed bayonets and leveled charged artillery pieces on the crowd. One participant recorded in his diary a singular reason for welcoming Lincoln's death. Although Booth's act was despicable, it relieved the southern soldiery from the oath many had sworn never to live under a government ruled over by "King Abraham the First." Now they could return home without perjuring their word.[2] News of the assassination in parts of the South was delayed, sometimes purposely, sometimes owing to the erratic condition of southern communications. The steamer *Sultana* brought the word to Baton Rouge, where it was wired to New Orleans on April 19, 1865. The city's particular status — a bastion of rebel sentiment and the centerpiece of the Union occupation effort — reflected a microcosm of southern sentiment. Black New Orleans reacted to the news with despair, and African American newspapers heaped damnation on the perpetrators. Ten thousand freedmen reportedly paraded in the streets, and the freedmen's press also turned the event to political advantage, renewing their calls for black suffrage and suggesting that Louisiana could become a "Negro State." Henry Clay Warmoth, one of the city's commanders and the future reconstruction governor for Louisiana, observed the rapid decay of relations between northerners and southerners following the assassination. He observed no "unfeigned mourning" among the rebels, and in fact the New Orleans papers gave explicit instructions to readers on how they were expected to observe Lincoln's death.[3] The result was, as Sarah Morgan Dawson confided in her diary, displays in which the quantity of bunting festooning a southern residence was often in direct proportion to the glee at Lincoln's death felt within its walls.[4]

This masking of true sentiment, this deployment of symbolic means to express simultaneously required obeisance and resistance, was only one form of opposition. Northern commanders who attempted to orchestrate fitting obsequies often encountered silent opposition. Before the assassination, Episcopal churches had been closed for refusing to pray for the welfare of the Union leadership. Now, Commanding-General Edward O. Ord ordered Richmond citizens to pray for the departed commander-in-chief. Some churches closed, and other ministers found themselves addressing nearly empty pews.[5] White southern responses to the assassination were mixed, with many fearing the results of Andrew Johnson's coming to power as much as the immediate vengeance of Union forces. However, on balance the evidence shows that the visible expressions of sorrow were deceptions. Either imposed under threat by Union authorities, or a willing "putting on" by southerners themselves, the assassination became the occasion for a great symbolic charade. It in fact suggests an underlying motive for the later genesis of the southern version of the Booth legend — the expression of political hostility through the distortion of symbolic forms, including the distortion of historical narrative.

Limited outbursts and covert opposition, however, were not the sole southern responses. In Texas, the rejoicing was open. By mid-April, the state was the Confederacy's last independent region, and the only place where "fire-eating" editors could speak freely.[6] Their reaction to the news of Lincoln's death was all the fugitive could have hoped for. The *Galveston Daily News* proclaimed Booth's act divinely inspired, and that his name "will be inscribed on the roll of true-hearted patriots along with Brutus and Charlotte Corday."[7] Other papers echoed the sentiment that Lincoln had been a despot and that Booth deserved acclaim for his political act. Unlike the northern dissident press, southern papers made the connection between the actor's classical antecedents and the political nature of the killing. The poem "Our Brutus," traditionally attributed to Texas judge A. W. Tyrell, included this stanza:

He hath written his name in letters of flame
    O'er the arch way of Liberty's portal,
And the serfs that now blame shall crimson with shame
    When they learn they have cursed an immortal![8]

Kate Stone, whose wartime experiences as a woman of the slave-holding South have been described by Drew Gilpin Faust, tersely noted the classical analogies: "Caesar had his Brutus, Marat his Charlotte Corday, and Lincoln his Booth." By insisting on the deed's political character, Texas opinion makers were able to remove its personal character. According to the *Texas Republican,* "There is no reason to believe that Booth in killing Lincoln was actuated by malice or vulgar ambition. He slew him as a tyrant, and the enemy of his country. Therefore we honour the deed."[9] Thus, at the same time they recognized the crime's political nature, Texans depersonalized it — the exact reversal of the treatment provided in northern opposition newspapers. Nonetheless, both recognized the distinction between a public and private morality, in which an action's recognized political nature excused any moral sin. In the South, Booth's political action allowed him to emerge as a positive figure, the romantic hero who acted from principle. Instead of being ambiguous, his image in the South was clearly exceptional, solidly in the mold of the imagined southern gentleman.

When not ascribing Booth's act to a political motive, southerners insisted that it was an affair of honor. The most enduring version of the honor thesis appeared only days after the act and has survived to the present.[10] Millie Rutherford, Historian General of the United Daughters of the Confederacy (UDC), featured the story in the January 1924 issue of her *Scrap Book* (subtitled *Valuable Information about the South*). As part of her project to provide a thoroughly southern history of the assassination, she strung together the legend of Booth's escape with the story that he had murdered Lincoln to avenge the wrongful execution of Confederate naval commander John Yates Beall. Beall had been captured conducting partisan operations in upstate New York, condemned as a spy, and hanged in February 1865. Friends and southern sympathizers intervened with Union officials in an attempt to save his life, but to no avail. He quickly became a martyr to the southern cause, and when Lincoln's assassination took place, it was speculated that a handful of his supporters had taken their revenge. In post-assassination Richmond it is likely the Beall theory served the useful purpose (from a southern point of view) of deflecting the growing belief among northerners that the Confederate government was involved in the murder of the Union commander-in-chief, while providing a reasonable (from a southern point of view) substitute explanation.[11]

Rutherford also pointed out that as an affair of honor, the assassination did not figure as a political act. Her explanation issued from later sources, the recollections of Confederate veterans in the 1880s and '90s who maintained they witnessed Beall's execution or were on intimate terms with Beall, Booth, and other parties connected in the affair. Some of these accounts appeared in the southern veteran's monthly magazine *Confederate Veteran* near the turn of the century, others in southern papers. The story painted Booth as a central figure in the attempts to have Beall pardoned. Upon Beall's conviction as a spy, Booth "went to Mr. Lincoln, stated these facts to him, and Mr. Lincoln acknowledged the lack of jurisdiction of the court, and error in exceeding their authority in condemning him." Other accounts related that Booth went as a supplicant on his knees to the president. Lincoln promised Booth that Beall would not be executed on the appointed date, and said he would talk to Seward on the matter. The military commander, General John A. Dix, resented the interference, and Lincoln reneged on his promise, thus making the rebel climb the gallows. In the wake of Beall's execution, Booth went insane, and "for what he termed the perfidy of President Lincoln toward himself and his friend Beall, at once swore to avenge his friend's death by killing both Lincoln and Seward."[12]

Another version of the honor thesis (though not strictly a legend account) was the spurious *Private Confession of J. Wilkes Booth*, first published in France (in French), and later in Birmingham, England. It purported to be Booth's self-exoneration, penned in the interval between his flight from the theater and his capture. Like the northern fictitious accounts of the same period, the anonymous author of the *Private Confession* borrowed liberally from George Alfred Townsend's *World* articles; but this author offered a very different interpretation from that of the northern writers. For Dion Haco and Ned Buntline, Booth's sense of honor lacked moral grounding. It was a superficial affectation and, combined with his vanity, was easily transmuted by the mumbo-jumbo of secret society dealings to bad ends.

The *Private Confession* tells a different tale. Following the first battle of Bull Run, a party of Union deserters headed toward the farm of a friend of Booth's in northern Virginia: "Their worst passions had become inflamed . . . , my friend's wife was in the grounds which fronted her husband's house . . ." The soldiers accosted the woman, and two of them bore her off to a nearby barn. The husband, nearby but out of earshot, discovered what was happening and valiantly struggled to free her from her attackers. The soldiers brutally murdered him. At this point Booth and the woman's brother happened on the scene and spotted one of the woman's violators crawling from the barn. They fired on him with their rifles, "but neither of them took effect. Then the flying wretch turned his hideous visage and gave a grim smile of satisfaction." They found the sister, alive but brutally raped. Together with a neighboring farmer, the three men swore an oath of vengeance over the body of the husband. Booth led the ceremony. Joining hands, they swore "to maintain an endless and ceaseless strife with those who are the enemies of our country. Death to the Federals! Death!" Raising their right hands, they registered the oath, swearing devotion to the cause and fealty to one another. Over the next four years Booth and his companions tracked down the Union rapist, murdered him, and waged a body count competition by shooting federals from the Confederate lines. Both companions were eventually killed, leaving Booth to murder Lincoln and note in the *Confession:* "I HAD KEPT MY OATH!"[13]

Crudely fashioned, the *Private Confession*'s alternating tale of vengeance and lengthy excerpts from Townsend's articles creates a disorienting effect on the modern reader. Viewed in the context of the southern code of honor, however, the tale makes better sense. It was the violation of southern womanhood and the brutal murder of a friend's kin that justified killing the president. Booth's honor in this case — his fidelity to his oath — was not the superfluous affectation of a dissipated actor. It was the expression of what Bertram Wyatt-Brown defines as southern primal honor, the continuation of an archaic system of ethics in the white South brought on by frontier conditions and the need to enforce mastery over black slaves. Three vital components of this honor — all evident in the story — were valor in the face of family and communal enemies, fierce retaliation for wrongs done to women, and oath-swearing as a sacred bond between non–family members.[14] Under the circumstances, Booth was compelled to act as he did, for not to have done so would have resulted in disgrace and his exclusion from the circle of white southern manhood. Unlike the prisoners at Johnson Island, Booth had no one to relieve him from his oath. He had to see it through, and the assassination as a matter of honor fully vindicated his action.

Although none of these contemporary accounts supported the theory of escape, they provided the template upon which the southern version of the legend would later be written. The southern version may also be seen as a prolongation of the cultural disobedience first practiced when fear of retribution and northern censorship masked the southern response to Lincoln's death. When the story of Booth's escape emerged it emphasized the protagonist's honor and in a few cases made direct reference to his political motivations. Most of the attention, however, as in the northern accounts, fixed on the fugitive's person. As in the North, the idea of Booth's exceptionality appeared, but it underwent a transformation in the hands of the southern crafters. For northern writers, Booth's exceptional physique served as the counterpoint to his sacrilege. Even Democratic dissenters hedged their adulation in their concern to depoliticize his act. In the southern tradition, no such controverted meanings were necessary. Booth's bearing and intellectual acumen signified his identity as a southern gentleman, plain and simple.

These dimensions found literary expression early on, in Arkansas veteran R. H. Crozier's fictional *The Bloody Junto* (1869). A hard-hitting, thoroughly unreconstructed legend account, it contrasted the honorable, cultivated bearing of its southern protagonists to the mercantile and cowardly mien of the Yankees. Its author borrowed liberally from Townsend's *World* articles, and even employed Senator Garrett Davis's comments to make its case. These superficial borrowings belied very different intentions, however. Like Haco's dime novel, *The Bloody Junto* proceeds from the premise that Booth's role in the assassination came about through his involvement in a secret society. A virtuous (though not flawless) Booth, graced with transcendent beauty, is president of a treasonous society that meets in Mary Surratt's damp cellar. The group, bearing the name in the book's title, has some forty members, all of whom are dedicated to preventing, by whatever means, the usurpation of constitutional liberties by would-be tyrants. Most of the members are southern, and all are gentlemen, carefully selected, "with the discrimination of a Napoleon Bonaparte," for their qualifications. They are men of education, who have fallen on hard times "for various causes which can easily be imagined." Readers familiar with standard accounts of the assassination may not recognize the figure of Lewis Payne, the hulking attacker of Secretary of State William H. Seward. In Crozier's book, Payne is portrayed as a sensitive soul, opposed to the part of the society's charter that stipulates death for any member who withdraws. His musings on this and other matters prompt a fellow conspirator to exclaim, "You have probably been reading Dante!" to which Payne replies, "I confess that I am not altogether free from a disagreeable impression induced by a perusal of that author." In contrast, the northern chairman of the group, DeGroot, keeps his wife and sickly child in squalor. He is a beetle-browed, insensitive, scheming coward, who eventually poisons the child to keep it from being an impediment to his ambitious plans. The best this northerner merits at Crozier's hand is a backhanded compliment for his father-in-law, who had failed in business. The reason for his bankruptcy: unlike the majority of New England Yankees, he "would not disinter the bones of his departed ancestors and convert them into buttons," nor would he engage in the "wooden nutmeg" commerce.[15]

Booth is portrayed as a "strange, daring, man" with a fiery heart, whose name is covered in "romantic infamy." No common murderer, he is possessed by "a mad love of distinction and by a crazy desire, . . . to rid the people of a tyrant." This description approximates that given in northern accounts. The difference has to do with honor. It is not Booth's cupidity, nor a vain allegiance to the bankrupt ideal of the southern gentleman that leads to his committing the crime. Instead, he is following political principles and is honoring his commitment to a plan to upset the government. Nor does he exhibit the dissipated traits Townsend sketched. Whereas the northern reporter recounted Booth's sexual predation, Crozier turned the tables by contrasting northern and southern womanhood. Before the war, Booth finds his Boston hotel "besieged by flippant New England women," their modesty prostrated, who have assembled to see Don Juan realized in the person of John Wilkes Booth. No southern woman, "laying claim to the least respectability, would have thus overstepped the barriers of true modesty and feminine delicacy." In contrast to the majority of his fellow stage players, Booth does not give into temptation, and when a Philadelphia girl offers herself to him, he says to her, "Remember who you are, and do not forget that Wilkes Booth is a conscientious man."[16]

In Crozier's telling, Booth is led to murder Lincoln through the machinations of Coldheart, a highly placed Union official, who learns of the Bloody Junto through the indiscretion of Flora Louvan, Booth's *amour.* Coldheart confronts the actor with his knowledge and gains membership to the group. The society is committed to honorable treason, but the Union official proposes a more drastic solution, the removal of government leaders and the establishment of a monarchy. This monarchy would recognize southern independence and preserve "conservative" constitutional principles to ensure states' rights and the rule of educated white men. Coldheart also plans to establish a table of nobility and entices Booth with the title "Earl of Washington." The junto agrees to capture Lincoln, Seward, and other moderate members of the cabinet in order to bring about a political revolution. When Richmond falls, however, the plans for kidnapping evaporate, and Coldheart now convinces the secret assembly that its only option lay in murdering the government leaders. They draw straws, and Booth is designated to kill Lincoln.

After the assassination, Booth flees on horseback with his new bride riding beside him. He asks her to change into men's clothing, which she does, but her horse falls on her leg, hastening the midnight visit to Dr. Samuel Mudd's. They finally arrive at Garrett's farm, and Flora has a premonition of death as they take shelter there. They are surrounded in the barn, which is set on fire, and the hapless Flora is shot by Boston Corbett. As the detectives drag her outside, Booth emerges, the sight of the fallen Flora making him "hardly human. His eyes were lustrous like fever, and swelled and rolled in terrible beauty, while his teeth grated like those of a wild animal." He picks up a long beam and, wielding it "with the ease of a Sampson," rushes the federals "with a wild, savage, deafening yell, that sounded more like the voice of a demon, or an enraged beast." The soldiers drop their guns, "and betook themselves to inglorious flight." Booth stands over the shattered form of his bride, who implores him to make his escape. He refuses: "Never! never! I shall die right here." But Flora convinces him otherwise. "Make your escape," she says. "You will captured if you remain here. It is folly to fight against so many. Live and avenge my death. That is my dying request."[17]

They part tearfully, and Booth heads south. He crosses the Mississippi at Helena, Arkansas, and disappears from sight. In the fall of 1866, a strange ship is seen in the vicinity of the Dry Tortugas, off the Florida Keys, where four of Booth's co-conspirators were imprisoned. Hoisting a Confederate battle flag, the ship fires a few shells at "those in charge of the prison at that inhospitable place."[18]

Contrived and ponderous in its literary aspirations, *The Bloody Junto* nonetheless conveyed a southern rendition of events by combining political convictions with honorable actions. Again, southern womanhood fell victim to the depredations of perfidious Yankees. Crozier's account, however, was shot through with gender anxieties, and the book's finale — despite the exertions of its hero — was decidedly uncavalier. In a violation of the southern code, Booth escaped while his damsel perished. His inability to protect his wife and his own flight were symbolic of the sense of failure many southern men experienced following defeat, revealing what Gilpin Faust has described as the inversion of southern gender relations brought on by the war.[19] Crozier's comparisons of northern and southern womanhood may be read as a plea to the latter to maintain their traditional deference to white manhood in unsettling times. Perhaps more to the point, Crozier enacted a theme recurring in subsequent southern texts. Honorable and gentlemanly, Booth the fugitive is a man without a woman. This image accords with the formula of the tragic hero, who by virtue of his crime is cut off from human community. In Booth's case, however, male camaraderie seems to compensate for this loss. Compared to the northern version of the legend, with its middle-class and domestic settings, the southern version is set in places of public transience — saloons, hotels, and ships. In late-nineteenth-century American culture, these places were largely male preserves and, along with the local courthouse, established masculine reputations though such activities as storytelling, drinking, and gambling.

The reports of Booth sightings appearing between 1867 and the end of the century carried this treatment forward. According to the best tally of assassination experts, there were actually fewer than a dozen such incidents, but their grassroots origins and their publication in major newspapers suggest that the legend enjoyed a long and continuous life in American subculture.[20] First were reports of Booth sightings in faraway lands. One such narrative appeared in the "Notes from the People" section of the *New York Times* in early 1867, and was repeated in greater detail in the *Louisville Journal* around the same time. The narrator wrote that he was staying in a Calcutta hotel the year before, where he had overheard two gentlemen talking about Lincoln's assassination. The first, "apparently a man of more than ordinary intelligence and of decidedly strong southern proclivities," turned out to be Captain Martin Tolbert, former commander of the notorious blockade-runner *Shenandoah* and presently captain of the merchantman *Bird of the Ocean.* Tolbert defended the conspirators against the verbal depredations of his companion, a Bostonian, who asserted that any man who called himself an American and sympathized with Booth deserved the assassin's fate. "The same fate!" exclaimed the southerner. He then told the Bostonian he would wager £500 that he could prove, within the space of six months, that Booth was alive and well. The northerner accepted the wager, and the men proceeded to a magistrate, where they formalized the terms and deposited securities. The two then embarked on a journey on the *Bird of the Ocean.* The captain brought them to Booth, who was living on the island of Ceylon (Sri Lanka), and the northerner paid the wager.[21]

In 1875, the *St. Louis Republican,* a Democratic paper, ran a story of Booth's sojourn in the Far East. Again, the narrative of his survival was transmitted orally: the newspaper's informant heard the story from a Confederate veteran named Carroll Jackson Donelson. After the war, Donelson had shipped out as first mate on a merchantman bound for Shanghai. In the South Seas, he led a watering party ashore the deserted Pelew Islands, where, much to his surprise, they came across an encampment of five men and a woman. This first to approach him was Booth, whom Donelson recognized immediately because they had been on intimate terms years before in Montgomery, Alabama. After Donelson promised not to reveal Booth's location for one year, the assassin related his adventure. After fleeing the United States, he made his way to China and served under an assumed identity with adventurer Frederick Ward in suppressing the Tai Ping rebels. Booth's valor came to the attention of the Chinese emperor, who bestowed honors on the fugitive southerner. Later, while living in the expatriate community, Booth performed *Richard III* in an amateur theatrical production. This was his undoing, as his mastery of the stage brought the Anglo-American audience to its feet. Amid cries of "Booth! Booth!" he fled the stage. His cover blown, the grateful Ward lent him a lorca (a hybrid sailing vessel combining a Western keel with bamboo sails), and Booth sailed for the South Seas.

In 1898, on the eve of the Spanish-American War, the *Chicago Times* printed rumors that Booth had again been spotted in exile, this time in Brazil. This prompted a Beloit, Wisconsin, resident, Mrs. J. M. Crist, to relate her saga of meeting Booth and *Alabama* captain Raphael Semmes aboard her husband's sailing vessel in late 1865.

They had put in at Havana and taken the two men aboard. Booth appeared drawn and tired, and Mrs. Crist gave up her cabin to provide him with a place of rest. In appreciation for her sacrifice, he gave her a locket, which she treasured.[22]

More stories of foreign journeys surfaced after the turn of the century, largely through the efforts of legend believers like Finis L. Bates and Clarence Wilson, who collected eyewitness accounts to support their own legend narratives. These included the statement of Dr. H. W. Gay of Mississippi, who recollected the visit of a Klansman chased out of Arkansas around 1869 by Powell Clayton's militia. The fugitive told him that Booth was alive and had fled to Mexico. There, Booth had enlisted in the forces of the Emperor Maximilian, and when the French puppet's fortunes took a turn for the worse, Booth escaped the squads of Benito Suarez by disguising himself as an itinerant priest.[23] Wilson related a story he had heard as a child from Samuel Colonna, a wheelwright in the Union part of Delaware, who told of meeting Booth a year or so after Lincoln's death. A federal veteran, Colonna had turned to the sea, like Donelson, when the war ended. On boarding a steamer bound for Mexico, he looked up on deck and spotted a man at the railing surveying the boarding passengers. He was obviously of superior intelligence, Colonna noted, and extremely handsome. His bearing and elocution marked him as a man apart. The two became friends and traveled the interior of Mexico together, where they took on overseer positions in a mining operation. Soon Booth's natural leadership became evident among the workers and the mine's owners. When Colonna decided to return to the States, he asked Booth to come with him, but the fugitive wistfully declined.[24]

In addition to picturing Booth as the exceptional and often womanless individual, these tales of exile often mirrored actual locations of the Confederate exodus. Many of the places where Booth was "seen," including Mexico, Brazil, and the Far East, were destinations for Confederate leaders escaping federal punishment and disaffected southerners who preferred exile to life in the slaveless states. Missouri cavalry commander Jo Shelby led his brigade across the Rio Grande into Mexico in July 1865, and then on to Mexico City. The most ambitious effort to found a Confederate "New Virginia" was Matthew Fontaine Maury's short-lived colonization scheme in Mexico under Maximilian. The experiment ended in failure when forces under the liberal Benito Suarez wrested control from the French intruder.[25] The factors that encouraged white southern emigration included the chaotic situation throughout much of the South in the months following defeat, rampant inflation, and the inducements of Central and South American governments, including free land, religious freedom, tax incentives, and relocation subsidies. In Brazil, the continuation of slavery also proved attractive to former slaveholders.[26] Although the total number who actually left the southern states remained relatively small, emigration societies actively promoted the various settlement schemes until the organizations were disbanded by federal authorities. Exile, or even the idea of exile, served tormented white southerners as a psychological salve in the decade following defeat, and imagining Booth in similar locations probably increased the therapeutic effect.[27]

Booth was also spotted closer to home. The domestic tales of survival bring to the fore the southern legend's defining characteristics of form — its orality and a retrospective quality. Many, if not most, of these tales came out years after they supposedly happened, often surfacing when legend promoters jogged the memories of old white southerners. The preponderance of oral transmission may also have reflected the censorship of the postwar period, when federal oversight of southern written opinion discouraged the kind of extreme vituperation southern editors were known to practice. This may explain why the few accounts that did appear in print adopted the journalistic device of secondhand reporting. No paper asserted Booth's whereabouts directly. Instead, stories were relayed second and even third hand, thus relieving editors of potential charges that they were directly advocating Booth's escape and the failure of federal arms. This oral tradition included the work of Booth impersonators, persons who pretended to be the fugitive or were assumed by others to be him. Unlike their earlier northern counterparts, the southern look-alikes faced no threats and appear to have relished the notoriety their misidentification brought. T. H. Alexander, columnist for the *Nashville Tennessean* in the 1930s, catalogued five cases of impersonation in the postwar South, including that of David George. While he shared in the skepticism regarding Booth's true fate, Alexander believed the impersonation phenomenon reflected the social and cultural conditions of the postwar South rather than any reality of escape. The impostors were for the most part "wandering fellows" stirred up by war and, with little prodding, local communities made them notorious. In a country deprived of romance and starved by the war's stern realities, Alexander explained, people imagined whatever relieved their boredom: "Doubtless there were hundreds of men suspected of being John Wilkes Booth all over the South in the sixties — mysterious wanderers who were fleeing from justice or from having taken the unpopular side of the war in their home environments."[28]

In Richmond, in the 1880s, people suspected that the Reverend James G. Armstrong, a Presbyterian divine, was Booth. The more romantic of his female parishioners reportedly titillated in the pews when he ascended to the pulpit. His high forehead and jet black hair, which he combed back to hide a scar on the back of his neck, mirrored the assassin's exceptional features. Armstrong was also a devotee of the theater, and quite fond of Shakespearean tragedy. And he walked with a limp, suggesting the leg wound suffered by the actor as he leapt from the president's box at Ford's Theater. The minister apparently did little to discourage the rumors. One anecdote recounted his testimony at an ecclesiastical trial. When asked point blank whether he was Booth, he replied, "I am on trial as James Armstrong, not as John Wilkes Booth."[29]

In the 1930s, elderly residents in Houston County, Tennessee, recalled a mysterious stranger who appeared in their midst two years after the war. He carried the name John W. Burks, and showed up on the 4,000-acre Brigham farm in April 1867. A "tall, distinguished stranger, a striking brunette with dark hair and very dark eyes," he was taken in by the farm's young matron, twenty-seven-year-old Georgia Brigham, who afforded him the typical open-handed hospitality of the Old South. She soon fell in love with him. Burks was noteworthy for his clothes, which were remarkable for the time and place. He owned several Prince Albert suits, a velvet suit, a red velvet vest, and more silk stovepipe hats than had ever been seen in that part of the country. For social events, he sported black velvet and a white jeans suit. At dances he always carried two revolvers, but was never provoked as he "was regarded with awe as a desperate man." During his four-year stay, Burks labored occasionally on the farm, but would not take wages. He never lacked for money, though, and once loaned $400 in gold coin — a very high sum in the impoverished South — to a Brigham relation. At times he drank, and once, while in his cups, admitted his true identity. High-spirited and gay most of the time, he occasionally fell into moods of despondency. It was during one such time that Burks confided to Georgia's maiden aunt his desire to marry the young lady, "but could not in honor do so as he was appearing under a false name." When he died prematurely from typhoid fever, Georgia was disconsolate. The elderly residents who finally recounted the story seventy years later waited until Georgia's passing to relate their tale to the outside world, "and they kept faith by their silence with the woman who wept over his grave on a gentle day in April of 1871."[30]

Similar to David George's biographical elaboration, these collective memories described the impersonators as physically exceptional, financially independent, and honorable men. They exhibited premodern personalities — given to mood swings, independent of the marketplace, and bound in their conduct by the code of the southern gentleman. Oral performance was again key. J. C. Burrus of Benoit, Mississippi, remembered the visitors to his father's plantation in Bolivar County some time after the war. The house was known as a rendezvous for couriers traveling to and from the Confederate Trans-Mississippi. It was also the headquarters for cavalry units including, according to Burrus, scouts for Henderson and Evon. One day, Burrus recalled, two men arrived on horseback, one younger than the other, both traveling under the name Marr: "The younger man would sit for hours and without saying anything, apparently in a deep, brooding mood, and then maybe for a time, would be one of the most entertaining men I ever listened to." He eventually moved on, crossing the river alone into Arkansas.[31] Traildriver Levi Thrailkill also related his encounter with the fugitive in the late 1860s, when he hired him as a muledriver on a wagon train bound for Utah. It was soon apparent the new hire had no inkling of how to harness a mule team, but he made up for this deficiency by entertaining the crew in camp with recitations from Shakespeare and the poets.[32] In 1925, Texas attorney C. L. Bass related his encounter with Booth in 1887, in Birmingham, Alabama. The fugitive was then working as a barkeep at the Ruby Saloon, on the corner of First Avenue and Nineteenth Street. In the years since encountering him there, Bass recounted, "I had repeatedly told friends of the unusual character that had tended bar, merely to illustrate that occasionally we find extraordinary men in lowly places." One afternoon, in the midst of financial hard times, the incognito fugitive and about twenty other men, "broken down real estate agents who had floundered through the big real estate boom of that period," congregated in a saloon adjacent to the Ruby for beer and the free lunch. Someone convinced the barkeep to recite, and after slight prodding he consented. He "stood forth, not as a dowdy bartender, but a genius in common clothes. In an instant he was transformed and his body, voice, and whole being vibrated with the intense emotion of a great actor, and he began those beautiful lines entitled 'I have taken my last drink, boys; I have taken my last drink'":[33]

> This is my last token of esteem!
> This the final of a fruitless dream.
> Then drink once more from the spirit glass!
> For this the ending! No more! No more!
> The tides are here and we must sever —
> Again to mingle greetings never!
> No more — 'tis the last drink together!
> We go, we go — we know not whither —
> Drifting! Drifting down fate's river.
>
> No more we'll meet in reckless pleasure!
> No more we'll tread to revel's measure!
> So here! Our soul more sadly pressed.
> One more drink — to lend the spirit rest.
> Yet drink no draft to parting pain;
> That parting meet with merry 'frain,
> For here our social tares shall wither
> To drift as lightened blosed of hether,
> As we go! We go — we know not whither —
> Drifting! Drifting down fate's river.[34]

This is how Booth appeared to those who saw him. Not a particularly political figure, nor given to avenging his honor, but a man who stood out from the crowd by virtue of his oratorical abilities and his presence. He was a lone figure, who either had no familial attachments or, if he did, had deserted them. He was companionless in the midst of male camaraderie, a person avoiding emotional ties out of fear they would compromise his safety. These were, however, recollections of who John Wilkes Booth was imagined to be, not contemporaneous observations. This view of the fugitive dated from the early decades of the twentieth century, and any sense we may make from it must take this chronological bifurcation into account. What did the image of a man from the Old South mean in the context of the New South? What were these people recollecting? The answer hinges on the character of Booth as a personality from the old school. At the same time he remained a symbol of white southern unreconstructedness, he served as a human relic of an imagined past, and as an echo of the war's effect on southern manhood.

The recollective, oral character of the stories presents another kind of challenge. In at least one case, cultural entrepreneurs concocted an oral tradition based on an earlier, written narrative. In north central Texas, a story centering around the town of Granbury holds that residents in Reconstruction-era Hood County suspected that a saloonkeeper, John St. Helen, was the fugitive Booth. Beginning in the 1920s, affidavits and personal recollections surfaced, in which the saloonkeeper was remembered as an eloquent, elusive, and honorable gentleman who hid his past. This story continues to the present: in the early 1990s, a theatrical production at the local playhouse was based on the legend. In fairness to the present-day inhabitants of Granbury, who also claim that the real Jesse James lies buried in their town, many approach the story with lighthearted skepticism. Borrowing lines from the play, Granbury's local historian asks: "What is history? It's just gossip, . . . We all tell the story the way we heard it. None of us were present when it happened — we're repeating what's been handed down to us."[35]

Despite a concerted effort to locate the Granbury story's origins, no evidence of an oral tradition earlier than the 1920s has surfaced. All accounts lead back to the published legend narrative of Finis L. Bates, whose exploits are the subject of the next chapter. First published in 1907, his story had as its central proposition the common identity of Booth, St. Helen, and David George, and Bates's friendship with St. Helen/Booth in the early 1870s in Granbury. There were prior instances of Booth sightings in Texas, as an article in the *San Antonio Express* from 1890 makes clear, but no mention of Granbury or of John St. Helen. The only evidence that St. Helen and Bates ever coexisted in the same town occurs in the brief and separate mention each received in an 1895 county history.[36] What evidently happened is that once Bates's version of events took hold across the Southwest, local residents began obliging interested outsiders with their recollections of the mysterious saloonkeeper. Not all confirmed his fugitive identity, but several did. This process was encouraged by the mummy's travels through Texas in 1928, when legend believer J. N. Wilkerson accompanied carnival showman Bill Evans and collected testimony from local residents. A reversal unique to literate societies ensued, in which oral tradition flowed from the prompting of written narrative and popular entertainment. This process culminated when the St. Helen legend made its way into the records of the WPA oral history project, where it assumed the authenticity of folklore despite its ersatz beginnings.[37]

The fabrication of the Granbury oral history is probably an extreme case, although one other tradition, centered in Burillville, Rhode Island, may also have resulted from the work of a legend author who seeded the oral oyster bed. Izola Forrester's 1937 account claimed she was Booth's granddaughter through a secret marriage with Izola Mills d'Arcy in 1859. Two Rhode Island genealogists have established a lineage, in name at least, between the putative bride and other members of the Burrillville community. They have also collected the recollections of old-time residents, who "remember" the story of Booth's marriage and his wife's solitary exile in their town.[38] Unraveling the Burrillville claim is even harder to do than getting to the bottom of the Granbury story, although the name "Izola" suggests that this northern expression of the southern legend may owe something to the immigration through the eighteenth and nineteenth centuries of Portuguese and Spanish seafarers to New England towns.

The Burrillville story also points out another interpretive problem of the southern legend: geographic provenance. This problem can be seen as far back as the non-legend "Our Brutus." As Thomas Turner notes, the poem's authorship has been traditionally assigned to Texas Judge A. W. Tyrrell, who supposedly wrote it shortly after the assassination. However, a copy found in the papers of judge advocate John A. Bingham (who prosecuted the Lincoln conspirators before the military tribunal) indicates that a Judge Arrington of Chicago may have penned the lines. The poem was later set to music by E. B. Armand and published in New Orleans around 1868. The cover of the sheet music version attributes the text to Brick Pomeroy's *LaCrosse (Wisconsin) Democrat,* one of the best-known northern opposition papers during the war (Figure 12).[39] Geographic provenance cannot be the determining factor in determining the legend's "southern" version. Northern cultural entrepreneurs produced much of the Lost

Figure 12.
E. B. Armand, "Our Brutus," sheet music, New Orleans,
circa 1868. (Sheet music cover 1271, Cage 430, Butler Collection,
Washington State University Libraries.)

Cause's iconography, from lithographs shortly after the war to the ubiquitous bronze statues of rebel infantrymen placed in town squares near century's end.[40] What made the texts "southern" was a combination of consistent narrative elements, a retrospective quality, and a reliance on oral testimony.

Near the end of the nineteenth century, retrospective accounts of a different kind surfaced, as northern veterans and persons associated with the assassination offered their memories of events. Markedly different from the southern narratives, these recollections renewed the questions over the details of the assassination and the assassin's capture. Assassination expert Steven Miller has carefully researched one instance of how oral accounts often gained credence through publication in newspapers, leading to the production of further oral testimony, as was the case of the Enid mummy. Miller's example is the famous (among legend devotees) Mrs. J. M. Crist/Wilson Kenzie episode of 1898. It began with the tale of a man named Ritter, who claimed to have helped Booth escape to Brazil, where they married sisters and established families. Ritter returned to the States following the death of his wife, but Booth stayed on, living under the alias "Enos" or "Unos." This tale garnered the attention of several Midwestern papers, and it appeared in the *Chicago Sunday Chronicle* in April 1898. The story was read by two residents of Euclid Street, in Beloit, Wisconsin, who proceeded to offer their own versions of Booth's escape. The first, as told by Mrs. J. M. Crist, was related previously. The second, Wilson Kenzie's retrospective eyewitness account of the events at the Garrett farmstead, alleged that the body in no way resembled Booth's: it had red hair and a ruddy complexion. Kenzie had been one of the Union soldiers detailed to accompany Lafayette Baker's detectives. When he and fellow trooper Joe Zizgen told the commanding officer of their doubts, they were told to shut up. Both men claimed to have known the actor while stationed with the Union occupation forces in New Orleans.[41]

Kenzie's account continues to fire the imagination of legend believers. It is a quintessentially northern account in its focus on the details of the capture and the allegation of a government cover-up perpetrated by Baker's minions. The point of interest for our purposes lies in how Crist and Kenzie coproduced their separate versions.

According to Crist's granddaughter, the stories first surfaced in the course of a neighborhood seance, with both Crist and Kenzie present, when the topic of Booth's escape came up. Mrs. Crist offered her story of Booth's escape and, to the amazement of her neighbors, Kenzie immediately seconded it.[42] In doing so, they produced a living instance of reunion literature, in which northern and southern versions of the legend began to merge.

5

FINIS L. BATES AND THE
"CORRECTION OF HISTORY"

———————•◦•◦•———————

*To officially find that it was a matter of no importance . . . whether Booth
still lived . . . when proof was offered to this end was to officially find that John
Wilkes Booth should go at large as far as these officials were concerned.*
(Finis L. Bates)

We now return to events in Enid, where the local story ebbed in February 1903, after viewing of the George/Booth corpse ceased and news
began to dwindle. The community's attention moved to other matters,
including local political disputes. The arrival of spring weather, with
the Fair God's caressing breezes and gentle rain, also meant that Enid's
hinterland residents turned their attention to agricultural pursuits.
There were a few, isolated notices relating to the corpse in the local
papers, including the revelation in April that the body was still above
ground. About the same time, the earlier-mentioned photograph of
George/Booth appeared in an embalming fluid manufacturer's full-
page ad. In the main, however, the story dropped from sight, and local
tradition has it that Penniman moved the body to the carriage house
of his home on West Cherokee Street.[1]

My earlier account, however, omitted a significant piece of the traditional story, as those familiar with it have undoubtedly noted. For
both critics and the faithful, the arrival on the scene of Tennessee attorney Finis L. Bates stands as the crystallizing event in the modern
legend's formation. His *Escape and Suicide of John Wilkes Booth* (1907),
published four years after his visit to Enid, related his sojourn there
and authenticated the George body as that of Lincoln's assassin. A
combination of personal narrative and historical exposé, *Escape and
Suicide* borrowed from both northern and southern traditions in constructing its proof. Despite its ludicrous moments, Bates's account

has served as a bible for modern legend believers, who believe he substantiated the rumors of Booth's escape by providing documentary "evidence" and a detailed and plausible account of events. The book reportedly sold over 70,000 copies, making it the legend's all-time bestseller.[2] There is little question his story displaced other versions of the legend, in part because of its ties to the mummy; and it has endured as the legend's dominant modern rendition, despite the withering attacks of critics. NBC's *Unsolved Mysteries* featured the work in September 1991, and Bates's "proof" became central to the claim by Maryland educator Nate Orlowek that the body buried in Booth's Baltimore gravesite might not be his. While the Tennessee attorney's historical inaccuracies undermined Orlowek's legal challenge in Baltimore's Circuit Court, the exposure the work received in the national media assured its place in the legend canon.

This combination of enduring popularity and controverted history has made Bates the bane of legend critics. Other accounts, notably popular writer Izola Forrester's claim to be Booth's granddaughter, are just as far-fetched, but have come in for much less censure.[3] The difference lies in the former's application of historical discourse to support controversial political conclusions. Forrester's account was romantic and, while vaguely revisionist in its portrayal of motive, did little to upset the mainstream commemoration of either the war or Abraham Lincoln. Bates, however, revived the ancient allegations of Union government conspiracy and grafted them onto the romance of the southern legend. He tied this historical account firmly to the Enid mummy and thus prolonged the sensation, as one student of the legend noted fifty years ago, by providing the body with a background.[4] It is the issue of history, and Bates's claim to correct it, that explains the furor his version provoked.

Over the years, debunkers have devoted considerable time and energy to proving his version wrong. Journalist William Shepherd spent two years collecting the testimony of Oklahoma residents, viewing the mummy, and interviewing Bates himself shortly before the latter's death in 1923. Shepherd found Bates to be both sincere and sane: "I listened enthralled as he spun me his yarn, in soft southern dialect, of those days." As for the legend, the veteran journalist considered it the most absorbing story in his twenty years of reporting, and "no mild rumor. It has penetrated the office of Harper's Magazine, as well as others, many times during the past twenty years."[5] Nonetheless,

Shepherd found the evidence flimsy and the handwriting comparisons used to substantiate the George-as-Booth equation unconvincing. North Carolina journalist David Rankin Barbee, no slouch when it came to conjuring up theories of Lincoln's assassination, spent years collecting evidence to disprove Bates's thesis. Barbee even conjectured at one point that Bates himself was Sanford Conover, the government informant who falsely testified following the assassination on Confederate involvement in the plot.[6] *Dearborn Independent* editor Fred L. Black published a series of articles in 1925 researched at the behest of Henry Ford several years earlier. Bates, who by then owned the mummy, offered to sell it to the auto magnate for $1,000. That Ford considered buying it is in itself an interesting fact, given his other cultural exploits of the period, including the anti-Semitic broadsides published in the *Independent* and Ford's re-creation of small-town America at Greenfield Village. He instructed his editor to spare no expense in establishing the artifact's legitimacy, and Black traveled to Oklahoma and Texas, where he conducted interviews with still-living participants. Their retrospective accounts discredited Bates's version of what transpired in Enid, and Black was able to prove that the attorney had resorted to forging a sworn affidavit in order to make his case.[7] More recently, historian James O. Hall, coauthor of *Come Retribution* and guiding spirit of the Surratt Society, wrote that he conducted extensive research on the topic in the 1960s and 1970s: "My files are huge," he said. "Out of all this, I concluded that David E. George could not be John Wilkes Booth."[8]

Bates's omission from my earlier chapter has nothing to do with the suspect nature of his evidence. On the contrary, his narrative provides a wealth of insight into the legend's development in early twentieth-century America. The omission stems from what was, I believe, a crucial misrepresentation on his part: that he arrived in Enid the third week of January 1903, at the same time Penniman ended public viewing, and that while there he contributed to the body's identification. There is little evidence to support this claim. The *Enid Daily Wave,* in fact, reported that the party from Memphis, Tennessee, had failed to materialize. Even if Bates came and went secretly, as his narrative asserts, the only evidence placing him on the scene at the time is a sworn affidavit and the retrospective accounts of Penniman and Ryan. He played no discernible part in the mummy's initial construction, although his desire to locate himself as close as possible to the mummy's origin is understandable in light of his subsequent actions: it helped him establish his prior claim to the body. Ironically, Bates's detractors have maintained this fiction, in spite of their detailed unpacking of his lies, probably because placing him at the source of the mischief served the useful purpose of providing a single-source scapegoat, thereby simplifying the explanation of how the Enid mummy came to be.

The more likely scenario — based on published sources — is that Bates first learned of George's suicide and the suicide's alleged identity as Booth in the January 18, 1903, edition of the *Memphis Commercial Appeal*. That he next communicated with someone (probably Penniman) in Enid stands confirmed by the subsequent notices in the *Wave* that he never appeared. Sources show that Bates had been attempting to prove that Booth escaped since the late 1890s, and in 1898 he had written the War Department offering proof that the assassin was still alive. George's suicide, as others have pointed out, was a fortuitous event for Bates, assuming he could connect the deceased drifter to his own favorite candidate, Texas saloonkeeper John St. Helen. Regardless of whether he went to Enid in January or not, the Tennessee attorney spent the next several months making his case. He collected sworn affidavits from Booth's nephew Junius Brutus Booth and actor Joseph Jefferson testifying to the likeness of a tintype of St. Helen and Booth. In April, he was interviewed by the *Commercial Appeal*'s city editor, accompanied by David Rankin Barbee (the paper's young telegraph editor), who later confided to another assassination devotee that he knew Bates personally: "The first story written about the Enid suicide being Booth he gave to *The Memphis Commercial Appeal* in 1904 [*sic*]; and at that time I pronounced it a fake."[9]

While Bates's January sojourn in Enid is questionable, there is no doubt he visited the town several months later; yet he avoided any mention of this later visit in his narrative (for reasons shortly to be made clear). One clue confirming the later trip comes from his own account of the alleged January visit, in which he mentioned the delays in reaching Enid owing to washouts on the railroad lines. But there were no washouts reported in January, and the only notable weather event for that month was a snowstorm that blew down from the Dakotas. There were, however, washouts at the end of May, and the Oklahoma Territory suffered torrential downpours. Enid endured a soggy Memorial Day weekend and experienced some flooding. Railroad traffic was "completely demoralized," and the *Wave* warned its readers of dangerous travel conditions owing to mushy ties and miles of track under water.[10]

According to the newspapers, Bates arrived on Friday, May 29, posing as George/Booth's "confidential lawyer" and as the Booth family's legal representative. He produced evidence in the form of a tintype portrait, the sworn statements mentioned above, and correspondence with the government — the same information presented in his book four years later. At the time, the documents' apparent authenticity coupled with Bates's squirely mien convinced many that his claims were true. Particularly effective was a letter from John Simonton, a War Department employee, in which Simonton claimed the government lacked conclusive proof that Booth had been killed. Here was the confirming proof sought earlier: "The Evidence Appears to Be Conclusive Beyond Doubt," announced the *Enid Eagle*. The *Wave* pronounced the case solved: "Mr. Bates has a number of pictures, and papers which goes [*sic*] to show that David E. George was none other than J. Wilkes Booth."[11] Bates gained custody of the body, and Penniman prepared it for shipment back east to the Booth family, or so it was reported. But not everyone was taken in. *Die Post,* under an item headed "Der Booth-Schwindel," noted the attorney's arrival and predicted that the body was headed for a museum and display at the St. Louis World Exposition. And the *Garfield County Democrat* soon ran an item headed "The Fraud of Penniman and Company Exposed."[12] The funeral parlor operator had opted (despite his later professions of ethical concern) to accept an offer for the sale of the body. Penniman's retrospective account indicates that it was at this point that the body was taken from its seated sanctuary in the casket room and laid out to receive further chemical injections. This was done, Penniman himself admits, in order to preserve it permanently, a sure sign of his and Bates's intentions. Unfortunately, the addition of two ounces of 40 percent formaldehyde to the solution had unwanted consequences. The lifelike result of the earlier work was botched: "The toxic effect of this treatment hastened dessication and within a few weeks the skin had the drawn and tanned look of an old mummy." So culminated the mummy's physical construction.[13]

Developments to this point show Bates acting the role of an enterprising showman. His efforts, however, did not stop at securing the body. What follows complicates the view of him as solely a huckster intent on profiting from the sensation. He gave interviews and issued press dispatches for dissemination to the larger regional dailies. This inaugurated a new round of newsmaking that again rippled outward from Enid to the larger world. After providing a brief account to the papers, he reserved the Opera House and announced his plan to deliver a lecture on the "life and death of John Wilkes Booth" on June 2 and 3.[14] During this time Enid kept its head above the flood waters, celebrating a soggy Memorial Day on Saturday, May 30. Bates's arrival was timed as part of his carefully planned program. He intended his historical presentation to be interpreted in the context of the Civil War's major rite of remembrance.

Enid's celebration followed the late-century norm in mixing solemn ceremonies of remembrance with festive activities. In a sense, Bates's mixing of carnivalesque enterprise and serious historical discourse only mimicked the mixing of activities acceptable in mainstream culture. The orientation of the celebration was northern, with the day of observance May 30 and the Grand Army of the Republic (GAR) presiding. The mayor's proclamation honored "the defenders of our nation's unity and glory." In the morning, the GAR and the Ladies' Circle marshaled at the Masonic Hall, where they were joined by a fife and drum corps and Company K of the territorial National Guard. Once formed, the parade proceeded to the cemetery, where relatives and the ladies' auxiliary decorated the graves of the fallen veterans. The venue then shifted to the Opera House, where speeches and patriotic music followed the reading of the Gettysburg Address. The ceremonies were firmly reconciliationist in tone, in keeping with the tenor of the times. The graves of Enid's two deceased Confederates were decorated along with those of the Union dead. And the *Eagle* reported that soldiers in gray paraded along with those in blue. Afternoon races at the Enid Driving Park competed for the attention of the more somber observances. The races featured a $1,000 purse for trotters and pacers. Planned as well were "exciting automobile races" and a motorcycle duel. The railroads offered excursion rates on all lines into Enid to promote the event. Unfortunately, the weather discouraged visitors, and the motormen refused to race owing to the condition of the track.[15]

Bates scheduled his lecture to coincide with the southern date for celebrating Memorial Day, June 3, which also happened to be the birthday of Jefferson Davis. The gist of his talk was reported by the local papers and corresponded substantially with the version presented in his book four years later.[16]

The tale began in 1872, when young Bates encountered John St. Helen while Bates was practicing law in Granbury, Texas. The two met in the course of a legal matter, when St. Helen refused to enter a courtroom to plead a minor offense. The young lawyer pondered the man's action and concluded that "his restless and uneasy manner was due to the long outdoor life on the plains, and that by force of habit he had acquired that restless and hunted, worried expression." His dark eyes spoke of desperation and a capacity for crime. But Bates was also struck by the noble bearing of his interlocutor, his easy, graceful attitude ("as if so by nature born"), and the eloquence of his parting words on their first meeting, "dramatically acted in eloquence by word, motion of the body, jesticulation [sic] of the hand and utterance of the voice, not before or since equalled by any other person" of Bates's acquaintance. St. Helen appeared unsuited for the life he led, a log-cabin merchant on the frontier. Bates wondered, "Who can this handsome man, this violent man, this soft-mannered man, this eloquent man, be?"[17] Despite their difference in age, the two became fast friends. St. Helen fascinated the younger man with his oratorical abilities, gentlemanly bearing, and apparent disregard for pecuniary gain. He regaled him with soliloquies from Shakespeare and the poets. Tennyson's *Locksley Hall* was his favorite recitation, but he could offer more hackneyed verse when the occasion demanded:

> Come not when I am dead
> To shed thy tears around my head.
> Let the wind sweep and the plover cry,
> But thou, oh, fool man, go by.[18]

On what he thought was his deathbed, St. Helen revealed to Bates his true name and instructed him to take a tintype portrait from under his pillow "for my future identification" (Figure 13).[19] With help from St. Helen's Mexican servant, Bates administered a vigorous brandy rubdown to restore the dying man's vitality. Miraculously, St Helen/ Booth recovered, and after convalescing several weeks revealed the details of Lincoln's assassination to his companion. Andrew Johnson goaded the actor into killing Lincoln, he said. They were co-conspirators in a plot to kidnap the president, but following Lee's surrender, they grew desperate. Kidnapping was no longer a possibility, as the

Figure 13.
Finis L. Bates's tintype of John St. Helen/John Wilkes Booth.
(E. H. Swaim Collection, Georgetown University Library,
Special Collections Division, Washington, D.C.)

Confederates had evacuated Richmond. Meeting at Johnson's hotel on Good Friday morning, they weighed their options. Booth was willing to accept defeat, but Johnson said to him angrily, "Will you falter at this supreme moment?" As Bates related the story, St. Helen/Booth then told him:

> "I could not understand his meaning, and stood silent, when with pale face, fixed eyes and quivering lips, Mr. Johnson asked of me:
> "'Are you too faint-hearted to kill him?'
> "As God is my judge, this was the first suggestion of the dastardly deed of the taking of the life of President Lincoln, and came as a shock to me."[20]

Johnson guaranteed Booth's safety by arranging for General Grant's absence from the presidential party that night at Ford's Theater. Fired by thoughts of patriotism and hoping to serve the southern cause, Booth agreed to carry out the murder. He bore no grudge against Lincoln, "for I had none against him as an individual," and saw his action in purely political terms. It would be the means of elevating Johnson, "a southern man," to the presidency, and Johnson had promised he would protect white southerners from oppression and the confiscation of their land. Lincoln's emancipation of the slaves had violated the constitutional property rights of the "southern people," and there was nothing to keep him from violating the Constitution further. Johnson convinced Booth that Lincoln would in the end confiscate the real estate of white southerners for redistribution to the freed slaves.[21]

St. Helen/Booth accepted this argument; its "reasoning at the time seemed unselfish and logical, and I agreed with him that the supreme moment for the displacement of President Lincoln had arrived."[22] But he had since lived with deep regret. He acknowledged to Bates his desire to find a confidant to whom he could confess his misdeed. Only God and the criminal knew the punishment of not being able to "unfold his mind to the ear which will listen with pity." He wearied of his solitary burden:

> "Yes, I walk in the companionship of crime, sleep within the folds of sin and dream the dreams of the damned and awake to go forth by all men accused as well as self-condemned. Ah, aweary, aweary! Shall I say that I would that I were dead? Yes, that I could on the

wings of the wind, by a starless and moonless night, be gone in flight to the land of perpetual silence, where I could forget and be forgotten, and whisper to my weary soul, 'Peace, be still.'"[23]

The unfortunate man added that he would gladly give his own life if Lincoln could regain his.

At the time, Bates said, he rejected his companion's story as the demented fancy of an otherwise charming and proper southern gentleman, and the two continued in their friendship for several more years. In the late 1870s, they went their separate ways. St. Helen/Booth drifted further west, and Bates returned to his home state of Mississippi. Twenty years passed. Then one day Bates, now a successful land title attorney in Memphis, Tennessee, found a recent edition of the Sunday *Boston Globe* inexplicably placed on his reception hall table. It contained the reminiscences of David Dana, the brother of publisher Charles Dana (founder of the *New York Sun*) and a Civil War veteran. In the spring of 1865, Dana related, he served with the third brigade of Harden's division, under the Twenty-Second Corps commanded by General C. C. Augur. They were assigned patrol duty in southeastern Maryland, and Lieutenant Dana commanded detachments guarding the river crossings into Washington. In early April he learned of a plot forming against the government and requested a battalion of regular cavalry to reinforce his military police patrols. His soldiers were ordered to ascertain the name and business of any person wishing to cross into the city during daylight hours. During the night, no passage at all would be allowed. On Friday midmorning, April 14, two men appeared on a road leading into the city, and Dana's guards placed them under arrest when they refused to identify themselves or their business. After an hour or so, they gave their names as Booth and Herold, but remained under guard. Later in the afternoon, unexpectedly and against Dana's recommendation, General Augur ordered all prisoners released and the pickets on the roads withdrawn. When Dana heard of the shooting at Ford's Theater late that evening, one of his guards, who knew Booth, confirmed that the assassin had ridden out some time earlier. Dana reported this to Augur, and found the general standing at his desk in tears. "'My God, marshal,' he cried, upon seeing me, 'if I had listened to your advice this terrible thing never would have happened.'"[24]

Bates recognized the similarities between Dana's account and what

St. Helen had told him decades earlier. St. Helen had admitted being stopped with Herold on the morning of the assassination as the two returned from reconnoitering their escape route in southern Maryland. He also corroborated Dana's information on his passage across the Navy Yard Bridge, where the password "T. B. Road," which Johnson had given him, satisfied the guard on duty. Subjecting Dana's recollections to a legal parsing, Bates concluded that St. Helen's twin epic of conspiracy and escape was in fact true. Augur's actions could only be explained in the light of Johnson's conspiracy, since he acted against Dana's advice to keep the pickets out in the face of confirmed plots against the president's life. The general's expression of grief was a "self-accusation," acknowledgment of Augur's foreknowledge of the plot and his role in abetting it by withdrawing the guards. Accepting Dana's story as true, then, the inevitable conclusion, "applying the legal rule, the standard by which we measure the words of men — if true in one thing, true in all, or false in one thing, false in all," led Bates to accept St. Helen's tale of escape in toto.[25]

The crux of the escape story centered on the identity of the body in the barn. Mainstream accounts held that following a twelve-day chase, Booth and Herold were surrounded by a detachment of the Sixteenth New York Cavalry in Garrett's tobacco barn. Disobeying orders to take the assassin alive, Sergeant Boston Corbett — a self-emasculated religious zealot — shot Booth through a gap in the barn's plank siding. But St. Helen/Booth told Bates that he wasn't in the barn at the time, and the person Corbett fired on must have been a swarthy field hand named Robey or Ruddy. This man had accompanied Booth and Herold earlier in the day, but in the afternoon Booth sent him back to retrieve some personal effects fallen from the actor's pockets when they crossed the Rappahannock. By the time the man returned, Booth had left at the urging of Mosby's cavalry scouts, and was heading west toward Fredericksburg. The field hand remained in the barn overnight with Herold and was trapped in the clutches of the federal force. It was on the basis of the personal effects found in the dead man's pockets, including Booth's diary and a bank draft, that the authorities declared that it was the assassin whom they had captured and killed.[26]

Convinced now that St. Helen had told him the truth, Bates tried to find his old comrade. Acquaintances from Granbury informed him that St. Helen had been in Leadville, Colorado, in 1879, and that he later drifted on to Fresno, California. Bates wrote the War Department asking if they were interested in confirming evidence that Booth was still alive. Officials responded with indifference. A few months later, however, Bates received the "voluntary statement" of a War Department employee (Simonton) who had seen Bates's letter to his superiors and who suggested to Bates that the government lacked proof establishing Booth's demise and burial. Again, application of the legal rule led Bates to the conclusion, based on the truth of the employee's voluntary statement, that the government had something to hide. War Department officials were guilty as accessories after the fact in Lincoln's death, since they failed to pursue the assassin even when faced with the evidence of his survival.[27]

Five years passed. Then came the news from Enid. Instructions found in George's pocket identified Bates as his confidential attorney. Penniman telegraphed the attorney on the morning of January 17, and the Tennessean left for Enid that afternoon. Owing to "many washouts over the Frisco System," it took Bates several days to reach his destination. He was met at the depot by the clerk from the hotel where George had ended his life. Bates said the clerk told him "that my coming was awaited with great anxiety by a large and much-excited throng of people from widely located sections of the country." There was a contingent of federal veterans in town, "who, it had been whispered about, intended to take the body into the streets and burn it, if it should be identified as that of John Wilkes Booth." An estimated fifty thousand people had viewed the body, and the crowd had grown so that Penniman was forced to close the morgue, "as it seemed the place would be actually picked to pieces by the souvenir hunters."[28] Bates assumed the disguise of a furniture house drummer and met Penniman secretly at the morgue. Together, they entered the room where the body lay:

> You ask what did I say? I don't know. Mr. Pennaman [sic] says I exclaimed, "My God! St. Helen, is it possible?" Then my manhood softened into sentiment and soul into tears. Spread the veil of charity upon the deeds of the dead, that mantle of death cast in the loom of sorrow and woven in the warp and woof of sighs and tears. Shaken with emotion for my dead friend, I had no thought of the crime that this man had committed while his body lay at rest, seeming to sleep in pleasant repose.[29]

Out came the tintype Bates had safeguarded these many years and confirmation from Penniman and his assistant that the body on the slab matched St. Helen's picture exactly. Together they examined the marks on the body — the disjointed right thumb, the scar above the eye, the slight nick in the right fibula — which, Bates asserted, identified it as the assassin's. Thus was established the connection between John St. Helen, David George, and John Wilkes Booth. Bates concluded his sentimental appreciation with a rhapsodic evocation of the dead man's physique. His neck rose from his chest and shoulders "as beautifully as the most beautifully formed women's, masculine it is true, but with that beautiful symmetry of form." It was the embalmer Ryan who pointed out this feature to him; Ryan had abstained from making the usual incision above the breastbone because he considered it "a formation of art too beautiful to destroy, even in a dead body."[30]

This, in outline, is the twentieth century's version of the Booth legend. Whether Bates presented the entire story at his talk at the Opera House in Enid is not clear. From the perspective of hindsight, it appears that Bates pasted his evidence together from bits and pieces he found in the *Wave* and Enid's other newspapers along with his own story of John St. Helen. The handwriting comparison, the deathbed confession, the scars on the body, St. Helen/Booth's sentimental regrets, even the allegations of official involvement — all were authored by Mrs. Harper and Isenberg's *Wave* in the period immediately following George's suicide. Bates's contribution was not so much the way in which he gathered these pieces into a semicoherent, albeit logically suspect, narrative, but the story he told with them. He fused the northern and southern versions of the legend, creating a peculiar brand of reunion literature, vouchsafed for by his book's dedication to the "Armies and Navies of the late Civil War, fought between the States of North America."

St. Helen/George/Booth remained the southern gentleman who acted on principle and a slight to his honor. He resembled the southern portrayals, where an honorable, if misguided, Booth was led to commit his crime through the machinations of a northern-affiliated man in power. In Bates's account, St. Helen/Booth's masculinity stood in marked contrast to the unmanly comportment of Johnson, who spoke with a pale face and quivering lips. St. Helen's oratorical abilities, his mastery of men in social situations, and his apparent disregard for money coincide with the descriptions of the exiled Booth contained in the southern narratives. By linking Booth to St. Helen, and St. Helen to George, Bates extended the southern story into the twentieth century. The setting in *Escape and Suicide,* like many of the scenes in the earlier accounts, was homosocial and transient. Unlike the reunion literature described by Nina Silber, with its portrayal of sentimental domesticity, this was not a domestic account, despite its effusive and gaudy sentimentality.[31] At the same time Bates painted Lincoln's assassin with the brush of the honorable vindicator, St. Helen's character stands as a memory to a world of male camaraderie located in boardinghouses, saloons, theaters, and public speaking platforms. Thus he repeats the double figure already present in Enid's own construction of the mummy, wherein George/Booth stood as an icon for white southern "unreconstructedness" as well as a reminder of the passing world of the imagined frontier.

St. Helen also, however, with his regret for his deed, stood for the northern memory of events, or at least an accommodation for the memory of northern trauma. Booth's survival put him in a limbo state, a kind of personal annihilation that was his necessary torment for killing Lincoln. His psychological nightmare was the distant echo of the mass trauma that erupted in the wake of Lincoln's murder; his suicide, the final price for killing the best man who ever lived. This northern memory also included the Radicals' suspicion of Andrew Johnson; the misbegotten president now assumed the full burden of the suspicions cast upon him in 1867. But Bates did not fully work out the political formula he inherited from Ben Butler. For Bates's purposes, Johnson acted correctly even if he failed in the measure of manhood; in fact, it is unclear why Bates decided to accuse the president most white southerners came to appreciate for his leniency toward them. Johnson became esteemed in the South for the very attributes Radicals despised him for. His defense of southern rights and betrayal of Reconstruction's political program became, retrospectively, the honorable reasons for which Booth acted.

The tale's two sides presented a southern rendition of events, but one in which the southern protagonist engages in a final act of atonement, despite the honor of his cause. It confounded the earlier distinction between northerners' seeing Booth's act as nonpolitical, and hence heinous, and the original southern celebration of it as eminently political and hence justified. In Bates's telling, the assassination was justified and yet remained sinful. By venerating Lincoln even as he defended the principles upon which he acted, St. Helen/George/Booth symbolized the white southern plea for forgiveness — on its terms.

But there was more bite to the tale Bates told his Enid audience, and this leads to the reason why he assiduously avoided any mention of the trip in his later book. Listeners objected to his interpretation, and he was warned not to repeat the talk, as scheduled, the next night. It was probably the federal veterans who objected most strenuously, and Bates heeded their threats. He canceled his second lecture and boarded the southbound train Wednesday evening — but not before delivering a parting shot, as described in the *Wave*: "this Booth identification was nothing to him any further than his employment by the Booth people, hence, the matter is closed between he [sic] and Enid and that in all probability he would never be called upon to return here again. The corps [sic] will be shiped [sic] out in a few days."[32]

Judging from the press commentary that followed, Bates, in giving his talk, risked grave repercussions. Uncharacteristically quiet, the Democratic *Wave* lay low, stating only its belief in the truth of the Booth claim, but demurring in supporting the lawyer's revisionism. It had not, its editorial voice reported, had the time to investigate matters thoroughly. The *Eagle* and the *Democrat* were forthright in condemning the affair, and even the *Kansas City Journal* (clipped by the local papers) weighed in. The notorious Booth fake was the product of an "immoral curiosity" without place in civilized society: "No state should permit the exploitation of such a rank speculation. A regicide is a national criminal." Bates, in his attempts to profit from the crime, was more sordid and cowardly than the actual perpetrator. In fact, taking Bates at his word, if he was George's attorney and harbored his crime, "he is *particeps criminis* with the murderer of Mr. Lincoln." He was an accessory after the fact and punishable as such. Perhaps if Bates were questioned more closely, "he might retract his story and tell how he happened to tell it, or divulge more facts that would throw further light on this interesting transaction. In either event the truth of history would not be a sufferer."[33] These were the same accusations Bates leveled against federal officials in his book.

None of the editorial commentary, however, impugned the south-ernness of his interpretation. Combined with the veterans' previous objections — at the time Mrs. Harper made her initial revelation — it seems likely that what rankled most were the insinuations of government involvement in the plot to kill its own president. Despite the partisan political content they regularly displayed, the papers on this occasion limited their commentary to the moral and legal aspects of Bates's involvement. The *Democrat* sounded a firmly reconciliation-ist note in affirming that old soldiers on either side could feel nothing but unmeasured contempt for the connivers of the ghoulish scheme. The war was over, and the "tattered remnant" of the most heroic army ever defeated "had succumbed to the inevitable[,] and the great heart of Lincoln was about to respond to [the] needs of the desolated and ruined south when this foolish fanatic, like a coward, sent his great soul into eternity and thus brought untold calamities on the southern people."[34]

For all his preparation, Bates seriously misread his public, perhaps due to the mummy's prior reception. His timing and delivery suggest he intended to present a reunion narrative, in which Andrew Johnson stood as the man everyone could agree to hate. The much-maligned seventeenth president would become the vehicle for uniting the southern and northern memories of Booth's act, by allowing the actor-assassin to retain his virtue and yet venerate the man he killed. Bates's allegations of Johnson's murderous treason, however, went too far. Even more galling were the insinuations that federal officers cooperated in the plot to kill their own commander-in-chief. Not only were these charges grossly ludicrous, they directly implicated the loyalty of the Union veterans by casting aspersions on their former commanders.

Why did Bates construct the legend the way he did, and was his provocation of the audience intentional? There is a poetic answer that accords well with Bates's own poetic sensibilities. It begins with the parallel figuration of St. Helen/George's masculinity and white beauty. Even when facing the corpse of a rather ordinary elderly white male, Bates reverted to the language of racial beauty found in the southern narratives and Townsend's postassassination biography. The characterization of St. Helen's physical beauty was repeated else-where in the written narrative, and Bates remarked upon the fugitive's beautiful black hair and high white forehead.[35] He also recalled the sentimental, poetic appreciation of death familiar in antebellum times. This lingering over the corpse and the evocation of racial beauty suggest that at the same time George/Booth stood for the memory of the war, Bates carried this memory further back to the evocation of the body from before the war. In this way George/Booth (for Bates, St.Helen/George/Booth) evoked the remembrance of a racial identity, as had the antebellum mummies. Joined to the allegations of treason among high officials, the appeal to ancient whiteness became the basis of a conspiracy theory implicating the government in the destruction of white racial destiny.

What Bates concocted, intentionally or not, was a major shift in the legend's meaning as memory. His synthesis of northern and southern strands allowed for the appearance of a "new" memory — one focused on the betrayal of government against its "own" people, resulting in the subsequent distortion of all history. The northern memory of the assassination had always incorporated a belief that the Confederate government or northern secret societies had had a hand in Lincoln's death. (In fact, the belief in a grand conspiracy involving the Confederate government stands as the dominant interpretation among current assassination experts.) Bates modernized this component by shifting agency to the national government at a time when a new nationalism and the beginning of positive federal government were significant forces. Concurrently, industrialization and the rise of the immigrant metropolis had begun to threaten the place of native-born white Protestants. Bates's effort to "correct history" thereby entailed one of the first instances of modern American conspiracy thinking, with its belief that the nation's government was at the center of a massive plot against its own people. His attempt to pass this vision off in Enid fell flat because the time was not yet ripe. He had to contend with the local boosters and the ardent nationalism of the Spanish-American War. The United States' assumption of world-power status as a result of this conflict, and the war's role in reestablishing the valor and loyalty of white southerners, added to the prevailing sentiment of adoration for the nation-state. Conspiracy theories existed galore, but they were directed against the usual cast of characters — the Catholic Church, the world Jewish conspiracy, Wall Street financiers, and secret organizations.[36] Bates's attempt to implicate the nation's government ran against the current; for this he was violently censured.

Bates's second major contribution to the legend was in detailing it. He was the first believer to carefully amass the detailed "evidence" from veterans' accounts, newspaper articles, affidavits from participants or persons who had known Booth, and artifacts such as the tintype. His collected evidence, along with the mummy, would comprise the legend's chief archive over the course of the twentieth century and would give rise to a community of legend believers who mined (and continue to mine) his papers to support their claims. For this reason Bates stands as a unique type of cultural entrepreneur in that he moved the legend from its informal, grassroots, and oral sources to a documentary footing. Even though much of his evidence is obviously contrived, it was the production of his archive, I believe, that brought him into conflict with subsequent generations of legend critics. By establishing his evidence in written form and by adopting the methods of documentary proof, Bates violated the separation between popular belief and historical discourse.

⤜⤛

As was the case following Booth's capture, the seriousness attending Bates's historical revisionism gave way shortly thereafter to farce. The *Wave* finally played its hand in August when it announced that Booth's body was to be exhibited at the St. Louis World's Fair alongside the other Oklahoma exhibits. The body would be encased in a large glass jar and would be fully dressed and seated in a chair. "A pair of fresh and beautiful jet black eyes will be provided for Booth from which an automobile wire will extend through the cork of the jar . . . to a point where a button will be placed." After an introduction, the master of ceremonies for the Oklahoma Building would hit the switch and make one of the body's eyes wink.[37] Earlier, the *Garfield County Democrat* featured an "Oklahoma Fish Story" in which the correspondent related his encounter with all three presidential assassins — Booth, Guiteau, and Czolgosz — on the banks of the Canadian River. After a round of good whiskey provided by the pop-eyed journalist — "the kind of stuff that the state of Kansas prohibits to be manufactured" — each assassin related his tale of escape. All had made it past their executioners through unwitting substitutes — in Czolgosz's case an automaton was led to the electric chair. The correspondent concluded on a populist note:

We are living now in an age of progress, when queer things are done when men become millionaires by a twist of a financial screwdriver that can't be seen, and the public wonders at such financial legerdemain, and why not a tincture of jugglery in our criminal matters? It was not but a generation or two ago, but what such men as Frank James and Cole Younger would have beaten upon the wheel, beheaded or hanged, but, instead of that, we see that they are posing before the public as showmen and are doing some good for themselves as well as others.[38]

THE LEGEND IN THE ERA OF
LINCOLN'S COMMEMORATION

———————•◦❯❮◦•———————

*History does not always tell us everything. Nature and
memory are more explicit and faithful. The record in lineaments
is sometimes more truthful than in documents.*
(Izola Forrester)

The Booth legend underwent a hiatus following the World's Fair caper
and the appearance of Bates's written account. Belief in the likelihood
of Booth's escape undoubtedly persisted, but the record of popular
print indicates that the story — or, at any rate, publication of the story
— faded after 1903. Other than a brief flurry when Bates's *Escape and
Suicide of John Wilkes Booth* was first published, printed versions of the
legend did not reappear until after the Great War. Likewise the body,
after the fanfare of the Enid finale, faded from view. Local legend has
it that Penniman ensconced George's remains in the barn of his residence on West Cherokee Street.[1] At some point Bates gained possession of the body and transported it back to Memphis, where "Booth"
inhabited a pine box in the attorney's garage.

When the legend and its physical artifact reemerged after the war,
they did so in new guises and new contexts. To begin with, there was
a shift from production to performance: less effort was devoted to
constructing new versions of the tale than to presenting the existing
story to a regional and national audience. The synthesis of southern
and northern variants that Bates had crafted, combined with the sensation of the mummy, provided the interwar period's dominant narrative. With one notable exception — Izola Forrester's *This One Mad
Act* (1937) — follow-on accounts adapted themselves to Bates's ren-

dition. Actress Blanche DeBar Booth, the daughter of John Wilkes's elder brother Junius, made the Sunday editions in 1925 with the story of her near encounter with her uncle while playing in Enid at the turn of the century. The following year, Tennessean McCager Payne claimed he was Booth's stepson through the marriage of his mother, Louisa, to the fugitive in Winchester, Tennessee, in 1872. When George committed suicide, Payne's uncle, who resided in neighboring El Reno, informed the family of what had happened, and the family corresponded with El Reno's mayor regarding the deceased man's estate. In Payne's account, Bates was accompanied to Enid by his sister, Ida, the daughter of John Wilkes and Louisa.[2] Likewise, the retrospective accounts of the southern older generation reasserted the themes and escape plotlines that had surfaced earlier.

What was new about the legend during this period was its increasing exposure to a national audience. Granted, the Enid story achieved national recognition through the dissemination of the press. In the 1920s and '30s, however, the story reached a national audience directly, through mass circulation periodicals including *Harper's Magazine,* the *Saturday Evening Post,* and *Life.* The legend also was part of the popular literary renaissance centered on the assassin and his act, and the period saw the publication of a dozen or so books on the assassin, including several accounts addressing the matter of his survival.[3] Nonetheless, at the same time it reached a national audience, the legend also became marginalized. It is this apparent contradiction — between its greater exposure on the one hand, and its relegation to the cultural margins on the other — that suggests the story's greatest significance during this time. The marginalization entailed a two-step process. Booth's escape lost the bulk of its original political significance — that is, it ceased to serve as a symbol for white southern intransigence and northern political dissidence. At the same time, the legend became the subject of a cultural commentary by believers and debunkers that served to place it outside the cultural mainstream. The legend and its believers came to be seen as representing a set of attitudes increasingly out of place in modern industrial America.

This shift was in large part a reflection of the larger swing in the commemorative economy of the Civil War and its martyr president. Booth's commemoration had always been tied to that of his victim, but the period between the world wars saw significant change on two fronts. First, the level of commemorative activity — whether in ink or stone — was unprecedented. Second, as the Civil War generation faded from the scene, the spirit of reunion between white North and South helped elevate Abraham Lincoln to the status of national deity. In the process, Booth's image suffered, especially in the attribution of meaningful political motives to his act. William Hanchett believes the public reaction to him split between adoration and hatred, with the assassin viewed either as tragic hero in the mold of Brutus, or as a sociopath, whose action lacked all meaning.[4] Booth's treatment in the early decades of the twentieth century would therefore appear to be a return to the immediate postassassination period, with one signal difference. The assassin's utility as an icon for white southern intransigence, and for white racism in general, became unnecessary with mainstream America's shift toward a revisionist interpretation of Lincoln as a racial conservative. With the legend no longer required to fill this symbolic need, both critics and believers began investing it with other content. For legend debunkers, the story became a vehicle, like the Scopes Monkey Trial of the same era, for a modernist critique of provincial America. Shorn of its former ideological intentions, opponents found in the story the workings of superstition, small-town morality, hucksterism, and the gullibility of the masses. For believers, the earthly shell of David George continued to embody the distrust of government first voiced in Bates's account. Even further, by disproving the mainstream version of Lincoln's assassination, the body provided an explanation for conservative America's disillusion with the shape of the American present. It served as an icon for history gone wrong, for a thwarting of destiny that some Americans believed had occurred with Lincoln's untimely death.

This shift, from regional tale to national sensation, and from a dissident political viewpoint to one reflecting the views of an increasingly marginalized cultural group, was itself part of the larger collision between regionalism and the new urban nationalism of post–World War I America. The legend's existence during this time was one example (albeit peculiar) of a broader movement that included the Southern Agrarians, pioneer festivals, the collection of Americana, the preservation of folklore (especially under the auspices of the Depression-era WPA), and the regionalist school in the arts.[5] This upsurge in the celebration of local pasts grew out of different motivations. In some cases it was inclusive, with the country's multiple heritages used to promote social cohesion and so forge a stronger sense of national identity. In other cases, it was exclusive, in that assertions of regionalism resisted the centralizing pull of nationalism and attempted to preserve a way of life, an identity, and a vision of the past and present seemingly at odds with the drift of mainstream American culture. The best-known intellectual expression of exclusive regionalism was John Crowe Ransom's essay in the Southern Agrarian manifesto *I'll Take My Stand* (1930). Ransom's defense of the southern way of life contrasted the imagined organic society of the past to the belligerent gospels of Progress and Service that defined modern American society. In his view, the antebellum South never embraced the principle that material production was the sole measure of an individual's worth or of cultural progress. Work was part of a whole that included leisure and sociability. The "arts" of the prewar South were "the eighteenth-century arts of dress, conversation, manners, the table, the hunt, politics, oratory, the pulpit."[6] The decisive victory of the North in the Civil War naturally impaired much of this southern tradition. Nevertheless, Ransom believed that the South in its poverty continued to maintain an alternate vision of human purpose. Now, in the early decades of the twentieth century, the hour of crisis had come, as the promoters of the New South had successfully injected the region with the industrialist plague. Whether the South could resist or not remained an unanswered question; but if it did resist, the preservation of an alternate to "malignant industrialism" would take place away from the urban centers, in rural areas and small towns. Ransom concluded by reaffirming Jeffersonian principles: the South's problem, in essence, was "the farmer's problem, and this problem is simply the most acute version of that general agrarian problem which inspires the despair of many thoughtful Americans today."[7]

Ransom voiced a specific kind of exclusive regionalism, one tied to the memory of an organic, hierarchical society in which manners and sociability mattered. The figure of Booth in the legend as a kind of premarket personality imbued with the arts of etiquette and oral persuasion suggests the connection between the legend and this precise intellectual explication. The legend served as the guttural cultural equivalent to what Ransom had written. In fact, its counterhistorical assertions went further than Ransom could go, in suggesting that the present ("malignant industrialism") stood as a kind of mistruth because Booth — in his eloquence, bearing, and natural aristocracy —

had survived. This was part of the explanation his body provided. Ransom also raised twentieth-century regionalism's central problem: the joining of the South's opposition to commercial-industrial America with a broader agrarian discontent in America. This linkage would hamper regionalism's influence as a counternarrative to modernism as it became associated with the racist viewpoints that usually accompanied the "Southern point of view." In the case of the legend a similar linkage, provided by the northern and southern versions of the tale, already existed. During this period, however, the legend no longer served its original ideological purposes; it worked primarily to express a broader discontent, supplying a regionalist counternarrative in its depiction of Booth as a premodern personality, endowed with the graces of a gentleman of the Old South. The display of George's remains also served as a tangible link to the past, or rather to the deceit of the past, and in doing so helped viewers explain their uneasiness with the present. Nor was the legend's impact restricted to rural areas, as Ransom's analysis suggested. Displeasure with the shape of the American present was shared by Americans from all walks of life, including some who occupied positions of power in the modern industrial order.

In order to get at this story, to understand how the legend of Booth's escape simultaneously reached its popular apogee while expressing an exclusive regionalism, this chapter begins by detailing the mummy's travels and then examines how the transformations in Lincoln's image during this period affected that of his murderer. It concludes by considering Izola Forrester's book *This One Mad Act* to demonstrate how the legend commemorated a romantic and noncommercial world where manners and oral performance still mattered.

After keeping the body of David George privately for a decade, Finis Bates began exhibiting it on his own and by renting it out to carnival entrepreneurs. According to the report of one legend informant, Bates toured through Texas in late 1920 with Wortham's Carnival.[8] It was in Texas that Bill Evans, known as the Carnival King of the Southwest, spotted the body at the Waco Cotton Palace. He struck a deal with Bates and rented "Booth" for $1,000 per twenty weeks, posting a $40,000 bond for the mummy's safe return.[9] The Carnival King ran a railroad sideshow across the Southwest that featured freak animals. He hoped the mummy would headline his attractions, but it did not fare well alongside five-legged horses. The showman concluded that "Booth" required more dignified surroundings in order to succeed. Unfortunately, his fortunes took a turn for the worse when a train wreck killed most of his live exhibits, and shortly afterward the mummy was stolen. Evans advertised a reward for weeks in the pages of *Billboard Magazine* and managed to recover the valuable cadaver after paying the thief a ransom of $500. He returned "Booth" to Bates and canceled the bond. In the meantime (the exact chronology remains unclear) Bates also tried to sell the curiosity to Henry Ford for $1,000. Legend critics have assumed that Bates's motivation in wanting to sell the mummy sprang from his despair at ever making good on the government reward money, a sizable sum that Bates considered due him because he possessed the corpse of the real assassin.

Another factor influencing Bates to sell his treasure was an article that was to be published in *Harper's Magazine*. William Shepherd of *Harper's* wrote to Bates in August 1922, requesting that he remove the body from exhibition as a condition of publication, lest *Harper's* be perceived as promoting a commercial venture. Shepherd wrote, in part, "You have been using the mummified body of John St. Helen for the purposes of drawing out, from those who may possibly know the real facts, all information regarding the matter." The magazine article "will multiply the desired publicity of the fact by ten thousand, and its articles will be copied and commented on editorially by hundreds of newspapers and magazines and spoken of by hundreds of thousands of citizens." The only rub was the continued exhibition of the mummy, which had to cease. Shepherd offered that *Harper's* could lease the body and then entrust it back to Bates's care, with the understanding that it would be retired permanently from exhibition. His concluding lines to Bates succinctly expressed the legend's cultural position during this period:

> We bear in mind that there is sufficient interest in your contention to justify us in giving great publicity to what you believe; and I presume that the whole matter now has resolved itself into the question whether you desire that publicity in almost the entire press of the United States through "Harper's", or whether you desire to secure questionable publicity by exhibiting the body as a sideshow in the Coney Island[s] of the United States.[10]

Bates's attempt to sell the mummy to Ford may have been intended to satisfy *Harper's* editors, but it also had a logic of its own. The Tennessee attorney probably knew of Ford's growing passion for Americana, the arts and artifacts of the American past. News of the interest of powerful collectors of the period would have trickled down through the ranks of dealers to the owners of curiosities, who would then swamp the collectors and their agents with offers. As noted earlier, Ford was interested enough (and uncertain enough) about the historical possibilities that he detailed his attorney and editor, Fred L. Black, to establish the artifact's authenticity. Black's careful disassembly of the Enid story dissuaded the auto magnate from considering the purchase further. Black's account also established Bates as the hoax's preeminent fabricator, largely on the basis of Penniman's retrospective testimony.[11] The connection between Bates and Ford went deeper than a mere potential business transaction, however, for at the same time Bates began exhibiting the body, Ford was contemplating his own culture project, a major museum of Americana that eventually became the Henry Ford Museum and Greenfield Village. Though Ford's project was primarily devoted to preserving America's industrial past, as Michael Kammen notes, it also expressed Ford's ambivalent stance toward the pace of social change and the structure of the American present. When it opened in 1933, the museum featured an eclectic mass of "democratic" objects, the remnants of ordinary lives rather than the products of high culture, reflecting its patron's anti-intellectualist streak as well as his nostalgia for small-town, Protestant America.[12] Together with Ford's other cultural adventure of the period, the anti-Semitic broadsides published at his direction in the *Dearborn Independent,* his passing interest in the mummy provides a first indication of its significance during this period. The Chicago Lincoln expert Otto Eisenschiml related in a letter to David Rankin Barbee that at the same time he was considering purchasing the mummy, Ford received an offer of proof that Jewish bankers had a direct role in Lincoln's death: "this was mincemeat for Ford, who was then at the height of his anti-Jewish campaign. I have not seen the evidence, but Black described it to me as ridiculous."[13] Ford's involvement forces us to recognize that the legend's significance during this time was not overwhelmingly "southern." Like the colonial-era structures uprooted from their foundations and trundled to Greenfield Village, the mummy served to commemorate a point of history, a point that assumed a special place in the present. No less than Ford's eclectic collections, the carnival exhibit of Booth's purported remains provided a counterpoint to the modernist world "outside." Ford's re-creation of small-town America was meant to evoke a place of com-munal harmony and racial-cultural homogeneity. The mummy, through its opposition to the dominant Civil War narrative, provided an outlet for the disenchantment that sometimes gripped even the most successful native-born Americans as they contemplated the changing social landscape.

Following Bates's death in November 1923, Evans purchased the body from his widow and hit the circuit once more in the hopes of cashing in on his prize attraction. He shifted his theater of operations to California, and it was at this time he constructed the carnival ex-hibit shown in Figure 1. Evans also gained a portion of the mass of "evidence" — the sworn affidavits and eyewitness accounts Bates had collected over the years, as well as portraits of the assassination's main personalities. Success again proved elusive, and sometime in the late 1920s he folded his tents and moved the whole show to Declo, in south central Idaho. Evans may have found the West Coast crowd too so-phisticated for the historical trumpery the mummy presented, but his move to an agricultural crossroads on the northern fringe of the Mormon desert did not mean he was giving up on the business.[14] The showman was searching for an audience, and like all skilled impre-sarios he understood that audiences have different personalities, reflect regional characteristics, and, depending on these character-istics, favor certain kinds of entertainment. Surrounded by the natural wonders of the region and close to the Oregon Trail, Declo was situated at a major intersection leading north from Salt Lake City and westward to Oregon. The Trail's upcoming centennial celebration, planned for 1930, may have convinced the Carnival King that the site had good tourist potential. He bought a small potato farm and estab-lished a roadside attraction, complete with an old Pullman car, at the town's main intersection.[15] From a showman of an earlier era, for whom the railroad served as the conduit into the American heartland, Evans grasped the transition to motorcar tourism that debuted in the 1920s. The Pullman served as a cafe, a dance hall, and a display room for his prize exhibit. He hired a young local girl to tend the mummy, and stretched an advertising banner across the main street that read,

"See the Man Who Shot Lincoln." Intrigued by the activities of this curious interloper, the town's residents wrote to officials in Washington, D.C., requesting information on Booth's demise. According to their retrospective accounts, they received only qualified answers in response, and so the mystery survived.[16] Travelers on their way to the Oregon Trail's sites in southern Idaho encountered this historical anomaly, one that did not easily mesh with the Trail's honorific celebration of pioneer fortitude. Notwithstanding his obvious pecuniary motives, Evans's roadside attraction, positioned like many others along the route to a major commemorative site, offered up an alternate narrative that distracted from the dominant theme. Outside the Pullman car, by the roadside, a calliope played endless tunes to catch the attention of passing motorists, and Evans offered $1,000 to anyone who could prove that the body was *not* that of Lincoln's assassin.

Whether business was good or bad, there is no definite record. In August 1928, a Kansas City legend enthusiast named J. N. Wilkerson passed through Declo on a motorcar trip to California and saw the mummy. He illuminated the Carnival King on the full history of Booth's survival, and the pair struck an agreement to take the show on the road.[17] Armed with Bates's affidavits and Wilkerson's historical knowledge, the two men loaded the mummy in a panel truck and made their way to Salt Lake City. In the Mormon capital, they cleared $200 before being run out of town for teaching "false history." In Texas, business was good until authorities in Big Spring seized the mummy as an unburied corpse. Tried and fined by the local justice of the peace, they moved on to Austin, incorporated themselves as the American Historical Research Society, and had their treasure certified as a mummy by the state's health officer. Their next stop was Odessa, Texas, where a recent oil strike had made everyone prosperous, and the exhibit's collection plate rang with the sound of silver dollars. The pair had finally hit pay dirt when a woman told Wilkerson of a retired judge in Lubbock who had direct information on Booth's life as a fugitive. Unable to resist the pull of history, Wilkerson convinced his partner to pack up and leave prosperity behind. Once in Lubbock, they found the jurist, who told of an encounter he had in 1901 in Guthrie, Oklahoma, with a stranger over breakfast. The stranger regaled him with stories of Booth's life after the assassination. The two became fast friends and spent the entire day together.

Wilkerson believed the judge had encountered Booth himself and decided that he and Evans should continue their inquiry in the towns mentioned by Bates three decades before.[18] Traveling through Hood County, Texas, the pair displayed the mummy and collected testimony. Informants confirmed St. Helen's courteous manners and grace. Old-timers remembered that St. Helen's two saloons in Granbury — the Lady Gay and the Blackhawk — had also been schools of etiquette, where rough-cut rowdies went to learn the ways of high society by observing the elegant bartender. (When the WPA Oral History project reached the area twelve years later, the soil had been well prepared.)

After Texas, Evans and Wilkerson headed back to the Northwest, where an encounter with overzealous local officials in Aberdeen, Washington, convinced Wilkerson he had had enough of carnival life. He parted company with the mummy and its keeper and returned to Kansas City. The summation of his researches, including the testimony collected from Texas residents, he eventually delivered as a lecture before the Lincoln Club in Chicago. In 1931, the Carnival King also made his way to the Windy City, where his promotional efforts garnered the attention of the Chicago Press Club. Members of the club convinced a group of local medical practitioners to conduct an autopsy of the body (Figures 14 and 15). The six doctors subjected George's remains to a thorough analysis, including x-rays, and determined that it did have the markings — arched right eyebrow, deformed thumb, thickened fibula, scar on the back of the neck — that legend adherents believed proved the body was Booth's. They also found the remains of a ring in the abdominal cavity, a signet ring with the initial "B" carved on it. The lead examiner, Dr. Orlando Scott, believed Booth had escaped and that "a substitution of bodies, inadequately identified, was used as a subterfuge to cool the wrath of the North . . . and thus prevent a renewal of hostilities." He also conjectured that because of his sentimental nature Booth may have swallowed the ring in order to protect it during his escape, and it became lodged in his gastrointestinal canal, where it remained for thirty-eight years. He recommended that Booth's assumed remains in a Baltimore cemetery be exhumed, in order to resolve the matter once and for all.[19]

In 1932, a year before he died in a Chicago holdup, Evans sold the mummy for $5,000 to John Harkin, who had worked as a tattooed man with the Wallace-Hagenbeck Circus and was a believer in alternate histories. Harkin and his wife loaded "Johnny" into an exhibition truck and headed for the road. Financial success was as elusive as ever, although they hit it rich in Shawano, Wisconsin, when Indians from the Menominee Reservation visited the exhibit in large numbers. Harkin discovered that some years earlier a white schoolmaster teaching on the reservation had told his pupils that Lincoln's killer was an Indian. When the mummy arrived and the local chief heard of its Caucasian identity, he ordered the entire tribe to attend the show. Ironically, this, the most explicit instance of the body serving as a racial icon involved a role reversal from what took place during the antebellum period, when Euro-Americans gazed upon the remains of Native Americans and ancient Egyptians.[20]

At their stops at towns and fairs of the upper Midwest, "Barney" Harkin acted as the barker and collected admissions, while Mrs. Harkin told Booth's story inside the makeshift exhibit. In order to save money, husband and wife slept in the back of their panel truck, with the mummy on the floor between them. Times were tough, not only on the economically depressed northern plains where they toured, but also for the Harkins personally. His Chicago real-estate properties plummeted in value after blacks moved into the neighborhood and whites fled. A creditor seized the mummy for debt, and Harkin was forced to sell his real estate in order to recover his prize. Then in 1937, the trio hooked up with Jay Gould's Million-Dollar Circus, a family outfit that toured the upper Midwest with a show featuring trained animals and human oddities. Gould found a formula to make the mummy pay, but as *Saturday Evening Post* writer Alva Johnston noted, the time was also ripe for doubting the official version of events. The same year also saw the publication of Otto Eisenschiml's *Why Was Lincoln Murdered?*, a controversial history of the assassination that accused Edwin Stanton of being the mastermind of the president's murder and possibly helping Booth escape. Published the same year, Izola Forrester's *This One Mad Act*, while less rabid in its political implications, also contested the government's version of events and added to the public debate over details of the assassination. The coincidence in time between this literary output and the mummy's successful touring was matched by a geographical convergence. Regardless of its southern echoes, the Booth legend and its material artifact during the interwar years found their center of performance in the western half of the country, and their literary center

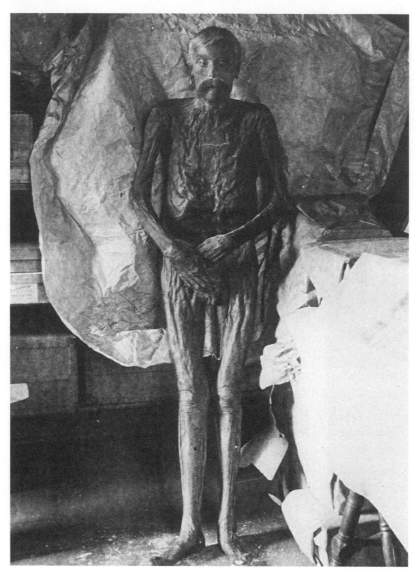

Figure 14.
The George mummy in the early 1930s.
(E. H. Swaim Collection, Georgetown University Library,
Special Collections Division, Washington, D.C.)

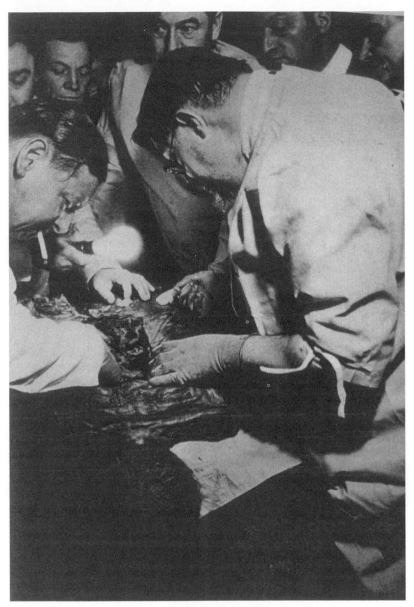

Figure 15.
Chicago medical examiners study the mummy. Pic magazine,
Sept. 2, 1941. (Photo courtesy of Michael Kauffmann.)

in Chicago. Merrill Peterson has noted the preeminence of Chicago in the "Lincoln enterprise" during this period, and it is not surprising that the same should apply for his murderer.[21] Important Lincoln collectors Oliver Barrett, Henry Horner (elected governor of Illinois in 1933), and Alfred Whital Stern all hailed from the Windy City. So too did authors Eisenschiml, Carl Sandburg, and Lloyd Lewis, all of whom became associated with the Chicago Civil War Round Table on its founding in 1940.

This geographical provenance also helps to explain the interwar legend's significance, even for those skeptical of the mummy's alleged past. Sideshows and carnivals remained staple forms of entertainment across America, in both rural and urban settings. In smaller towns and the countryside, they remained what they always had been, traveling enterprises. With the progress of motor transportation following World War I, the smaller exhibitions forsook the railroads and waterways and took to the road, either singly or as part of a caravan. Like their predecessors a century earlier, these shows featured live freaks, extreme performances like snake eating, and museum shows displaying a range of human and natural "curiosities." The Booth mummy had many companions in the sideshows, some of whom were genuine mummies, others wax effigies. Nearly all of these displays belonged to the crime/horror tradition, as by the end of the nineteenth century the venerable Egyptian mummies had largely retreated to the high-culture precincts of university museums and anthropology collections. A traveling history and crime museum photographed near Fayetteville, North Carolina, provides one instance of the genre, and reveals the ramshackle nature of Depression-era traveling entertainment.[22]

The routes Evans and the Harkins traced in their search for paying customers, however, shed the most light on the place of the Booth mummy in this cultural environment. Their efforts to locate an audience never led them southward, or at least not to the Old South east of the Mississippi River. Instinctively or mistakenly, these cultural entrepreneurs located the story of the assassin's escape in the Plains and the Southwest, in those regions hit hard by the ecological and economic disaster of the agricultural depression, and where the tradition of the social bandit remained strongest. The combination of destitution and ingrained iconoclasm provided ready soil for the legend's next iteration. The meaning now attached to Booth's escape was not dissimilar from what had motivated Henry Ford's fleeting interest: it echoed the destitution of the frontier promise as it asserted the betrayal of government leaders. The indictment here went much further than that originally voiced by Bates and his Enid associates, in which government conspiracy was alleged to have let the real murderers escape. Now the charges implied a conspiracy to disrupt the shape of the American present. In this light the drifter's remains could be read in one of two ways: Booth himself thwarted America's destiny in killing Lincoln, and the mummy provided a tangible link to this betrayal; or those who covered up the assassin's true fate also disrupted the shape of America's future by creating a false history. In either case, the cadaver provided an explanation for history gone wrong, for the decay of the frontier myth.

The mummy's travels thus help affirm the legend's transformation over time. From a political counternarrative in the postassassination period to a cultural and political counternarrative of the South in the Gilded Age, the legend now expressed the deep discontent of a group of Americans with the shape of their present-day society. Any interpretation of the legend during this period, however, must reckon with the conjunction between the commemoration of Booth's escape and the commemoration of Abraham Lincoln. The two had always been linked, though the legend's southern and early twentieth-century manifestations showed how independent of the assassination the representation of Booth could become. In contrast, the interwar fascination with Lincoln was paralleled by a fascination with his murderer, and the degree of attention devoted to both parties was unprecedented. In Booth's case, the production of literary works and exposure in popular print has already been noted. When positioned against the backdrop of Lincoln's own commemoration, the shape of the legend in this period becomes much clearer.

As Merrill Peterson points out, Lincoln's apotheosis began the morning of his death, but through the end of the nineteenth century, his appeal as a national icon had its limits. Lincoln remained a "partial hero," without a place in the hearts of a large portion of his countrymen.[23] The white South ignored and despised him, despite the fact that many former Confederates felt he would have softened the blow of Reconstruction. Even in the North, his image lacked consistency.

Union loyalists advanced the dominant and most compelling image — that of the savior and martyr for the Union cause, whose blood, like the thousands of soldiers who passed before him, was shed to preserve God's chosen nation. Alongside this rendering, there emerged the figures of the Great Emancipator, the First American, the Man of the People, and the Self-Made Man, and they did not always strike a consistent note.[24] Among his biographers, a conflict emerged between those dedicated to creating a national demigod, and those who stubbornly fought to retain Lincoln's earthier touches. Lincoln's attitudes toward slavery and the black race also engendered a debate, between former abolitionists who viewed the Emancipation Proclamation as a signal document in the history of moral progress and those who saw it solely as an expedient for winning the war.

By the turn of the century, these disparate renderings had begun to resolve, and by the time of the centennial of his birth in 1909, Lincoln's commemoration had assumed the preeminent place in American collective memory it would hold for the next half century. When the exact apogee of this commemorative effort occurred is hard to gauge, but indications point to the interwar period. Jim Cullen finds the golden age of Lincoln culture to be the 1920s and '30s, as marked by the literary contributions of Carl Sandburg, Albert Beveridge, William Barton, and James Randall.[25] Peterson considers the "tide of reminiscence" to have crested during the centennial, but he finds the years between 1926 and 1933 to be a "manic period for biographies of all kinds," matched by the output of heroic sculpture.[26] If monumental sculptures are taken as the measure of the nation's devotion, then the dedication of the Lincoln Memorial (1922) and the completion of Mount Rushmore (1937) affirm the primacy of the interwar era. More important than fixing the chronological point of apotheosis, however, is grasping its definition. Most apparent was Lincoln's transition from sectional hero to national icon. At the time of his centennial — despite his profile's being placed on the U.S. penny — Lincoln remained a principally northern hero. White southern acceptance, however, as Bates's narrative showed, was growing, and this appreciation was tied to the ongoing reconciliation of white North and South. In the process his image was transformed in one significant way. The Great Emancipator faded from view and was replaced by the image of the Racial Moderate, who would have opposed the radical Republican plans for racial equality had he lived. This image reflected developments in the larger commemoration of the war, where by century's end a reconciliationist and white supremacist vision of the conflict had overwhelmed the remembrance of racial conflict and emancipation. With rare exceptions, the focus of white remembrance elided the history of slavery and contemporary racial conflict. Lincoln's ascent to the pantheon of national memory required that his image be stripped of its former allusions to racial justice.[27]

In this context, the memory of the assassin as a figure of white racial beauty or as an icon for white supremacist politics became secondary. What need was there for it? Booth and his victim moved closer together in their viewpoints toward the black race, and the killer's animosity toward the Emancipator lost its motivation. The classic expression of the reconciliationists' Lincoln was Thomas Dixon Jr.'s *The Clansman* (1905) and its screen adaptation, D. W. Griffith's *Birth of a Nation* (1915). Much has been written about both these works, including Woodrow Wilson's description of the film as "history written with lightning." These works depicted Lincoln as "a friend of the South," whose aim of preserving a white republic unraveled following his assassination by the racial leveling policies of Senator Austin Stoneman (Thaddeus Stevens in disguise). The two men's contrasting attitudes were graphically presented in the book's illustration of a twisted, clubfooted Stoneman saying to the yet living Lincoln, "The South is conquered soil. I mean to blot it from the map."[28] Lincoln had no intention, in Dixon's telling, of allowing the freed slaves to compete politically or socially with the forgiven rebels. His plans, however, were thwarted by Booth's ill-timed act, leading to the Radical takeover and the "horrors" of Reconstruction.

The reconciliationists' Lincoln also coincided with the position of the revisionists, who viewed the war as resulting from the excesses of "ideologues" infesting both sides of the Mason-Dixon Line. Among professional historians, leading revisionists included James G. Randall, whose 1934 address "Has the Lincoln Theme Been Exhausted?" is credited with launching the professional historical study of the sixteenth president. The most influential popular history was Claude G. Bowers's *The Tragic Era* (1929), a partisan and anti-Republican interpretation of Reconstruction that heaped abuse on Stanton and the Radicals.[29]

The revisionist interpretation of the war and its leader achieved its greatest influence in the late 1930s, at the same time Lincoln's commemoration approached its zenith. The amalgamation of the image of Lincoln with the reconciliationist vision of the war and the perennial myth of the Lost Cause yielded a mainstream perspective that facilitated Lincoln's national appeal by eliding the issue of race. In its most extreme popular rendition, this amalgam also gave rise to the idea that the Radical leadership was implicated in its chieftain's murder. Conspiracy theories surrounding the Lincoln assassination, as William Hanchett noted, have always been tied to national political developments. In the beginning, southern leaders bore the onus; later, Andrew Johnson's falling out with Congress led to accusations of his involvement. During the revisionist era, it was the radical Republicans' turn, by virtue of their implacable demands for punishing the South and equal rights for the freed slaves. In its bestselling formulation, Otto Eisenschiml's *Why Was Lincoln Murdered?* (1937), Secretary of War Edwin Stanton stood accused of masterminding his president's murder. In the process of ferreting out the anomalies and inconsistencies that he found surrounding the assassination, the Austrian-born chemist turned historian also suggested that Booth escaped.

Eisenschiml's theory rested on a series of events occurring just before and after the murder. General Ulysses S. Grant and his wife, who had accepted the Lincolns' invitation to the theater that evening, suddenly changed their plans and boarded a train that afternoon for New Jersey. Stanton refused Lincoln's request for his aide, the stalwart Major Thomas Eckert, as an escort. After the murder, all telegraph service out of the city was interrupted, save for the War Department's lines, thus preventing news of the assassination (and of the assassin's identity) of being broadcast at the earliest possible moment. Oddly, the wires were not cut but only the batteries grounded, indicating that "the interruption was a strange coincidence or else that the task was performed by experts who had due regard for the interests of the government."[30] Equally puzzling was that every avenue of escape out of the city was quickly sealed, on Stanton's orders, except for the route Booth was most likely (and did in fact) take. The assassin fled across the navy yard bridge into southeastern Maryland, where he successfully eluded his misdirected pursuers for the next twelve days. The expedition that finally caught up with him at the Garrett farmstead was itself surrounded by a great deal of mystery. Lafayette Baker's intuitive knowledge of Booth's likely whereabouts was a fraud, as he had filched the intelligence from another army commander and invented the story of an "old negro" informant to cover his own tracks. Equally suspicious was the War Department's failure to prosecute those who had sheltered Booth and Herold during their flight. Eisenschiml concluded that it was almost as if "an invisible guardian angel were watching over his [Booth's] every step and shaping fortune in his favor."[31]

Even Booth's supposed end in the Garrett barn begged the question as to why he was not captured alive. Tradition had Boston Corbett firing the fatal shot, but only one person present at the scene ever corroborated his claim. Ballistic evidence indicated the shot was probably fired at close range, from inside the barn, not outside, where Corbett allegedly stood looking through the gaps in the plank siding. Eisenschiml inferred that it was Colonel Everton Conger, one of Baker's men, who shot Booth, and that he did so in order to prevent the assassin from ever revealing the larger plot. Eisenschiml ended his discussion of the capture with a query: "Who was shot at Garrett's farm on the night of April 26, 1865?"[32]

The method of inferring conclusions from a mass of circumstantial evidence links *Why Was Lincoln Murdered?* to a venerable tradition of conspiracy theory — not limited to Lincoln's assassination — and has long been criticized by members of the Lincoln studies community. The more interesting aspect was Eisenschiml's political inclination, which hinged upon the author's unrelenting characterization of Edwin Stanton. From the opening pages, where the secretary's entrance into Lincoln's last cabinet meeting ended "the pleasant flow of informal conversation," the war minister was made to seem a dismal and threatening figure. Stanton, Eisenschiml asserted, attended cabinet meetings only rarely, and when he did come, he always came late:

> It was his way of indicating the superiority he felt over his colleagues, if not over Lincoln himself. Gideon Welles distrusted him intensely, considering him an unscrupulous intriguer. . . . Small of stature, with a long beard that he kept perfumed, the Secretary of War had an air of sterness; but Welles always believed this outward semblance concealed the heart of a coward.[33]

Worse than arrogance, cowardice, or fragrant coiffure, Stanton was the leader of the Radical abolitionist contingent, whom Eisenschiml charged with devising a comprehensive plan early in the war to thwart the commander-in-chief's intentions and override the Constitution. They were moved by the zealotry of their cause as well as a political goal: to assure the continuation in power of the new Republican Party by whatever means. During the war's early stages majority sentiment in the North favored lenient treatment for the rebelling states, if they returned to the fold quickly. They would retain full sovereignty, including the preservation of slavery within their bounds. Under these terms, the Democratic Party would regain power. This outcome, Eisenschiml asserted, was unacceptable to the Radicals, and Stanton worked deliberately to prolong the war in order to turn public opinion against the South. He sabotaged McClellan's preparations, forcing him to launch a campaign before the general was ready, bleeding divisions from the Army of the Potomac, and foredooming the gallant Little Mac to defeat. Similarly, in the West, Stanton employed General Halleck to stay Grant's hand following the repulse of the Confederates on the second day of Shiloh in April 1862. Halleck took over Grant's army and turned what would have been the rapid decimation of Beauregard's tattered forces into a cautious, toothless crawl toward Corinth, Mississippi. Observers at the time noted the change and could make no sense of it. That summer, despite his demonstrated ineptness, Halleck was promoted to general in chief of the Union forces and returned to Washington. According to Eisenschiml, it was the Radical leaders who elevated him, as just reward for his role in prolonging the campaign.[34]

The equation changed, however, following the election in 1864. With his incumbency assured, Lincoln's lukewarm stance toward slavery — despite having signed the Emancipation Proclamation — and his intention of showing mercy toward the defeated rebels alarmed the Radical leaders. The final straw came in late March 1865, when Lincoln advised Grant, as Richmond was about to fall, to "let 'em up easy." This was anathema to Stanton and his party, who expected to exact a full pound of flesh from the defeated rebel states:

> How many desperate meetings took place to devise a means of overcoming what, to the Radicals, was outright treachery? There was no use arguing with Lincoln, who could be as stubborn as a mule. There was no beating him in the game of politics or at the polls. Many a Radical may have hoped that Lincoln might die so that his own political and financial existence could endure; for

short of killing the president there did not seem to be any chance of stopping him.[35]

Kill him they did, although Eisenschiml was careful not to accuse the Radicals directly, but to let his inferences do the talking. In the end, untold bloodshed fell upon the head of the Secretary of War and his minions, for in pursuing their political object, the Radicals sacrificed thousands of lives, northern and southern, and murdered the Union's savior. This was the revisionist message, and Eisenschiml's treatment of it was a direct echo, across two generations, of Civil War copperheadism of the virulent midwestern strain. On the southern side, Stanton's disdain for parliamentary procedure, his willingness to adopt extralegal measures, and his lack of human charity echoed the characterizations of Crozier's Coldheart and Dixon's Stoneman. As Eisenschiml occasionally reminded his readers, truth is stranger than fiction, though his portrayal of Stanton and the Radicals followed closely that of their fictional predecessors. Also of note was a change of role. At the turn of the century, Finis Bates had indicted the War Department for allowing Lincoln's murderers to go free and for complicity in Andrew Johnson's plot to remove the president in order to protect white southern rights. In Bates's version of events, the treason of government facilitated the murderer's escape, but no harm was imputed to America's subsequent history. Although Eisenschiml retained a part in his theory for the hapless Johnson, he reversed the equation. Now government was subverted by those entrusted with its care to protect the plans of a Radical minority who were striving to ensure their own power and their own plans for racial leveling. The white man's kingdom was demolished from within. Historical destiny had been maliciously rearranged, and Eisenschiml also gave voice to the lament of thwarted destiny.

Despite some displeasure at Eisenschiml's rough handling of Stanton, reviewers omitted any mention of his work's ideological implications. Paul Angle, librarian at the Illinois State Historical Society and a major figure in early twentieth-century Lincoln studies, carefully dissected the argument against Stanton but felt the book's greatest contribution was in pointing out the "almost unbelievable inefficiency of the War Department. And for this at least Edwin Stanton was responsible." Another reviewer noted, "Mr. Eisenschiml is just and impartial. He has not tried to write a sensational exposé." And

Paul H. Buck, whose own *Road to Reunion* appeared the same year, considered it a work "so sincere in purpose, so honest in scholarship, and so completely documented that it commands the utmost respect from the most meticulous student of history."[36] Revisionism was in the air, and while readers may have objected to Eisenschiml's premise, they rarely noticed, much less objected to, the underlying political stance.[37] Incredibly, as will be seen in this study's concluding chapter, Eisenschiml's basic thesis remains the dominant Lincoln conspiracy theory and still works to transmit the revisionist interpretation of the Civil War.

Where did Booth and the tale of his escape figure in this revisionist landscape? The simple answer is that neither had important roles to play. Eisenschiml's appeal to the legend was gratuitous, intended only as one more teaser in a line of shocking inferences. Logically, Booth's escape made no sense to the plot, for if Stanton were guilty of the things he was charged with, he would have seen to the erasure of the one character who could have spilled the beans. More to the point, Booth lost a measure of his significance as his victim's image reformed. This does not mean that the older vituperation of Lincoln did not survive. Midwestern poet Edgar Lee Masters's *Lincoln: The Man* (1931) was one example. Masters reviled Lincoln as a centralizing usurper, the founder of monopoly and bureaucracy in America.[38] In the South, Lyon G. Tyler and Millie Rutherford kept to the unreconstructed viewpoint, fighting Lincoln's deification on every front. Tyler raged against the attempts by northern popular historian William Barton and others to tie Lincoln's bloodlines to Virginia's first families. And Rutherford's *Scrapbook* maintained the portrayal of the actor as having acted from honor. But these were increasingly minority viewpoints, as Rutherford discovered in the aftermath of her Historical Commission's report to the Confederate veterans' 1922 reunion. It intoned the Lost Cause credo, stating in part that the "War between the States" had been "deliberately and personally conceived and its inauguration made by Abraham Lincoln, and he was personally responsible for forcing the war upon the South." The veterans greeted the report with cheers, but southern newspapers condemned it. As one editor remarked, it was no longer necessary to vilify Lincoln in order to honor the Confederacy.[39] Lincoln was gaining stature in the white South, in part due to the revisionist view of his racial politics. And the corollary to this was a change in his assassin's repute. With the Radicals held accountable for the woes of Reconstruction, Booth ceased to function as the vindicator of the southern cause. His status as an icon for white supremacy, in this context at least, lost its pungency.

What, then, did Booth stand for? Hanchett's observation — that he was either hated or adored — provides a partial answer. But in view of the mummy's travels, and the political transformation that rendered Booth's significance as an icon for white racist politics secondary if not insignificant, the terms should be modified: he was either patholo-gized or sentimentalized. Some found his act so completely devoid of meaning they could only explain it in terms of mental illness. Others found in him the vestiges of a premarket world, in which orality, so-ciability, and detachment from commercial concerns held sway. In the first case, the depiction of Booth as insane resembled the treat-ment he received in the northern dissident press after the assassina-tion. However, the later version dispensed with the politics of insanity that had helped to drive the original depiction of the actor as mad and vain. What remained, and what became the actor's principal useful-ness during the interwar period, was his image as a personality from a bygone America. Booth became a regionalist icon, but it was a re-gionalism that refused cooperation with the larger national com memorative economy of the period. As monuments to the martyred president were raised, and as biographers, popular writers, and jour-nalists portrayed Lincoln to an eager public, the remains of the Ok-lahoma drifter were hauled around two-bit towns of the troubled agrarian West. This countercommemoration, this funeral procession without terminus, certainly attracted much less attention than did the Lincoln apotheosis, but was representative nonetheless. It satisfied a deeper cultural logic, what popular author Lloyd Lewis described as the oppositional pairing of Booth and Lincoln. In *Myths after Lincoln,* published the same year as Bowers's *Tragic Era* (1929), the Chicago journalist drew from the mythological structures of Frazer's *Golden Bough* to argue that Booth served as Lincoln's nemesis twin in the folk-mythological pantheon. As Lincoln was elevated to immortality, so was his assailant.[40]

This creation of god and antigod was itself the imperative of folk psychology, and it also represented the particular conditions of Ameri-can democratic society. Booth and Lincoln, as immortal figures, were created to fulfill a need. Having forsaken the dying gods of their "mother races," the European colonists in the New World strove in vain for three generations to give birth to a folk-god. The likely candidates — George Washington, Thomas Jefferson, and Andrew Jackson — were all found wanting for one reason or another. The Father of His Country was too austere, and the Sage of Monticello was "too much a creature of the brain, always tampering with intellectual heresy." Andrew Jackson, though heroic, was too eager to shed blood. On the evil side, Americans found temporary solace in the perfidy of Benedict Arnold and Aaron Burr, but their crimes had only amounted to treason, insufficient in itself to classify them as arch-villains. Booth, however, was more promising, despite his paltry life as a ham actor: "he had done one act of demoniac infamy; he had killed America's patron saint, and was, therefore, the Cain, the Judas, for whom the myth-wanting patriots had longed." This explained why, regardless of the evidence amassed by historians and the government, his soul could never be laid to rest. He became the "folk-story Judas" of America, condemned to doing what the traditional betrayers of mythology always did: wander the earth in friendless infamy.[41]

Lewis's mythological explanation, however, served as the peroration to an account that explained Lincoln and Booth's "immortality" as the product of political motives and mass cultural effects. The real logic to the myths after Lincoln (and after Booth) was not the structuralist workings of timeless folk psychology, but a political contest that saw Lincoln's deification serve the needs of his political "enemies." Lewis perceived how modern myths often served political objects, that they comprise what Roland Barthes later described as forms of "depoliticized speech," in which the apparently natural, preordained, or inevitable arrangement of images, words, or concepts works to camouflage ideological content.[42] But Lewis's act of exposure was betrayed by his own revisionist overlay, and it is this revisionism that again forms the basis for understanding what the legend stood for, even in the eyes of one who professed to disbelieve it.

In *Myths after Lincoln,* Stanton and the Radicals suffered the kind of character assassination they had previously been subjected to in the work of Dixon, and would later in the assault of Lewis's Chicago confrère, Eisenschiml.[43] In the journalist's telling, a pervasive mood of goodwill erupted throughout the North at the announcement of Lee's defeat. On the home front, the people, "all at once, had forgiven their Southern brothers for everything, for the years of dole and woe, grief and taxation, which, as they thought, the Secessionists had forced upon them." In this atmosphere of peace and reconciliation there were the occasional Union supporters "who clung to the old grudges, refusing to join in the saturnalia of glee."[44] These "bitter-enders" insisted on punishment for the South and revenge for the horrors of the war. But they stood in the minority, as the mass of the northern public preached "forgive and forget" and the "tender-hearted" Lincoln was the hero of the hour.

Lincoln, said Lewis, had always pursued a double strategy — of de-feating the South, but then of allowing the defeated rebel states back into the Union with the least damage done to them. But he was op-posed in his mercy by the "black-clad Radicals of his own party." This group became furious at the suggestion of leniency toward the South: "In its ranks were fanatical Sadists who wanted to hang the 'rebel' leaders; in its ranks, too, were fanatics of a nobler breed, 'Abolition-ists' who demanded that everything North or South be sacrificed to the great cause of negro citizenship. It was the 'dusky brother,' not the Union, that claimed their warm hearts." Now, with Lincoln's murder, they saw their chance; for them, the assassination was a godsend. As for Stanton, he took charge at Lincoln's deathbed, ready to smash the South again, and ready to assume the power he felt was rightfully his. All along, the "mad incorruptible" Stanton had considered himself the real ruler of the nation, "guiding with his superior brain the weaker, softer will of Lincoln, and now his hour had come." He be-came the nation's dictator and succumbed to the influence of the Radi-cals. A good lieutenant, he was a lousy chief, and the proximity of death made him slightly unhinged.[45]

The problem for the Radicals became one of overcoming Lincoln's moral influence among the northern public, especially regarding his merciful attitude toward the defeated rebels. They therefore imme-diately contested both Lincoln's legacy and the image of the slain president. At the forefront of the effort to impose the Radical vision were the northern Protestant preachers, especially those from the East, who instead of consolation preached revenge from the pulpits on Black Easter. The vicars of Christ's mercy called "more loudly than the Radicals . . . for the doom of the slaveholding South." Their words carried great weight with the northern public owing to the clergy's "dazzling power," a power they would lose in the decades leading up to Lewis's own time "as the cities grew, enabling men to hide themselves in teeming crowds and thus be free from the scrutiny of pastors and neighbors." Since the colonial era, ministers had acted as leaders in matters political as well as religious. Although plenty of hard-headed, free-thinking skeptics of the Jeffersonian stripe had rejected their presumed leadership, "there were greater groups of wood-choppers, merchants, and farmers to ally themselves with the women in revering the clerics as leaders of thought."[46] Lewis tied this political assault to a manifestation of cultural recidivism, a turning away from manly Jeffersonianism to settlement femininity. The nation's manliness would only be recovered with the eclipse of small-town Protestant morality by the modern urban center.[47]

In consoling their congregations, the clergy also had to convince the northern masses that Lincoln's death was for the best. This they did by arguing in biblical terms that Lincoln was the country's Moses, fated not to enter the Promised Land. God had removed Lincoln at a providential moment, for his gentle soul was not the proper one for the harsh task of Reconstruction. A sterner hand was needed, that of Andrew Johnson and the Republican Congress. The clergy's greatest service to the Radical cause was raising Lincoln to sainthood, to the status of the "dying god" who expired in order to protect his people. The clergy's mystic picture of Lincoln perfectly suited the needs of the Radicals, "who regarded the people as simpletons and idiots for their admiration of Lincoln, [and] were content that the masses should have Lincoln dramatized for them as a saint, . . . too unworldly to manage the political battle that must come with the invidious, treacherous South." The Radicals encouraged the mythologization of Lincoln in order to gain earthly power: "It was though a cosmic trade had been accomplished, giving Lincoln the glory of a blind and beautiful god, and giving his enemies the Republican party. He had the crown, the Radicals had the power. He was dead on the mountain, they were loose in the promised land of Dixie."[48]

In the process, the eastern preachers and their political overlords obliterated the picture of who Lincoln really was. They effaced the image of the rangy frontiersman, the common man who outfoxed the effete politicians of the East, the untutored settler's boy who outshone the university talent with his oratory and prose. In his place they constructed the otherworldly saint, a superhuman deity unfit for the rigors of political infighting, hovering above the nation to protect it. Lewis tapped into the contemporary bifurcation of Lincoln's image, and although he twisted it to suit his purposes, his awareness of the political content embedded in Lincoln's varying iconography leads directly to a consideration of the legend's place in the larger narrative about Lincoln and the history of the war.

Sociologist Barry Schwartz has analyzed the mutating image of Lincoln in the early twentieth century, concluding that by the end of the Great War a crystallization of two contrasting images — the Man of the People and the Great Man — took place. The rustic Lincoln collided with the heroic one, and in the tussle between these two narratives, the latter version gained sway. By the 1920s, Schwartz observes, Lincoln had become a demigod, and throughout the period he symbolized political power and centralization.[49] The expression of this image included Daniel Chester French's seated patriarch in the Lincoln Memorial. In contrast, the controversy surrounding George Barnard's "stomach-ache statue," so named by critics because it portrayed a beardless and rangy Lincoln standing with hands folded in front, indicated the continued presence of dissent against the hegemonic image of the hero.[50] There remained the two contrasting Lincolns, reflecting a cultural dualism, "the kind one finds in a society that values both equality — the familiarity that makes people alike — and hierarchy — the powers that distinguish them."[51] Lincoln, in his diversity, served as a means of reconciling contradictory tendencies in American culture during the early modern period, as the nation was making the transition from rural to urban. It was also a time when the state assumed unprecedented power over the lives of individuals. In this context, the figure of Lincoln served as a memory site where conflicting social and political views could to some extent be reconciled. In this way Lincoln's disparate commemoration served to promote social cohesion, even while the debate over his image raged on.

And it did rage on, as the assassination narratives described so far in this chapter have shown. But rather than focusing on Lincoln's split commemoration as allowing the nation to adjust to changing social realities, a more useful explication of what his image meant to Booth's is provided in Jim Cullen's reading of Carl Sandburg's opus, and of what Cullen terms the Sandburg work's central paradox: that Lincoln is both of the world and never quite in it. Sandburg crafted a poetic vision in which Lincoln's rootedness on the one hand and his detachment on the other were his preeminent features. This duality interlocked with another equally important one: the regional-national dialectic that Cullen believes served as a recurring motif in post–Civil War America's search for a national character. The 1920s and '30s, he noted, saw a flowering of regionalism in the arts and literature. The duality that Sandburg composed was his attempt to resolve the two strands; it was his effort at forging an inclusive regionalism, "to compress the entire nation into one single figure, a man who would 'carry in his breast Cape Cod, the Shenandoah, the Mississippi, the Gulf, the Rocky Mountains, the Sacramento, the Great Plains, the Great Lakes, their dialects and shibboleths.'"[52] Cullen believes that Sandburg's purpose in taking this position was to reassure an anxious American people who were uneasy over the unprecedented growth in governmental authority during the 1930s. Lincoln stood as the previous example of a leader who had assumed unprecedented powers but retained his allegiance to the people, his rootedness in the local.

Booth also stood rooted in the local. His commemoration, however, found its place in the exclusive regionalist opposition to the nationalizing ideology that Lincoln stood for. Unlike Sandburg's "folk," Booth's own folksiness included no attempt to adjust to the conditions of the modern order. He stood as a denial of the present, and Sandburg appropriately described him as the "Outsider," an appellation with roots in the early northern characterization of the assassin as the "other" within, but more descriptive of the actor's place in the contemporary memory of the president and his assassin. Sandburg's pathologization of Booth emphasized his split personality, his ability to be the spectator to his own actions, "a spectator fascinated and spellbound that he himself could see it all before the world saw and himself not shrink back from it."[53] Such a characterization helped move the Booth legend from being the expression of a minority political viewpoint to that of a marginalized cultural narrative. Just as Lewis concocted his revisionist interpretation of the legend's origins in Lincoln's own mythification, he marked the waypoints of cultural exclusion: priests, woodchoppers, small-town merchants, and sodbusters.[54] The legend had its roots as much in the decline of Jeffersonian independence as in the superstitions of the "folk." But now the advent of modern urban life had eroded the power of the priests. The legend also was a relic. Legend believers would not have disagreed, and would have found virtue in their vision of the world Booth represented. Their countercommemoration did not differ markedly from that engaged in by visitors to Greenfield Village and Williamsburg, who found in these places' antique houses and furnishings relief from the press of modern America. Just as Lincoln's dual image helped reconcile the anxieties of small-town Americans to the realities of the modern order (as well as serving as an assimilationist figure for recent immigrants), Booth's image stood for regionalism's harder side, one that refused inclusion.

Although Booth stood for regionalism's harder side, his portrayal in the prolegend literature of the period emphasized a sentimental and romantic account of events, in which the pathos of Booth's remorse rose to new heights. Granted, there had always been those who saw the assassin in a romantic light, but the Booth of the 1920s and '30s was an exemplar from the past, and his survival stood for the preservation of an imagined past and of premodern identities.[55] Also worth noting, although difficult to decipher with much accuracy, is that, like Bates, the producers of prolegend accounts during the 1920s and '30s hailed from border states. Bernie Babcock, author of *Booth and the Spirit of Lincoln: A Story of a Living Dead Man* (1925), was born in Ohio and moved to Arkansas as a young girl. She grafted a spiritualist interpretation of Booth's wanderings onto the legend version provided by Bates. In her book, Booth in his postassassination travels confronts Lincoln's ghost, whose only communications to him are the merciful tones from the second inaugural address — "with malice toward none, with charity for all." These spiritual encounters finally drive the tormented fugitive to his rendezvous with strychnine in Enid, Oklahoma.

A more original work was Izola Forrester's *This One Mad Act* (1937), which remains the best-written and best-researched prolegend account. Like Babcock, Forrester was a professional writer who specialized in children's fiction. Her credits also included several movie screenplays. Forrester hailed from West Virginia and moved to the regionalist center of Chicago. There is no indication, however, that she was connected with the Chicago writers on Lincoln discussed earlier, perhaps at least partly because of their difference in age: Forrester was born in the late 1870s, and *This One Mad Act* was written near the end of her career.

Drawing largely from previous legend sources, Forrester argued that Booth was the tool of the Knights of the Golden Circle and that his escape was due to their assistance. She did not accept Bates's finale, however, and believed the assassin perished in 1879 in England. Her unique contribution to the legend was her assertion that she was Booth's granddaughter through a secret marriage that took place on the eve of the Civil War. It was this aspect of her book, combined with its extreme retrospectivity, her constant dwelling on the memories of past family events, that makes Forrester's work significant. Her commitment to recovering memory in this fashion, and of locating history in domestic, private, and local events (instead of in public sources) accords very well with Susan Stabile's recent work on remembrance among eighteenth-century American women. In analyzing commonplace books and other artifacts of selected women from the early republic, Stabile concludes that unlike men, who tended to focus on communal events, women located the national past in domestic and familial spaces.[56] Her observations appear to apply equally well to women of a later generation. What this points out is the gendered aspect of the legend's performance, and how Babcock and Forrester used the story of Booth's survival as a vehicle for expressing modes of knowledge increasingly discredited in the modernist mainstream. Furthermore, Forrester's relation of the tragedy visited upon her family by Booth's "one mad act" may be read synecdochically as standing for the tragedy visited upon the white "family" of America, a tragedy that could only end by ferreting out the true agents of the assassination. Forrester argues throughout her text that the recuperation of memory provides the only means of healing the familial wound. Memory, not conventional history, provides the means of working through the trauma.[57]

Forrester's conviction that her grandmother, Izola Mills D'Arcy, was Booth's wife provides another case of oral tradition after the fact. As Forrester told it, her grandmother, the daughter of a New England sea captain and his Spanish wife, met Booth in Richmond in 1858 or 1859, and the two fell passionately in love. Marrying secretly (owing to her parents' disapproval of Booth's profession), the two established a homestead in the Shenandoah Valley just before the outbreak of hostilities. While Booth spied for the Confederacy — in addition to acting and investing in Pennsylvania oil properties — the older Izola bore him two daughters in their Virginia retreat. Together with their faithful mammy, Aunt Sarah, Izola fended off Yankee intruders and fed cornbread to Confederate soldiers bivouacked nearby. When news of the assassination came, Izola was forced to flee and found refuge with friends in Baltimore. In 1868 she traveled to California with her daughters, and was briefly reunited with "her darling." Booth, forced to move on lest he be found out, left Izola once more in the care of friends. Pregnant with a son, she returned to New England and settled near Burrillville, Rhode Island, on the Connecticut border. She re-married, raised her family, endured the recriminations of northern relatives, and upon her death in 1881 was buried in a local cemetery. The presence of her remains coupled with Forrester's account has given rise to a local legend tradition; local boosters admit that, whether true or not, the story is good for tourism.[58]

Regardless of the truth of the story, it is the quality of remembrance in Forrester's telling that matters. She crafted a memory text, in which persons and physical mementos allowed her to find the truth of her own past and present. The portrait of Booth in her grandmother's house "attracted me because the eyes appeared to follow me, but also because of its youth and peculiar, melancholy beauty — beauty of a for-eign quality, aloof, rather haughty, with a brooding sadness in his dreamy dark eyes." The portrait, in fact, summarized the family's own physical and social position, as they were theater people possessed with the attributes of dark beauty and premodern personalities. Her grandmother, the matriarch, possessed a magnetic personality and always dramatized life. She spoke in a "lofty, grandiloquent manner." She was endowed with a dark, radiant beauty. "Her complexion was rich and warmly colored." The combination of pre–Gibson Girl, pre-Nordic beauty applied as well to Izola's mother, with her dark hair and long white arms. She was quiet and aloof and conveyed a "half-foreign stateliness which seemed to separate her from other women." Likewise, her Uncle Harry, conceived during the California visit, pos-sessed "raven black hair, and dark eyes that could be piercingly sharp, or soften with infinite understanding." Both were restless personal-ities who eschewed the fixities of domestic existence for the uncer-tainty and adventure of life on the road. Harry led the life of a mod-ern-day minstrel, "a gentleman drifter, the Villon type of true

Bohemian."[59] He could neither earn nor keep money and lived a precarious existence on the margins of the entertainment world.

It was as a friend and performer that this son of Booth most resembled his father, and most resembled Booth's depiction as a charismatic oral performer whom both men and women found irresistible. Although once married, Harry had amicably divorced, and he lived a life of voluntary simplicity, "content with very little, books to read, sauntering about the city, and his love of music." A tall man at six foot two, his clothes were threadbare, but he always appeared dignified. He was known throughout turn-of-the-century New York, from Harlem to the Bowery, in "well known haunts like the Cairo, and the Lion d'Or, Scheffel Hall over near Third Avenue, and Kid McCoy's saloon on Fourteenth Street," where he often appeared as an impromptu singer of popular ditties. Harry, like the father he never acknowledged, was a master of oral performance and a friend to all. He succored the homeless and the down-and-out, both physically and emotionally: "And I made them cry, my dear," he would say feelingly. "Old down-and-outers. Girls who can never go home. I made them break down and cry when I sang, 'Shall We Gather at the River,' and 'Put Those Little Shoes Away,' and 'Silver Threads Among the Gold.'"[60] When he died prematurely (like Izola's mother) at the age of forty-eight, the city's cast-off humanity filled the church to pay their last respects. As Izola left the service one old-timer asked to accompany her to scatter his ashes:

> "Everybody loved Harry," the old fellow said, tears rolling unashamed down his cheeks. . . . "There was some of us who thought we knew who he was, but he never talked about it, you know. One night, down in McCoy's saloon, an old Southerner said to him that he looked exactly like John Wilkes Booth, and Harry just stared at him, and bowed, and said he must be mistaken."[61]

The bow, not the words spoken, was the confirming gesture. It was the mark of the old school, the sign of respect from one gentleman toward another. For Forrester, Harry was a strange personality, one who combined the qualities of the "beloved vagabonds of the world" with the burden of his parentage. The combination exiled him for the duration of his life "in a no-man's land of human existence."[62] But he was a familial and familiar personality whose fate replicated that of the family as a whole, for all of Booth's progeny were condemned to stand outside the mainstream for his singular act.

This is his granddaughter's understanding of the matter, but in describing the difference, the foreignness, and the dramatic temperament of her people Forrester was also engaging in an act of commemoration that marked the passing of an older American society to the author's own present. Commemoration of the war recalled the rise of modern America, which hatched bittersweet memories for her. On the one hand, Forrester remembered her childhood in the 1880s as a time when sectional hatred of the war "was slipping into the visualization stage, where presented to the public in novels and dramas, it had begun to take shape as an episode of history instead of news of the day." Still, there remained strong resentment, in New England especially, against anyone who had been a rebel. Once, as a schoolgirl in Boston, Forrester innocently announced in class her grandfather's name and said he had died for the South. Her teacher kept her after school and warned her never to speak of it again. She remembered the South as a place where her mother always felt more comfortable, where she dropped her caution and seemed to relax as she never did elsewhere, and where her traveling company shed the old legitimate dramas played up North for light opera, "delightful operas, whose gay melodies became intermingled in my memory with the rare old gardens . . . , magnolias in bloom, and rose vines tumbling over narrow galleries."[63] Forrester placed her fond memories in a southern setting, as did many northerners in the early twentieth century, who found relief there from the pressures of modern existence.

Forrester wrote also of other memories, not only of her family's appearance and character, but also memories drawn from the relics they left behind. When she raised the lid of her mother's traveling chest "there swept from it, like a liberated genie, the fascinating blend of fragrance that was so intimately associated with her in my own mind." Each article brought back the memories of the wonderful old days when her mother and she had traveled together and when life proceeded with celebration and dramatic flair. In a scrapbook left by her grandmother she found a curious collection of "clippings, keepsakes of old pressed flowers and ferns, traceries of rose-tinted seaweed, sprigs of pale jessamine, political cartoons — it was like listening to disconnected motifs of many themes." Again the aural allusions, listening to the past through its physical artifacts, and the juxtaposition of tragedy with sentimental charm. Forrester embarks on her own reconstruction, inspired by the words of her mother's old friend: "History does not always tell us everything. Nature and memory are more explicit and faithful. The record of lineaments is sometimes more truthful than in documents." Thus, against the official remembrance of Booth's deed, the meager, scathing, and damning edition of his life, she constructs a countermemory. She reverses Booth's negative image with the remembered words of her grandmother and her own memory exercises to allow his goodness to reemerge and to make his evil born of political passions fall away. John Wilkes Booth was, after all, a family man, and his act was the product of the times, nothing more. In the words of Forrester's adoptive father, Booth's crime had nothing to do with his family, nor did his family bear responsibility for his crime.[64] The tragedy of Harry, her grandmother, and her own mother's alienation should therefore be passed over — as should also, by implication, the tragedy of the larger Southern family.

In Forrester's account, Booth's survival had two purposes. His escape served as the vehicle for a remembrance of things past, a precommercial past of captivating personalities, personal interaction, and the scents and sounds associated with a more civilized time. Her version of the legend was undoubtedly nostalgic — and fitting Booth into this mold required some shoehorning, despite the existing image of him as a tragic hero. To achieve it she borrowed from the available narratives of the assassin's comportment and dark beauty. The waning of his political significance in the early twentieth century allowed Forrester to complete the picture. Revisionism allowed her to craft a domestic tragedy. Booth became a "family man" whose errancy had cost his descendants their place in society and enforced their separateness. But this separateness was not all bad. Booth's survival and the mementos that proved it, including the features and personalities of his descendants, provided a more compelling logic than history ever could. For Forrester, Booth's escape and subsequent life established the primacy of memory over historical narrative. Moreover, the truth of the past was always a family matter, locked up in the memories of individual members, to be shared discreetly or lived out without words, in nature and lineaments. Documents could never know it. In an era of objective historical understanding, Forrester's approach to the past was increasingly marginalized. Like Babcock's spiritualist rendition, Forrester's memory account helped keep Booth in an alternate framework, a regionalism of the mind at odds with the modernist impulse.

Forrester, however, had no place for the mummy in her account. Nor did her version of events convey the sense of disruption to American destiny found elsewhere. The conservative American who is the subject of the next chapter did express, in no uncertain terms, what this disruption entailed.

CLARENCE TRUE WILSON AND THE "THINGS THAT ARE TO BE"

In the United States there are three political parties,
the Republican, Democratic, and the Methodist Church.
(Ulysses S. Grant)

This chapter examines the legend belief of Clarence True Wilson (1872–1939), a Methodist minister and leading Prohibition advocate. Wilson's involvement in the Booth legend coincided in time with that of the figures explored in Chapter 6. Although Wilson based his legend belief on many of the same sources as the characters discussed earlier, several factors make his contribution especially significant to the legend's modern development. First, his involvement in the story of Booth's escape was extensive, and his relations with other believers — through the exchange of correspondence and legend documents — reveal the the legend's interior workings and what may be termed its "archival community" in modern times. Second, his status as a spokesperson for conservative Protestant America provides an excellent background for understanding what the Booth escape story stood for and its place on the broader cultural map of early-twentieth-century America. Third, and most important, while his account of Booth's escape and wanderings relied heavily on Bates's version, the Methodist minister drew upon his evangelical outlook to invest the story with an explicit historical and religious interpretation not found in other popular accounts.

Wilson's involvement with the Booth mummy also calls into question the assumed opposition between carnival sideshows and more "respectable" forms of cultural expression. The Methodist minister viewed the mummy on at least one occasion, and probably more than once. According to Russian literary critic Mikhail Bakhtin, carnivals and related forms of popular expression stand opposed to "official" culture and serve as venues where narratives and identities prohibited in mainstream culture can stand forth.[1] In the case of Booth's mummy and the memory it represented, both stood outside the mainstream commemoration of the Civil War and Lincoln during the interwar period. However, cultural marginalization does not necessarily entail a separation of cultural forms, as Wilson's involvement demonstrates. His devotion to the legend at the same time he led a mainstream Protestant organization confounds Bakhtin's notion of a separation between the two types of culture. Wilson's mixing of the religious and the profane is consistent with the legend's appearance throughout its history, where its reverent, political nature was periodically controverted by cultural entrepreneurs to ludicrous and bawdy ends. Reconciling the Methodist divine's foray into the world of popular death displays with his religious persona accords with the "lived religion" perspective advocated by David Hall and Robert Orsi. In their view, an individual's or a group's religious practice can entail elements deemed "popular" with those considered traditionally "religious" without posing any contradiction.[2] Both elements contribute to the elaboration of a comprehensive worldview, which adherents use to make sense of their life experience and to resolve the tensions and contradictions that often accompany this experience.

What is interesting in Wilson's case is that his particular worldview was coming apart during the period in question, and he used the legend in an attempt to keep it together — to address the threat he perceived to America's destiny as God's Chosen Nation. A dedicated public Protestant in the opening decades of the twentieth century, Wilson defies the notion of a "two-party system" in religion: he was neither fundamentalist nor modernist in religious matters. His was a postmillennial vision in which moral reform stood as the key to the coming Kingdom on Earth. The son of a Methodist preacher, Wilson came of age in the decades following the Civil War, a time that witnessed both America's transformation into an industrial power and Methodism's greatest period of growth.[3] Despite the anxieties that accompanied the gradual dissolution of Protestant small-town culture in the last decades of the nineteenth and the opening decades of the twentieth century, mainstream evangelical Protestants like Wilson remained optimistic regarding America's providential destiny. The key to this destiny, they believed, lay in the progress of moral reform. And the centerpiece of the Protestant reform movement during this period was the effort to ban the sale and manufacture of alcohol. Through the opening decades of the twentieth century, "dry" sentiment gained ground, and by 1917 prohibition laws had been passed in thirty-four states. With passage of the Eighteenth Amendment establishing national Prohibition in 1919, many religious spokespersons assumed that the hour of final victory was at hand. Over the course of the 1920s, however, the Great Experiment floundered, as millions of Americans flouted the law and the eruption of bootlegging and mob violence led many to argue that the cure was worse than the disease.[4]

This growing opposition to Prohibition, along with the continuing transformation of America into a modern, urban, and secular nation, meant that Wilson and like-minded Protestants found their evangelical optimism increasingly strained. Historian Leo Ribuffo has noted the "apocalyptic disposition" of conservative Christians during the Depression era and their efforts to root out infidelity in order to protect the Christian Nation's destiny.[5] Wilson, with some variation, fit this mold. It was fitting that his efforts on behalf of the cause of Prohibition and his legend involvement coincided in time, for in one sense, Booth's escape proved to Wilson the infidelity of selected personages in America's past, and this past shaped the present and the future. Like the right-wing religionists described by Ribuffo, Wilson's discomfiture with the shape of the present included an eschatological component. Unlike liberal Protestant thinkers, whose adaptation to modernity led them increasingly to perceive the end-times as an open-ended process of development, Wilson maintained a traditional view of Christ's imminent return. But he also rejected the premillennialist interpretation favored by fundamentalists and other conservative Protestants.[6] He struggled to maintain the traditional evangelical postmillennialist view of the world's ending: Christ's return, while imminent, was rendered more likely by society's moral improvement, not its degeneration, as the premillennialists predicted. Caught between optimistic and pessimistic interpretations of the world's final days, Wilson's attempt to reconcile his worldview with the changing realities of modern America was not easily accomplished: he could neither accept the changes as gradual improvement on the liberal plan, nor see in the present the signs of impending doom. Complicating matters even further, Wilson, like right-wing

Christians such as *Dearborn Independent* editor (and occasional preacher) William J. Cameron, maintained a strong commitment to the twin credos of Anglo-Saxon racial superiority and Anglo-Israelism. As Ribuffo and more recently Michael Barkun have demonstrated, twentieth-century Christian Nationalists continued to espouse the physical links between Anglo-Saxons and ancient Israelites.[7] Wilson's Anglo-Israelism, while less vicious than that of his contemporary, Gerald L. K. Smith, nonetheless raises the possibility of how the legend, and particularly the embalmed remains of John Wilkes Booth, functioned within his cosmology. While undoubtedly a villain, "Booth" also served as a tangible link to a past age of heroic deeds and racial purity.

In summary, Wilson's eschatological and race beliefs suggest that the legend served him in his effort to reconcile his worldview with the present and that his viewing of the mummy included, however dimly, the racial attributions practiced by antebellum viewers. In order to flesh out these suggested interpretations, we must first consider his legend involvement in greater detail. In addition to viewing the mummy, he produced three drafts of a book-length manuscript entitled variously *On the Assassin's Trail* and *Trailing Lincoln's Assassin*. On his frequent Prohibition speaking tours he gave a lecture called "The Mystery of John Wilkes Booth's Escape" and took the opportunity, when traveling, to pursue the same kind of oral history research as J. N. Wilkerson did. Wilson corresponded with Leslie Traylor, a Texas legend gadfly who also corresponded with David Rankin Barbee and the medical examiner who autopsied the mummy in 1931. In Caroline County, Virginia, where the Garrett farm once stood, Wilson interviewed aging residents who corroborated the story of Booth's escape. In Enid, Oklahoma, he interviewed Frank Fairgrieves, a retired drayman and former saloon habitué, who recalled how David George once intervened in a poker game to relieve a card sharp of his winnings and returned the money to a tenderfoot with the admonition "Young man, beware of the other man's game." By Wilson's accounting, he spent $12,000 of his own money over a period of fifty years investigating Booth's escape, collecting sworn affidavits and other "evidence." He cultivated a friendship with Finis L. Bates and eventually obtained a good portion of the elderly attorney's material, possibly in exchange for his services in helping Bates remarket his story. His efforts led to the publication of the article "Is History Wrong?" over Bates's byline in the August 1923 issue of *True Confessions* magazine. Upon the attorney's death Wilson became his literary legatee and undertook the rewriting of *Escape and Suicide*. In a letter to Mrs. Bates he assured the widow she would "be pleased with what I have done with your work, because I have not changed it or changed Mr. Bates' style." Unfortunately, he was less successful than his predecessor in getting the work published. Despite Wilson's hiring an agent, his multiple reworkings of Bates's story were all rejected. Wilson recognized that the criticism against the book had to do with his unrelenting attack on Andrew Johnson as a conspirator in Lincoln's murder: "they say [my terrific onslaught upon Andrew Johnson], . . . will not be acceptable and they do not want to be responsible for putting out facts that show that a man who was once President of the United States gained his position by conspiring with plotters." Wilson's solution to this editorial problem was to change all references to Johnson in his final draft to "Mr. V.P.X." Needless to say, this modification did nothing to increase the work's appeal to publishers, and *Trailing Lincoln's Assassin* remained unpublished.[8]

Other legend devotees viewed Wilson as an interloper, a Johnny-come-lately out to steal "evidence" and artifacts. William Campbell, an Oklahoman whose own legend account appeared in 1922 under the title *John Wilkes Booth: Escape and Wanderings until Final Ending of the Trail by Suicide,* wrote to Blanche DeBar Booth, a younger relative of the assassin and an actress in her own right, of Wilson's visit to him in 1924: "I was lead [*sic*] to believe, . . . that the visits were of a social trend. . . . However, I fortunately caught on to the fact that he was visiting for another pur[p]ose. . . . As a consequence the items I had gat[h]ered didn't leak to any great extent." Wilson's snooping, Campbell concluded, was tied to his plans to put out a revised edition of the "Bates book." Campbell, who was editor and publisher of the *Waukomis (Oklahoma) Hornet* at the time of George's suicide, was absolutely right.[9]

Wilson's cavorting with the cadaver was also known to journalists, who used the information in articles critical of the minister's cultural politics. The *Literary Digest* asserted that Wilson brokered the sale of the mummy to Bill Evans for the widow Bates, and the *Christian Cen-*

tury, the leading liberal, nondenominational religious journal of its day, even alleged that the Methodist divine owned the body.[10]

The journalists' barbs were not without provocation, for at the same time he pursued the assassin's trail, Wilson also headed one of Protestant America's most influential lobbying organizations. As general-secretary for the Methodist Episcopal Board of Temperance, Prohibition, and Public Morals (MBTP), he was among those leading the charge in what religious historians describe as Protestant America's final attempt to reform America.[11] Ostensibly engaged in Christian education, the board was in fact a lobby, devoted to grass-roots mobilization and close political persuasion. Wilson had cut his teeth as a Prohibition advocate while still in his teens and served as president of the Oregon Anti-Saloon League from 1906 to 1908. From meager beginnings in 1910, when he began serving the MBTP, Wilson built the organization up through his boundless energy, effectiveness as a public speaker, and talent for organizing. By the 1920s, after moving from Topeka, Kansas, to Washington, D.C. — where it could more effectively oversee the implementation of national Prohibition — the Board had come to assume second place only to the Anti-Saloon League among politically influential Protestant organizations. The *New Republic* considered it "the most up-to-date of the new church lobbies," brazenly engaged in influencing political opinion to achieve political ends.[12] The MBTP's advisory members included North Carolina senator Josephus Daniels, California senator Charles Randall, dime-store magnate S. S. Kresge, and New York retailer J. C. Penney. Its activities included the publication of tracts and a monthly journal. A weekly "clipsheet" sent out to the nation's press and a reported twenty thousand clergymen kept them informed of legislative developments in Washington pertinent to the Board's agenda. This agenda included not only Prohibition, but also the whole rubric of causes associated with the Protestant antimodernist crusade of the period. Cigarette smoking, dancing, heavy petting, unassimilated immigrants, Catholics, and New York City all came under the fire of Wilson and his staff. Although still drawing from evangelical Protestantism's earlier commitment to antebellum abolition and other humanitarian reforms, by the 1920s the Methodist leader's vision of America's destiny was heavily tinted with nativist and antimodernist leanings.

Wilson's crowning achievement came in 1924 with the dedication of a $750,000 headquarters for the MBTP on Capitol Hill. Located directly across First Street from the Capitol grounds, and a stone's throw from the location of the future Supreme Court complex, the Methodist Building drew the ire of secularists, who accused Wilson and the Board of violating the separation of church and state.[13] Even more irritating to the secular modernists and liberal churchmen was the general-secretary's penchant for inflammatory rhetoric. The Board's monthly publication, the *Voice,* often cut loose with statements designed more to arouse the faithful than to further reasoned dialogue. In 1925, for instance, the statement "The only good bootlegger is a dead bootlegger," a paraphrase of General Philip Sheridan's opinion regarding Native Americans, enraged moderates on both sides of the liquor divide. A year later Wilson, borrowing from Anti-Saloon League rhetoric, declared that Prohibition was the reason for America's unprecedented prosperity and its good government. Before Prohibition, he was quoted as saying, "the rum element was in control of Congress." That prestigious assembly's sergeant-at-arms had supposedly confided to Wilson that in the bad old days his chief duty had been to "walk members up and down and get the drunks to their homes." Printed in the *New York Times,* these accusations were read by contemporary congressmen, one of whom accused the minister on the floor of the House of speaking a "dastardly canard" sprung from his "intemperate brain where it was concocted without an atom of truth."[14]

Wilson's public persona was indeed a mixture of respectable churchly mien and obstreperous discourse. Sporting a goatee and a pince-nez, the dapper Methodist circulated among the nation's political and religious leaders. At the same time, he was a veteran street campaigner who laced his oratory with folksy aphorisms and quotes from Mr. Dooley. Like the legendary Booth, the minister was the product of an age of public oral performance, although in his case the venue was the pulpit and not the saloon. He hearkened back to an evangelical tradition that prized the spoken word. Before gaining "respectability" in the mid-nineteenth century, Methodism frequently challenged social conventions and logical proof in its quest for personal holiness and social perfection. Peter Cartwright and the earlier divines eloquently described by Christine Heyrman were the spiritual predecessors Wilson acknowledged in his appeal to the days "when pulpits thundered the things that are to be," when "definite re-sults attended our preaching and far-reaching revivals blessed the church."[15] Despite his mainstream theology and denominational al-legiance, and his pouring on of statistics to prove a point, Wilson held to a model of public discourse that emphasized conviction over fac-tual truth and moral suasion over rational deliberation. This was his Methodist heritage; the early Methodist identity in America also included a penchant for crossing the social boundary between "respectability" and the profane. David Hempton describes this crossing in different terms, as Methodism's interior dialectic, the combination of discipline and order ranged against "a sensuous and subversive dimension."[16] Despite what other observers have noted as Methodism's shift toward social respectability beginning in the mid-1800s, Wilson vouchsafed the preservation of an earlier tradition. He also believed firmly in the public authority of the pulpit — another Methodist inheritance — and argued incessantly for the right of reli-gion to intervene in politics. One reviewer called him the "most sen-sational moral and political reformer in the United States," whose outbursts and habit of dissembling could be traced to his days as an itinerant speaker, "when he campaigned among rude folk who looked for edification as well as amusement to circus side-shows and itiner-ant medicine men."[17]

This description reveals its author's modernist bias against small-town, rural culture, and was one of a kind with Lloyd Lewis's summa-tion of the clergy's power in the nineteenth century. But it recognizes Wilson's mixed rhetorical performance, a crucial point to under-standing how this church leader could mix carnival sideshows with denominational orthodoxy in order to affirm his moral vision. Al-though he was skilled at dispensing scientific rationale when needed, and although he maintained a public posture emphasizing commit-ment to fact and logic, Wilson was actually beholden to rhetorical and epistemological models that were increasingly discredited in the 1920s and 1930s. For him, the spiritual took precedence over the ma-terial, moral suasion was just as authoritative as scientific reason, and a speaker's authority flowed from this moral font. History, in this scheme of things, remained a moral enterprise, with individual events always subordinate to the unfolding of God's larger plan. Wil-son continued to participate in what Dorothy Ross characterizes as a prehistoricist philosophy of history, in which material causation remained subordinate to the workings of providential destiny.[18] It is not surprising that a religious thinker would continue to view history in this fashion, even when the larger secular culture turned to more naturalistic frames of reference. Wilson's understanding of history also evinced a conspiratorial interpretation, one in which, as Gordon Wood explains, events were attributed to the "concerted designs of willful individuals," not to impersonal forces.[19] Wood contends that the prevalence of this mode of thinking in the eighteenth century represented an important step in the Western understanding of its social reality, and highlighted the contradiction between the growing complexity and impersonality of Western society (which made earlier, personal explanations implausible), and the attempt of Enlightenment thinkers to explain human actions in terms of universal laws. During the revolutionary era, the conspiratorial interpretation was a means by which educated persons ordered and gave meaning to their political world. For a later generation, however, this mode of interpretation entailed a rejection of historicism, by insisting that both individual actors and the overall progress of history evinced a moral design. To those with such a frame of mind, Booth's survival was the sign of a larger moral purpose.

The tale of Booth's escape supported Wilson's interpretation of the Christian Nation's moral progress at the same time it helped conceal the conflicts in his vision. On a first level, the assassin survived in order to suffer more fully. Contrary to the southern version of events, in which Booth's survival stood as an expression of vengeance, vindication, and white unreconstructedness, Wilson made the assassin live on in order to suffer moral retribution. History demanded as much. Booth had killed the immortal and good Lincoln, and had imposed on the country "that drunken maliprop, Andrew Johnson, who made of our period of reconstruction, which should have been a love-feast, a scene of more bitter memories and more unforgettable outrages than the entire four years of Civil War." While some may have thought it was better to survive under any circumstances than to be shot like a dog as Booth allegedly was, they did not grasp the full weight of his agony: "This ambitious and proud aristocrat . . . wandered for thirty-eight years concealing his identity, hiding his shame, seeking surcease from sorrow but in vain. He became a suicide without a glimpse of hope for any better world." Those who considered this fate an easy out did not properly reckon with the teachings of the "new psychology," in which psychic agony easily surpassed the pain of simple physical surcease. Even his corpse was deprived of a resting place; it has wandered about, being exhibited "as if the soil itself that gave the immortal Lincoln birth . . . refused to be polluted by the internment of Lincoln's assassin."[20] Thus Booth remained in limbo, unburied and unreconciled, and Wilson brought forward to the present one element of the legend's original northern interpretation, born of the assassination's trauma. His telling, however, had a certain twist, for Wilson folded a revisionist interpretation of the war into his account. Booth's act thwarted the "love-feast" that should have taken place through the reconstruction and reunion of white North and South. As we have seen, Wilson was by no means the first person to formulate this idea. The interesting point is that despite his evangelical heritage and frequent appeals to Methodism's role in the fight for the abolition of slavery, his legend account evinced the revisionist tendencies noted in the previous chapter.

How, then, did Booth's body serve to reconcile Wilson's conflicted view of history? On the one hand, the mummy stood as evidence of a bad past and better present; on the other, it was one of the last physical remnants of the age of heroes. Following Bates's lead, Wilson alleged that Booth had escaped as a result of a conspiracy originating in the highest levels of government. The cover-up was headed by Secret Service chief Lafayette Baker, in order to protect his share of the reward money, and in order to prevent a second Civil War, which would have erupted had the public learned of the vice-president's involvement. Andrew Johnson, who "acceded to his position through the perpetration of a plot that robbed the country of its greatest character and most noble son," was, according to Wilson, a drunkard.[21] Johnson's inebriation at his vice-presidential swearing-in was an acknowledged fact.[22] Wilson, however, took matters further, describing an alcoholic tête-à-tête between Booth and "a man high in official circles, who for this story shall be Mr. V.P.X.," at the Kirkwood Hotel (Johnson's residence) on the afternoon of the assassination. Booth, a poster boy for alcohol in Wilson's rendition, drank a decoction of "brandy, French absinthe, and a Bermudan wine they were just importing."[23] The general-secretary remained committed to the "Andrew Johnson did it" thesis, but with one significant shift. Johnson's original accusers came from the radical Republican camp, and their allegations of his involvement were tied to the effort to impeach

Johnson over his reconstruction policy. In Wilson's interpretation, Johnson assumed the role of the Radicals, who were claimed to have turned Reconstruction into a nightmare by insisting on black political equality. The "bad past" Wilson tied to the legend consisted of an amalgam of corrupt politics, alcohol in high places, and a transposed revisionism in which Johnson replaced the Radicals he in fact so vehemently opposed.

The evocation of this bad past served to accentuate the goodness of the present, and this was arguably the mummy's greater use in Wilson's scheme. If the body served as the physical remnant of deceit and tragedy in government, it also stood as a confirmation of humankind's progress under the aegis of the Christian Nation. The general-secretary's heirs made the connection between his religious world-view and nationalist sensibilities clear in their forward to the final draft of *Trailing Lincoln's Assassin:* "Dr. Wilson's religion . . . was vitally related to his desire to serve the nation. To him any form of treachery, past or present, was something to be exposed to the public good and the development of a national conscience."[24] He rooted his Christian Nationism in the assertion of an unbroken chain between Mosaic law and the U.S. Constitution. Even the number of original colonies corresponded to the ancient Israelite polity: the twelve tribes were actually thirteen because the House of Joseph was composed of two parts.[25] Moreover, wrote Wilson, the prophet Isaiah "was given a vision of America as playing a conspicuous part in the providence of God among the nations of the earth." The United States had become, he argued, the greatest theater for reform in the history of humankind.[26] But alcohol stood as the ever-present danger, the force that threatened to undo all the work of previous eras. It was the Anglo-Saxon dilemma, for the survival of the race required "deliverance from the bondage to Alcohol, of Body and Soul, of State and Nation."[27] In the period preceding and immediately following passage of the Eighteenth Amendment, Wilson rested easy in his confirmation of the promise of the present. Prohibition, he argued, was the root cause of America's unprecedented prosperity, as proven by the numbers from the 1932 Statistical Abstract, which the wet press attempted to suppress: more cars, more milk and fresh vegetables, more high school graduates, fewer lynchings, fewer deaths by automobile, and — cleaner politics. The final draft of *Trailing Lincoln's Assassin* concluded on a postmillennial note:

We are living in better days. We have better men in public life. . . . The world grows with the progress of the suns and our children will have a better world to live in than we have had. They will never see piracy on the high seas, an African slave trade, duelling, slavery, polygamy, cannibalism, the lottery system, legalized gambling, and the legalized liquor traffic in their generation. These will be the nightmares of a horrid dream but forgotten in the brightness of an awakening new day.[28]

Thus Booth's suffering and the legend as evidence of a corrupt past served to confirm an optimistic interpretation of history's moral progress despite the challenges offered by modern conditions. Booth suffered as he should have, and conspiratorial politics had given way to good government. But there was a textual blip here that points to a very different assessment of what the legend stood for. The phrase "legalized liquor traffic" was crossed out in the typescript and written over in pen with the words "opium trade, or dope and narcotics legalized." Between the time Wilson composed his conclusion and the manuscript's final edits, the Eighteenth Amendment was revoked, so the conclusion had to be modified to reflect this change. But Wilson did not choose to alter his optimistic assessment of the future, at least not here. Other writings of his, however, reveal unease and anxiety over the quest for moral reform and national destiny. The pages of the *Voice* were filled with dire incantations. Not only the repeal of Prohibition, but also the proliferation of cigarettes, motion pictures, and wild dancing was threatening to unravel America's promise. Wilson placed responsibility for these scourges on unassimilated immigrants, Catholics, and "centers of congested population," such as New York City.[29] As his heirs noted in the final version of the manuscript, Wilson believed that Booth "thwarted destiny" in killing Lincoln, suggesting another interpretation for the legend's meaning and the power of its corpse. The past was not bad, despite the Methodist's rhetorical demonstrations and postmillennial convictions. While the past may have witnessed corrupt politics abetted by alcohol, it was also the age of Father Abraham, and Wilson worshipped at the altar of Abraham Lincoln. Lincoln was "good and immortal," his was "the noblest name of any statesman in human history," his name "the moral magnet for all the other millions of the civilized world." Wilson's Christian Nationism had its roots in Anglo-Israelism and his own colorful interpretation of Isaiah's prophecy. But its avatar was Abraham Lincoln, and beyond Lincoln the entire generation of Civil War heroes, including his own father and Methodist bishop Matthew Simpson. These were men who had thundered from the pulpits. Wilson's vision of the past affirmed their role and that of the pulpit in assuring "heroic, ethical leadership, that the future may be just as progressive and glorious."[30] This past and the existence of these figures also stood for larger social and cultural values, including a homogenous "Americanism," the undisputed rule of native-born white males in the public sphere, and the public power of the clergy. The destiny Booth thwarted was not only the immediate future, the Reconstruction period, but also the future of a certain kind of America, one centered on evangelical Protestantism, moral valor, ethnic homogeneity, and a masculine priesthood.

Even as Wilson launched his building campaign and fought ceaselessly to defend the Noble Experiment, the pages of the *Voice* revealed his conviction that sinister forces were afoot. Not only immigration and the social evils begat by the Lost Generation, but also conspiracy threatened to unravel America's promise. In the same year Wilson first visited the mummy, an editorial in the *Voice* proclaimed, "One of the most colossal conspiracies against the Government of the United States that has ever been faced in our history . . . is that deliberate plan of the liquor men, the American Tobacco trusts, the anti-Sabbath leagues, and the moving-picture producers to make odious the enforcement of the Volstead Act."[31] Further, as the campaign against Prohibition mounted in the 1920s, Wilson came under increasing criticism for his meddling in politics and his reactionary cultural viewpoints. Several journals pointedly referred to the Board's insistence on regulating personal conduct while it neglected the more serious issue of Methodism's involvement with the Ku Klux Klan. Unfortunately, there was little in Wilson's public statements to discourage this view. In his testimony before the Senate during the Prohibition hearings in early 1926, he repeated his message regarding Prohibition's moral and material benefits before moving on to accuse immigrants of derailing the effort. He accused the liquor industry of "importing" European immigrants to the United States for the sole purpose of engaging in bootlegging.[32] Likewise, the pages of the *Voice* during this period included articles on "Americanism," Romanist plots, immigration, and the political fight for Prohibition. The

Voice also kept close tabs on the congressional vote during passage of the 1924 Immigration Act. And in the midst of all this appeared advertisements for Booth legend literature. Alongside titles from the Methodist and Cokesbury presses, the *Voice* announced, the Methodist Building's bookstore carried titles such as *Escape and Suicide of John Wilkes Booth* and *The Suppressed Truth about the Assassination of Abraham Lincoln.*[33]

In sum, the Booth legend served as a backdrop to Wilson's growing disillusion as the 1920s wore on. Despite Booth's arch-villainy, his body served as a tangible link to the heroic past. Hence, for Wilson the mummy had contradictory meanings, standing at once for the "bad" past of moral turpitude and the "good" past of the heroic fathers. Further, the mummy's existence as a sideshow exhibit did not preclude its being taken seriously by Wilson. Its position on the cultural margins in fact mimicked the minister's own situation, as evangelical Protestantism's public authority continued to erode in the 1920s.

The carnival exhibit that featured the Booth mummy displayed a board with the words "For the Correction of American History" painted on it. This was a quintessential expression of the Lost Cause, but it may have taken on broader significance in the culminating period of America's urban and ethnic transformation. Much as the blend of moral justice and historical revisionism formed the basis of Wilson's legend belief, the mummy's function "for the correction of history" moved beyond its originally southern focus to incorporate broader cultural anxieties. In the immediate context of the mummy's display, the statement ostensibly referred to rectifying the "incorrect" accounts of Lincoln's assassination, which in turn carried strong political implications, including charges that government leaders had committed treason and then covered their tracks. This was surely a disturbing notion, but one that was familiar enough in the late nineteenth and early twentieth centuries. But for Wilson, who was determined to fathom the forces that were intent on undoing Prohibition and moral progress, the "correction of history" also referred to redirecting (at least in the imagination) the progress of American history since the end of the Civil War. Here is the key to resolving Wilson's historical revisionism and his moral agenda. The "correction of history" for Wilson entailed the reassertion of a narrative in which the autonomous self, evangelical moral hegemony, and ethnic "homogeneity" continued to hold sway. The mummy, by "proving" the falsity of mainstream historical narrative, helped ease the tension between evangelical Protestantism's traditional optimism and the growing pessimism of conservative Protestants during the early decades of the twentieth century. And part of the mummy's power for Wilson lay, in a figurative sense, in its affiliation with the ancient white bodies of yore and, through them, the ancient Israelite nation. In short, as the material proof of conspiracy (a conspiracy that disrupted America's destiny), and simultaneously as an evocation of the venerable Euro-American myth of racial-religious origins, George's mummy affirmed the moral interpretation of history at the same time it served as a memory of ethnic, religious, and moral purity in a world its viewers believed had increasingly gone awry.

THE LEGEND IN
THE PRESENT TENSE

*Today, as always, there are too many people who have a vested interest
in preserving a standardized version of history. Instead of welcoming new
discoveries, as genuine historians should, they ignore or even try to suppress
fresh evidence that tends to contradict conventional accounts. This is
particularly true, and a tragedy in itself, of questions at the heart of
the Abraham Lincoln drama.*
(*Leonard F. Guttridge and Ray A. Neff*)

As I sat down to write this final chapter, the legend made its latest
foray into mainstream culture with the publication of *Dark Union: The
Secret Web of Profiteers, Politicians, and Booth Conspirators That Led to
Lincoln's Death* (2003).[1] The book's full title fairly summarizes the
plotline, which entails a variation on the Eisenschiml thesis and includes the story of Booth's escape.

The book has raised protests from historians on both substantive
and methodological grounds: for alleging that Lincoln's death resulted from a broad conspiracy and for basing these allegations on
suspicious (perhaps even fabricated) sources. In many ways — to be
detailed more fully below — *Dark Union* and the reactions it has provoked epitomize post–World War II Lincoln conspiracy theorizing. It
is therefore a fitting subject for considering the legend's current
existence. A preliminary assessment is that the contemporary legend
has inherited many of the characteristics of the revisionist-inspired
literature of the interwar period. The evocation of Booth's personality continues to recede in favor of Booth the fugitive, thus indicating
a conspiracy within the government. As a result, the legend per se has
lost its prominence and often serves merely as a garnish to the theory
to which it is tied. Regardless, both the legend and its associated

theory of conspiracy in government now participate in what Robert Alan Goldberg and others have analyzed as the master conspiracy narrative in contemporary American culture.[2] Finally, *Dark Union* wonderfully demonstrates the internal economy, or what was referred to earlier as the legend's "archival community," that has persisted from its emergence in the early 1900s. The spiritual descendants of Finis L. Bates, Otto Eisenschiml, Clarence T. Wilson, and others continue to develop a limited set of "evidence" through correspondence, publications, and oral communications, all the while maintaining that they are "correcting history" or revealing the truth. This conflicting claim and practice — as this chapter's epigraph highlights — gives *Dark Union* and allied works the ironic quality that is another hallmark of conspiracy theories in general.[3]

Before considering the book and its meanings in detail, it should be noted that the story of Booth's escape entered a period of decline following its popularity in the 1920s and '3os. While it undoubtedly persisted at the grassroots level, the Booth legend's literary appearances dwindled, and the mummy disappeared from view. The reasons for this were partly generational. Clarence True Wilson died in 1939, and his cohort of legend devotees was passing from the scene. Perhaps, too, marginal productions like the legend and associated conspiracy theories do not fare well during periods of concerted national effort. Such was the case in World War II America, and one would expect theories alleging betrayal by the nation's leaders to be given short shrift. The few pertinent books and articles appearing in the 1940s were uniformly critical of Booth, the legend, and its fabricators. Interestingly, Lloyd Lewis's *Myths after Lincoln* was reissued in a pocket-sized Armed Services Edition. Modernist disdain joined with nationalist ire to exclude the regionalist tendencies expressed by the story of the assassin's survival.[4]

Times change, however, and with the times, so do cultural priorities and the memories of the past. Lincoln conspiracy theories made a comeback in the late 1950s, as did stories of Booth's escape. Both have enjoyed a more or less continuous existence ever since, and *Dark Union* represents the culmination of this contemporary renaissance. What do the book and its production reveal about the legend's current lease on life?

Authors Leonard F. Guttridge and Ray A. Neff propose that Lincoln's murder originated in a kidnapping plot that itself sprang from a secret deal hatched in 1864 to trade southern cotton for northern bacon and greenbacks. The covert "pork-for-cotton" arrangement involved northern speculators, southern agents, and various side personalities, including John Wilkes Booth. Added to this combination were the radical Republicans, who, although not directly involved in the cotton deal, hated Lincoln (according to the authors) for his supposed leniency toward the South. These three groups — northern cotton speculators, southern agents, and radical politicians — had separate motives in orchestrating Lincoln's removal. For the speculators, the motivation was simple greed, as they stood to make fantastic profits by reselling southern cotton and by selling northern goods to the famished South. For the southern agents, it was a matter of survival. By 1864, the Confederate armies were in desperate need of provisions, and with the northern blockade of southern ports interdicting most foreign commerce, trading with the enemy seemed the last, best option. For the radical Republicans, the motivation was pure political hatred. By late 1864, they were determined to remove Lincoln from office for his obstinate refusal to obey congressional dictates in managing the war and for his lenient policies toward the South. This volatile mixture of greed, political passion, and obvious southern interests led to an "unholy alliance" between three seemingly inimical parties.[5] In a final twist, the kidnapping plans were abandoned when Lee surrendered and all parties reconciled themselves to the inevitable consequences of victory and Lincoln's triumph. Tragically, Booth — who had earlier been relieved by the plotters of his leading role in the abduction operation — went ahead on his own and assassinated Lincoln out of malice.

The problems with this argument, accepting it on the authors' own terms, begin with the respective roles assigned to Lincoln and Edwin Stanton vis-à-vis the cotton trade. Lincoln, according to the authors, accepted the trade as a necessary evil and authorized trading across enemy lines by signing cotton passes. Stanton, who functions in *Dark Union* as he did in Otto Eisenschiml's work, as the Radicals' main man, was resolutely opposed to the trade for obvious reasons: any support rendered to the enemy increased the Confederates' capacity to fight. So far, Guttridge and Neff's account has a basis in fact. Lincoln did condone the trade; and Stanton, along with others, opposed it. The authors abandon the trail of historical reasonability, however, in further developing their argument. According to them, when Stanton first learned of the secret cotton deal, he summoned the president to his home on a Sunday morning. His opposition to the trade was well known: "At cabinet meetings the secretary had opposed the very idea of it. His words that Sunday morning, and Lincoln's, can only be imagined."[6] Following his confrontation with Stanton, the president was forced to renege on the passes he had signed and issued orders to enforce the blockade. The northern speculators found their trade blocked, despite the presidential guarantees. Worse, on Stanton's orders, federal provost marshals seized 25 million pounds of meat intended for the southern armies from the warehouses of A. T. Stewart, a northern merchant and (according to Guttridge and Neff) the bacon end of the deal.[7]

The northern speculators somehow came to believe that removing Lincoln from power was essential to moving the cotton. In November 1864, one of the principals gave an associate (according to the authors' unverified special source) a message that if the president and his secretary of state were abducted for a fortnight, "the Congress, we are assured, could and would act in the manner of the Executive. We are further advised that our contracts would be recognized in toto."[8] Aside from the fact that the correspondent was poorly advised on the rules of presidential succession, this scenario assumed that once Lincoln — who tolerated the trade and signed the passes — was removed from the picture, Stanton — who opposed the trade and worked to stop it — would fall into line. Indeed, Guttridge and Neff confirm this assumption: "The money men Barnes [the cotton deal factotum] represented were now more positively than hitherto at one with Lincoln's radical foes."[9]

And what did this solidarity between radical Republicans and northern dealmakers lead to? Even before the conclusion of the pork-for-cotton "superdeal" in October 1864, Booth was engaged by the cotton men to plan an abduction. In August, he journeyed to Washington, where he linked up with William P. Wood, superintendent of the Old Capitol Prison and, according to the authors of *Dark Union*, Stanton's most trusted subordinate.[10] About the same time, a "secret conclave" of three dozen industrialists, publishers, and political extremists met at the home of New York attorney David Dudley Field to decide the fate of Abraham Lincoln. The latter's renomination for the presidency and his tenderheartedness toward the rebels made action imperative. Details remained secret, but declarations attributed to senator Henry Winter Davis (co-sponsor of the Wade-Davis reconstruction bill vetoed by Lincoln that summer) implied drastic action. Ridiculing those who viewed Lincoln as the nation's savior, he warned: "They will soon be convinced that he was on his way lower down and not intending to stay here much longer."[11]

This secret conclave, Guttridge and Neff imply, led to the strangest alliance in Civil War history — or in world history, for that matter. Accompanied by Wood, Booth crossed over the Potomac to a rendezvous with Confederate partisan commander John Singleton Mosby. There they discussed the kidnapping plan, with Wood and Booth seeking Mosby's help because his men specialized in the capture of high-ranking Union officers. The wily guerrilla, fearing a trap, remained suspicious. But Wood and Booth assured him "that many Republicans thought . . . Lincoln was a losing candidate and wanted him removed. His departure would benefit both the Confederacy and the Union." Mosby later recollected (according to the authors' special source) that "certain elements" in the Republican party "had decided that the best thing would be for Lincoln to be taken prisoner by the Confederates and a treaty worked out to the advantage of both sides."[12]

In summary, the plotline of *Dark Union* would have us believe that radical Republicans, northern cotton speculators, and Confederate agents consorted in Lincoln's kidnapping. This is in itself an amazing proposition. What is more amazing is that the shrewd northern businessmen, finding their trade blocked by the War Department under Stanton, would elect to remove Lincoln — who condoned the trade by signing the necessary cotton passes — in order to get the bales and bacon flowing. Furthermore, the radical Republicans and Stanton — who insisted on the South's utter destruction and supposedly wanted Lincoln dead for his leniency — made a deal with southern agents "to the advantage of both sides." True, Guttridge and Neff mention that Lincoln was, by early 1865, vacillating on the idea of trading with the enemy, which might explain the motive of the northern speculators. But according to their sequence of events, the plot was fully organized and in motion well before Lincoln expressed a change of heart concerning the cotton passes. Guttridge and Neff also characterize the conspiracy as "slipshod and improvised," but did this extend to its basic raison d'être?[13] How could these powerful and intelligent men of affairs have so missed the basic point? Lincoln was amenable to the trade, and his passes were honored by Union officials in the field. Would it not have been simpler and infinitely less risky to allow the cotton to flow and then discredit Lincoln, even impeach him (as is suggested at one point) in order to secure his removal? And were the Radicals so intent on their hatred for Lincoln that they abandoned their stated goal of destroying the South in order to make common cause with the Confederacy? They hated Lincoln for his supposed leniency toward the South! Surely this was a plot worthy of Shakespeare, although whether the bard could have imagined antagonists — as the Radicals are described — so twisted up in hatred as to forsake their own political interests remains an open question.

Dark Union has provoked censure, not so much for its logic as for its use of suspect sources. A lengthy article in *North & South* magazine by Lincoln assassination experts Ed Steers Jr. and Joan Chaconas contested the book's evidence point by point.[14] James McPherson, distinguished historian and recent president of the American Historical Association, criticized *Dark Union* in the January 2004 issue of the association's news magazine. Lamenting the continued production of theories alleging a broader conspiracy in Lincoln's death, the veteran scholar deplored *Dark Union*'s reliance on unproven sources and its claim to have uncovered what historians have missed. Asking why we should concern ourselves with fictional accounts masquerading as history, McPherson asserted that it is such accounts' insistence on their presenting the only truth that necessitates intervention. Otherwise, "thousands of readers will continue to believe them if historians merely ignore or dismiss the book without seriously engaging its egregious claims."[15] In concluding, he lightly noted that the acquisition of Guttridge and Neff's research materials by Indiana State University's (ISU) Rare Books and Special Collections Division would prove more useful to writers of fiction than to historical researchers. Nonetheless, in McPherson's closing words one detects a note of unease with the aura of legitimacy granted to the materials through their accession to a university's archives.

Faced with these criticisms, the other side was not slow to respond. The weeks following McPherson's piece saw a flurry of broadsides defending the validity of *Dark Union*'s evidence. First in the breach was David Vancil, head of the Rare Books and Special Collections Division at ISU's Cunningham Memorial Library. Archivists generally remain circumspect regarding the contents of the materials they hold, restricting their evaluation to issues of provenance (where the collection came from) and the collection's value to posterity. But Vancil defended the validity of the Neff-Guttridge Collection's most controversial piece — the alleged papers of alleged detective Andrew Potter — on the basis that a person named Andrew Potter once existed.[16] He also defended the collection's authenticity by comparing Neff's integrity and diligence in research with the "rush to judgment" and haphazard methods of his detractors.[17] In March, the *History News Network* (HNN), an online news service hosted by George Mason University, posted a rebuttal by *Dark Union* coauthor Leonard Guttridge, in which he responded to the "diatribe" of the Steers-Chaconas article with a barrage of factual minutiae that did very little to strengthen the book's argument or respond to the critics' complaints of unverified sources. In the end, Guttridge located Steers and Chaconas's unwillingness to accept the book's testimony "in their apparent refusal or inability to explore the period in Lincoln's career as chief executive when he struggled with a dilemma relatively few history books even mention."[18]

Where does all of this lead? In one sense, nowhere. In conspiracy theory, arguments over evidence are usually fruitless and always endless. Theories surrounding Lincoln's assassination, like those surrounding Kennedy's a century later, feed off ambiguity and controversy. In addition, the attack on the credibility of "traditional" historical studies voiced by *Dark Union* and predecessor works is also part of the conspiracy theory dynamic. On multiple fronts — its improbable logic, its use of suspect evidence, and its attack on the veracity of conventional accounts — *Dark Union* draws upon a venerable tradition whose modern progenitor was Finis L. Bates. It is this lineage that gives the book its logic, and it is to this lineage we must look in order to discern the contemporary legend's cultural and political functioning. Guttridge and Neff's contribution (though they may not recognize it) rests in how their work encapsulates the history of Lincoln conspiracy theories since the 1930s, as well as the legend's distinctive features in present-day America. As noted earlier, the legend of Booth's escape has assumed a secondary role, functioning primarily as proof of official betrayal. Attention has shifted from the figure of the assassin to the details of the intrigues among the supposed leaders of the plot. Most contemporary Lincoln conspiracy narratives describe the assassin in fairly flat fashion. Gone is the captivating personality, the man above the crowd who could beguile listeners with his oratory. Booth, as often as not, appears as the "patsy" in contemporary incarnations, or merely as a spurned co-conspirator acting out of simple malice.

Second, the legend in the present has prompted the opposition of historians and public officials. Contemporary scholars show less patience with theories that impugn, without solid evidence, the behavior of government officials or mainstream historical accounts. The contrast to the earlier criticism of the legend (and allied conspiracy theories) is worth noting. When Bates proposed his revisionist history in Enid, the public and the press drove him out of town. They rejected his account for its moral implications, not for its faulty evidence. They did so in part because the level of solid information on the assassination remained low. The absence of a comprehensive history provided the space where counterhistories like the legend could exist, allowing for an interplay of historical discourse and popular cultural performance. But Enid's citizens readily perceived the affront to the loyalty of the Union government under which the federal veterans had served, and to the nationalist narrative. By the 1920s, the situation had reversed. Legend critics like F. L. Black, William G. Shepherd, and Lloyd Lewis lambasted the Bates story for its fraudulent evidence. Their modernist temper led them to question the facts of the case more closely, and Bates's tintype and handwriting comparisons were found wanting. They rarely attacked the legend for its political content, however, focusing instead on the perceived cultural backwardness of its believers. Nor did professional historians enter into the fray. James Randall's famous essay on the state of Lincoln studies sounded the call for the scholarly appreciation of the nation's sixteenth president, but it did not address the conspiracy theories. Even Eisenschiml's outrageous allegations failed to elicit an outcry from professional historians. Their review of his work addressed its methods without acknowledging its challenge to historical understanding. The revisionist atmosphere of the interwar period erased disagreement. Legend detractors and legend defenders might argue over Booth's true fate, but they hardly differed on the larger issue of the Civil War's meaning in American history. Because of this consensus, the critique of the legend focused on the distortion of fact rather than the political judgments implied in the assertion of Booth's survival.

The situation changed in the present era. The Booth legend and the conspiracy theories to which it is tied have become repoliticized — but for new reasons. William Hanchett noted Booth's renewed political identity as one result of Lincoln's partial desanctification over the past forty years. As long as Lincoln stood as a saint, only a demon could have murdered him. But with the reevaluation of Lincoln's views on slavery and African Americans over the past forty years, Booth has also become a more realistic character. His actions, while still dastardly and tragic to the nation, are seen as having sprung from understandable motives. Actor Rob Morrow, who portrayed the assassin in a 1998 TNT special, underscored the new treatment. Booth, though misguided, killed Lincoln because, Morrow opined, "he believed he was doing something essential and important, that society as we know [sic] it was at stake. . . . In the 12 days between the time he did it and was hunted down, he was shocked to see himself vilified."[19]

The same period has also seen the professionalization of Lincoln studies and greater scholarly attention to the assassination. Hanchett noted the late arrival of the historical profession to the topic, which remained, in his estimate, open to amateur interpretation for too long. Writing in 1983, he concluded optimistically, "the scholarly studies forthcoming ought to put an end to the malignant influence of the sensational books that have deceived the public so long."[20]

Hanchett's faith in the progress of knowledge, as *Dark Union*'s appearance makes clear, has not been realized. But Hanchett recognized another side of the problem — what he saw as the growing divide in postwar America between the popular and the professional understanding of Lincoln's murder. He laid at Eisenschiml's doorstep much of the responsibility for the "growing irrationality" in the popular interpretation of events. The accusations against Stanton assumed the dimensions of the Orwellian Big Lie, so audacious in scope that it generated its own credibility. Even nonconspiratorial accounts, such as Philip Van Doren Stern's *The Man Who Killed Lincoln* (1939) and journalist Jim Bishop's immensely popular *The Day Lincoln Was Shot* (1955), were flavored by the innuendos decocted by the Chicago chemist in his 1937 "classic."[21] Much as Bates's account serves as the principal modern version of the legend, Eisenschiml's thesis dominates contemporary Lincoln conspiracy theory. The present-day line begins with Theodore Roscoe's *Web of Conspiracy* (1959), in which the popular writer repeated the theme of Stanton's guilt and argued for secret service chief Lafayette Baker's involvement in covering up the plot. Roscoe admitted in his preface that his treatment was hypothetical and (like Eisenschiml's approach) proceeded by inferring conclusions from a mass of circumstantial evidence.

Next came Ray Neff's discovery of secret messages in bound volumes of *Colburn's Service Magazine*. Like Finis L. Bates before him, Neff has maintained a perennial devotion to "correcting history." His discovery in the late 1950s of secret ciphers attributed to Lafayette C. Baker in the old journals created a sensation when reported by *Civil War Times* in August 1961.[22] Both Neff and the journal were careful to qualify their support for the documents' authenticity. Nevertheless, excerpts from the ciphers painted a vivid picture of Stanton's perfidy and the involvement of other northern officials:

> In new Rome there walked three men, a Judas, a Brutus, and a spy.
> Each planned that he should be king when Abraham should die.
> One trusted not the other but they went on for that day,
> Waiting for that final moment when with a pistol in his hand,
> One of the sons of Brutus would sneak behind that cursed man
> And put a bullet in his brain and lay his clumsey corpse away.
> As the fallen man lay dying, Judas came and paid respects to one
>   he hated,
> And when at last he saw him die, he said,
> "Now the ages have him, and the nation now have I."[23]

The original cipher lacked punctuation, capitalization, and stanza form. The rhyming patterns, however, indicated that whoever wrote the lines was attempting to compose verse. "Judas" of course referred to Stanton, and "Brutus" to Booth. The "spy" was Baker, who Neff believed was eventually poisoned for his knowledge of the plot. There is reason to doubt the cipher's authenticity, even if the volume did belong to Baker. The last stanza alludes to a saying attributed to Stanton — "Now he belongs to the ages" — supposedly uttered by him when Lincoln expired. Though reported at the time, the remark did not gain much notice until the 1920s.[24] Furthermore, Neff's authentication of the ciphers relied on the transcript of a hearing held in 1872 to determine the validity of a codicil to Baker's will, which Neff discovered in the Philadelphia hall of records. The transcript was discredited by historian James O. Hall, who demonstrated its several factual errors and improbabilities. Regardless of the ciphers' authenticity, at the time their discovery marked a new stage in the development of the

Eisenschiml thesis by introducing hard evidence into what had been a circumstantial case.

Following Neff came popular writer Vaughan Shelton, whose *Mask for Treason* (1965) took the evolving thesis of Stanton's guilt one step further and argued for Baker's active involvement in the plot. Shelton produced his own evidence: a letter from R. D. Watson to John Surratt (Booth's co-conspirator) shortly before the assassination that Shelton contended was actually written by Lafayette Baker! After discovering the letter at the National Archives, Shelton forwarded copies to graphologists, who confirmed that its penmanship matched samples of Baker's writing. Graphology, however, is not the same as forensic handwriting analysis. The former asserts the ability to read personality traits from a person's handwriting. Graphological testimony is not admissible in courts, nor has graphology achieved the status of a professional science. But it fits in perfectly with other alternative sciences that are often called upon to validate conspiracy theories, including phrenology and palm reading.

The professional reaction to the new evidence uncovered by Neff and Shelton ranged from tentative acceptance to explicit criticism. First on the list of the historians' doubts was the reliance on transcripts instead of original documents, followed by questions regarding the validity of graphological analysis.[25] Regardless of their doubts, however, no professional historian or public official intervened directly to challenge the counterhistories proposed by Eisenschiml's successors. Stanton and the Radicals remained indicted in the court of conspiracy opinion. Despite the intervening decades of civil rights activism, Eisenschiml's revisionist thesis — with its implicit denial that the Civil War or Reconstruction had any meaningful purpose in American history — held tight.

This would change in 1977, with the appearance in film and print of *The Lincoln Conspiracy*. Written by David Balsiger and Charles Sellier Jr., whose prior credits included *Grizzly Adams* and *In Search of Noah's Ark*, the feature film and accompanying paperback combined the previous treatments into one narrative. Ray Neff's Potter papers (as yet unavailable for public scrutiny) served as an essential source, and Neff worked as a consultant on the project. The most sensational piece of new evidence was the purported transcript of the Booth diary's "missing" pages, which the movie's producers claimed to have obtained from a dealer in Americana. These pages, and Potter's records, revealed an insidious three-way plot involving northern officials, northern speculators, and southern partisans. Like *Dark Union,* which clearly borrows from the earlier work, *The Lincoln Conspiracy* assumed the erasure of ideological commitment in a blizzard of corruption. Inspired by the American public's cynicism toward its leadership in the wake of Vietnam and Watergate, *The Lincoln Conspiracy* also fed off the widespread skepticism over the Warren Commission's verdict on the Kennedy assassination. Public disbelief in the commission's findings had led to the establishment of a House Select Committee on Assassinations in 1976, to the annoyance of those seeking to protect the nation's historical narrative from marginal and conspiratorial productions. Here, ironically (or maybe expectedly), the legislative branch of government tripped up the efforts of executive branch officials. In failing to untangle the facts of JFK and Martin Luther King Jr.'s murders, the committee did nothing to dissuade the production of counterhistory. Its final report concluded that *probably* Lee Harvey Oswald did not act alone, and *probably* the president was the victim of a conspiracy.[26]

The movie did remarkably well, and the mass-market paperback reached over a million copies in print. It made the *New York Times* best-seller list for seven weeks running.[27] Such popularity alone might have sufficed to raise the ire of professional historians. But the producers added fuel to the fire by asserting the failure of history in bringing out the truth, stating in the book, "Traditional historical writers have perpetuated an inadvertent cover-up by using 1865 government data and documents as gospel." Balsiger and Sellier, taking their cue from the revelations of the Warren Commission investigation and the Watergate cover-up, assumed that the government's statements might be false: "If the government's statements are true, they can be authenticated through papers in private collections."[28] Thus public history was said to depend on private verification, and despite the separation of four decades Balsiger and Sellier appealed to the fidelity of private sentiment over public record, as Izola Forrester had done in her family drama. Even more challenging to professional sensibilities were the authors' claims to having overcome historical uncertainty through the application of modern scientific techniques. In addition to the humdrum of archival research, *The*

Lincoln Conspiracy allegedly made use of psychological stress evalua-
tors, chemical testing, and special light photography.

It was this last item that sparked professional and official reaction,
when Ray Neff, under an arrangement with the movie's producers,
obtained permission from the custodians of Ford's Theater to examine Booth's diary. He photographed the diary's pages using special
light techniques and turned the photos over to Balsiger and Sellier,
who then claimed that the photos revealed more "historical discrepancies."[29] Along with information culled from their transcript of the
missing pages, the diary's pages proved the existence of a plot involving "70 prominent people . . . , and the pages contain some
cipher-coded names, including the names of prominent Stanton
aides."[30] The rumors of Neff's photographic mission, along with the
matter of the missing pages, circulated through the Lincoln assassination community months before the movie's release. It prompted
several historians to petition the Department of the Interior (DOI),
parent organization to the National Park Service, for the diary's complete examination by a competent public authority. After first being
refused (on the grounds that the diary was in bad shape and could not
sustain another photographic analysis), the historians turned to political pressure. Correspondence from National Park Service files indicates that Hubert Humphrey and Walter Mondale intervened on behalf of the petitioners, and in June 1977 the DOI turned the diary over
to the FBI Crime Lab.[31] FBI technicians subjected the diary to a page-
by-page analysis using their own special light techniques. Their report, currently available online at the FBI's Freedom of Information
Act Electronic Reading Room, found no evidence of secret writing.[32]
They did confirm that pages had been removed from the diary (actually a daybook of the kind still used today) at intervals, as indicated by
the tear marks against the volume's binding. They also compared
samples of Booth's handwriting — from his "To whom it may concern"
and "Dear mother" letters, which were provided by the National
Archives — to verify that the writing in the diary was his. (It was.)

The Crime Lab was also requested to photograph every page of the
artifact, as National Park officials had decided (or had been instructed) to prohibit future examination of the book by outside parties. When news of the findings and the FBI's involvement leaked out,
reporters clamored for information. *Washington Post* columnists

Haynes Johnson and the team of Jack Anderson and Les Whitten covered the story from opposite sides in the August 3 edition. *Civil War Times Illustrated,* sporting a name change and a new editor, retracted its former support for the Neff-Shelton allegations and published a lengthy critique of *The Lincoln Conspiracy* in its August and November issues.[33]

The most severe censure of Balsiger and Sellier came a year later, when Lincoln scholar Harold Hyman delivered the keynote address at the Abraham Lincoln Association's annual symposium. His talk, "With Malice Towards Some: Scholarship (or Something Less) on the Lincoln Murder," derided *The Lincoln Conspiracy* and kindred productions as "the d — — dest trash and fiction." The phrase was originally that of John P. Usher, Lincoln's Secretary of the Interior, who wrote in 1885 to lament the distortions then circulating over the life and death of his former chief. Hyman had his own reasons for lamenting the most recent eruption of what he saw as fiction. *The Lincoln Conspiracy,* as its book sales demonstrated, had gained both notice and acceptance from the general public. No doubt the movie studio's promotional efforts, which included selling block discounts to school groups (!), and the fact that Lincoln Memorial University awarded Balsiger and Sellier honorary doctorates, had something to do with the book's success. Clearly, the line separating counterhistory and mainstream historical study was being trampled on, and Hyman sought to reinstate it with a careful dissection of *The Lincoln Conspiracy*'s deceptions and errors. His analysis skewered the book's scientific pretensions; and since many of the sources used in *The Lincoln Conspiracy* have been recycled in *Dark Union,* Hyman's findings remain relevant. Of 1,081 footnotes counted, 500 — almost half — cited unreliable or unverifiable sources, including previous conspiracy works (those by Eisenschiml, Roscoe, and Shelton) and the unverified transcript of the "missing" diary pages. Another 225 of the 500 came from Neff's collection of Potter papers and other documents, which were at the time completely unavailable to outside scrutiny.[34]

Hyman's explanation of the forces driving the continued production of conspiracy literature asserted a parallel between historical writing and contemporaneous events. The short-term factor — the distrust in government following Kennedy's assassination, Vietnam, and Watergate — had made it difficult for contemporary historians "to insist on the basis of verifiable evidence, that exposures of Nixonian corruptions are not implicit proofs of analogous earlier cover-ups." Further back in time, Hyman found a partial basis for the evolving conspiracy mind-set in developments within the historical profession itself. The advent of professionalism in the last decades of the nineteenth century brought with it the adoption of social scientific theories. Darwin, Freud, and Marx — regardless of their explicatory powers — replaced individual choice with impersonal determinism. The result, Hyman believed, had deeply affected the New Historians of the Progressive Era, "and gave seeming credence to conspiracy theses on many subjects." During the 1920s and 1930s, disillusionment over the Great War and its outcome led historians to weave "analogic threads" into their Civil War and Reconstruction narratives. World War II had the opposite effect: the "good war" caused historians to rediscover "the possibility of morality in conflict, of useful victory, of constructive reconstructions, and of heightened racial justice even during a global war."[35] Attitudes changed again with Vietnam; disillusionment with the nation-state had historians appealing once more to the conspiratorial vision of Charles Beard and the New Historians.

The historians, Hyman seemed to say, rubbed off on the amateur producers. A development that Hyman did not mention, but that was equally important to the problem of historical interpretation in modern America, is that at the same time historians were adopting new scientific methods, other professions — lawyers, doctors, chemists — were also professionalizing. This professionalization, which began in the late nineteenth century, gave rise to a species of conspiracy authors who, while not trained in historical research, felt that their own specialties provided the keys to unlocking what the historians had missed. Laboratory scientists and lawyers appeared the most eager to take up the challenge — witness Bates, Eisenschiml, and Neff (a retired professor of public health at Indiana State University).

This idea of the interrelationship of professional historical discourse and popular counterhistories is central to my own analysis. Where I take issue with Hyman's analysis is on the matter of periodicity — the waxing and waning of conspiracy interpretations depending on concurrent political experience. Although the legend has undergone multiple developments in the 140 years of its existence, it has also demonstrated a strong degree of permanence. The mummy drew upon traditions and memories reaching back to the antebellum period. In the legend's northern version, the trauma of Lincoln's assassination encouraged a need for repeated enactment of the murderer's annihilation and reinstatement. In its southern form, the legend drew upon a perennial devotion in the post–Civil War South to the imagined traits of the prewar, premarket gentleman of the "old school." Though it is true that short-term ideological impulses were essential to defining the legend's significance at different periods, these perennial forces cannot be discounted.

Hyman's analysis also suggests the continuing battle for interpretive control within Lincoln studies and the history of the Civil War. Unlike other areas of American history, these two areas remain the province of gifted (and not so gifted) lay practitioners as well as professionals. The line between the two groups is admirably permeable, and Civil War journals continue to feature the work of professional and amateur historians long after the latter have disappeared from most historical publications.

This situation both contributes to and reflects the American public's continued fascination with the Civil War. It also guarantees accessibility, not to mention financial benefits, for writers on Civil War topics, as Civil War histories remain the most readable of historical genres. The downside, for those who argue for the field's fuller professionalization, is that amateurs continue to assert their rights in ways that professional scholars at times find disconcerting. *Civil War Times*'s espousal (and subsequent retraction) of the Baker cipher theory shows how fluid the line is dividing reasonable interpretations from more audacious productions, such as Neff's and Schick Sunn Classic (producers of *The Lincoln Conspiracy*). Alan Nolan's lament over the pervasive myth of the Lost Cause, noted in the introduction to this study, is the most obvious example of the tension between the professionals and the amateurs. The conspiracy theories are the extreme manifestation of this tension, serving in part as a rejection of the professionals' aspiration to interpretive control. Balsiger and Sellier's critique of the traditional historical enterprise has already been noted. Vaughan Shelton decried historians' lack of "positive results" in explaining what instigated Booth's actions. The result, in his opinion, was that after a century of scrutiny we were no closer to understanding the true causes of the assassination.[36] Guttridge and Neff berate historians' "vested interest in preserving a standardized version of history." Instead of accepting new evidence that promises to revise our understanding of the past, "they ignore or even try to suppress fresh evidence that tends to contradict conventional accounts."[37] As the epigraph at the beginning of this chapter underlines, "traditional" historical narrative has failed to provide the true explanation of why Lincoln was killed. These same sentiments were voiced a half-century or more earlier by Bates, Wilson, Forrester, and Eisenschiml. The record in lineaments is more faithful; truth is stranger than fiction; and Booth, having thwarted destiny, must wander the earth. Despite the claims of its professors, history fails to explain the memory of trauma, nostalgia — and revisionism.

History's "failure" — in the opinion of conspiracy theory adepts — to explain the drama of Lincoln's death suggests the deeper logic that sustains modern Lincoln conspiracy theories and further suggests that *Dark Union, The Lincoln Conspiracy,* and allied works are more closely related to Oliver Stone's *JFK, The X-Files,* and *Roswell* than to mainstream accounts of Lincoln's death. In fact, Kennedy's assassination in November 1963 permanently transformed the terrain upon which these theories operate. Long-standing accusations of Catholic complicity in the assassinations of several presidents became immediately anachronistic and even obscene.[38] More broadly, to the extent the trauma of Lincoln's demise still lingered in American collective memory, the murder of JFK irrevocably supplanted it. Kennedy's assassination (accentuated by the later killings of Martin Luther King Jr. and Robert Kennedy) served as America's principal trauma until the 2001 terrorist attacks on the World Trade Center and the Pentagon. While Lincoln remains enthroned in the pantheon of heroes, the tragedy of his death seems, to present-day Americans, far removed. This does not mean, however, that the earlier assassination (and with it the story of Booth's escape) has lost all import in contemporary conspiracy culture. Many readers know of the litany of coincidences between Lincoln and Kennedy — both elected in the year '60, both succeeded by vice-presidents named Johnson, etc. — that to contemporary conspiracy theorists link the two events.[39] There are also structural similarities between the Lincoln and JFK assassination theories (Oliver Stone's being the prime example of the latter group) that heighten this affinity. In both theories, the president figures as a benevolent individual who would have done the "right" thing if he had been allowed to live. He was destroyed not by outside forces, but by "insiders," powerful enemies in the seat of government who not only betrayed the people's elected representative, but the nation as well. The radical Republicans betrayed the nation by carrying out their program of destroying the South and imposing black civil rights — so the theory implies. In Kennedy's case, the claim is that the military-industrial complex reversed his decision to withdraw from Vietnam and launched the country on a ten-year nightmare. Although dated, the earlier assassination contributes to a cumulative trauma that ultimately may be rooted less in actual events than in a conviction of history gone wrong. The Booth legend and its allied conspiracy theories contribute (albeit on the margins) to the conspiracy master narrative in postwar America. Insidious, unseen, and omnipotent organizations have usurped government and killed the people's champion. And while the older tales of deception may lack the punch of *JFK* or *The X-Files,* they contribute to the body of lore that serves millions of Americans as a principal framework for making sense of the world.[40]

Beginning with Richard Hofstadter's critique of conspiracy theory as right-wing political paranoia, scholars have explored more fully its potential ideological and counterideological intentions. Recent takes include viewing conspiracy theory — with its insistence on the operation of unseen forces — as the political "other" in a democratic polity, where in theory political decision-making occurs in the open. Postmodern theorist Fredric Jameson sees conspiracy theory as a poor person's "cognitive mapping" of a society that has become too fragmented, too complex, and too large to be understood in terms of local forces and relations. Individuals not privy to the inside workings of multinational corporations and the superstate (that is, most of us) use conspiracy theory in an attempt to make sense of the world. A third interpretation sees conspiracy theory as both an expression of and resistance to "agency panic," the anxiety over lost personal autonomy many people feel in a society dominated by large, impersonal, and unsympathetic institutions. Both of the foregoing resemble Gordon Wood's historical explanation of conspiracy theory in the eighteenth century as a response to the increasing impersonality and complexity of social relations. On the religious side, conspiracy theories serve some premillennialist Protestant teachers in their warnings of impending doom.[41]

While sharing these meanings, the Lincoln theories remain unique because they are the most historical of American conspiracy theories.

They are concerned about the past in ways that theories of alien abductions and supernatural "insider" governments are not. It is this orientation, and the desire to find out the "truth" where regular history has failed, that gives them their quality of memory — or, more properly, countermemory. The "remembering" of Stanton's crime and Booth's escape speaks to the trauma of the original event, one that uncannily continues to resurface in American culture despite almost a century and a half. Lincoln theories perpetuate a more general collective trauma by endlessly replaying the assassination at the same time they promise a final accounting. But the final accounting never comes; so the theories, like the original northern narratives of Booth's person and whereabouts, sow ambiguity even as they claim truth. Eisenschiml's leading questions and *Dark Union*'s mystifying logic are not simply the products of unsteady sources or erratic minds. They serve a rhetorical and epistemological purpose: they deny "traditional" history in order to preserve a direct memory of the event that may never be obtained through factual accounts. Lincoln, Booth, Kennedy, Oswald — the trauma is reformatted as time progresses and new tragedies are heaped on the old. Despite its narrative of progress, there is a deep wound in American culture that refuses to heal. Lincoln's death merges with that of John F. Kennedy, Martin Luther King, Robert Kennedy, and the many other political assassinations in this country's recent history.

If the legend and its allied conspiracy theories only served to preserve a faithful memory of traumatic historical events, however, they would remain innocuous, hardly deserving of the recent assaults by historians. After all, very few, if any, current urban legends, myths, and counterhistories come in for the censure of the Booth and Stanton stories. To be sure, contemporary Lincoln theories manifest an antistate bias, but so does the narrative of the Master Conspiracy, with its allegations that big government serves the interests of a global super-elite instead of the people. But the Lincoln theories go further, and they arouse opposition for two reasons. First, they are more potent because they are the most historical of conspiracy stories. What they condemn is not the operation of present institutions, but the mainstream memory of the past and its historical narration. Historians naturally have a professional interest in protecting their terrain from destructive intrusions, but the opposition goes deeper. Assaulting the past through the medium of conspiracy theory also threatens the present. Lincoln conspiracy theories in the present era function as disruptive countermemories. And just as legend believers like Clarence True Wilson saw in Booth's survival a disruption to America's providential destiny, contemporary legend critics voice concern over its impact on the popular understanding of the nation's past. Their orientation is without a doubt more secular than the Methodist minister's, but their commitment to preserving the integrity of the nation's history from slanderous affronts is just as deeply felt. Especially in the wake of Vietnam and Watergate, maintaining the public's faith in the integrity of the nation-state has taken on increased significance for historians and other guardians of the nation's past.[42]

But the danger posed to the people's faith in their national government may be the lesser of two evils. More disturbing, at least in my judgment, is how contemporary Lincoln theories use the trauma of Lincoln's death to transmit down to the present the revisionist ideology expressed in Eisenschiml's *Why Was Lincoln Murdered?* and nonconspiracy works like Lewis's *Myths after Lincoln* and Bowers's *The Tragic Era*. Whether Guttridge, Neff, and other postwar theorists are aware of their role in this regard is doubtful — though Guttridge's recent claim that "Nowhere does *Dark Union* charge that Secretary of War Edwin M. Stanton 'did it'" is disingenuous.[43] Certainly, the racial crudities found in the early-twentieth-century works are gone, and recent authors fail to draw out the ideological implications of the story they tell. Nonetheless, a few passages from *Dark Union* confirm its pedigree:

> The radicals, ultras, unconditionals, Jacobins — whatever label they wore — were bent on limiting Lincoln's power and, if necessary, robbing him of it. (46)

> "Armistice would be the death of our cause." So wrote one of Stanton's intimates to a fellow radical. "*No armistice* was one of the distinct points on which Mr. Lincoln was re-elected." Stanton needed no such reminder. To keep the guns firing, Mr. Lincoln had to be watched, controlled — if necessary, circumvented. (86)

> Obeying an urgent summons from the secretary of war, three political radicals were soon in his office, Congressman George Julian, Senator Zachariah Chandler, and John Conness, senator from

Massachusetts [California] . . . The reaction in his office was as if a smoking bomb had landed there . . . "We have Booth's diary," said an obviously shaken secretary, "and he has recorded a lot in it." Chandler thumbed through the little red book, anxiously mumbling. Conness snatched it from him, scanned its pages, and moaned repeatedly, "Oh, my God. I am ruined if this ever gets out." (175)

What does this restatement of the revisionist portrayal of Stanton and the Radicals imply, and what should we make of its survival into the post–civil rights era? The answer is disconcerting. Against Hanchett's assertion that revisionism faded away at the same time Neff began his quest for the only truth (with his discovery of the Baker ciphers in the late 1950s), *Dark Union* forces us to recognize revisionism's continuing endurance as a countermemory of what the Civil War stood for.[44] Furthermore, it does so by joining the memory of the war as a conflict without purpose (and of the radical Republicans as bereft of human charity or moral conviction) to the memory of the trauma of Lincoln's death. This is the book's most egregious claim, and it goes far beyond the distortion of historical evidence.

CONCLUSION

Over the course of its 140–year history, the story of Booth's survival, appearing in multiple guises, has served a variety of political, cultural, and ideological purposes. How the legend and the mummy were created and put to use has been too multifaceted to permit complete resolution. Nor can we disregard the sensationalism that has often accompanied their ideological and political elaborations. This combination of factors makes it difficult to place a final value on the legend's meaning in American culture. Does it stand for white southern racial intolerance, another aspect of the "unregenerate" attitudes in Dixie a century ago, and of the more recent neo-Confederate surge? Or does it stand for the growing mistrust of a sizable group in American society toward its government? Should we conclude that the legend represents the failure of historical knowledge, as many of its critics maintain, and the manipulation of this ignorance by sensationalist self-promoters? Does it present a threat to the national narrative with its accusations of treasonous murder by political leaders entrusted with the nation's care? Do Booth and his mummified body evoke, in some deep yet vague way, the "remembrance" of ancient whiteness for Americans of European descent?

The short answer to these questions is yes — on all points. The legend continues to perform "serious" cultural work even as it appears in the most misbegotten theories of treason. Booth continues to stand, in the eyes of some people, as a regional hero who gave the South the last word, or else as a tragic hero whose one misstep brought calamity upon the nation. The evocation of his white beauty, though emphasized much less in recent incarnations, carries the echo of a white racial consciousness whose origins date to the first settlement of British North America.

Despite these multiple functions, however, we can identify certain features that may establish the legend's overall meaning and place in American culture. First, there is the trajectory of its production and performance over the past 140 years. The 1920s and '30s witnessed the apogee of this trajectory, as measured by popular literary output and exposure in national media. The literary renaissance of the Depression era drew upon oral and written traditions stretching back to the days following Lincoln's assassination. And in our own day, the story survives on the margins of a larger conspiracy culture. Lincoln assassination expert Steve Miller has told me that he fields inquiries from believers, disbelievers, Booth family members, and the generally curious weekly. Publishers continue to find a ready market for books on the assassination and the theories that allege to explain Booth's actions. The legend, past and present, defies the pessimism of cultural critics who see the present age as one of degraded memory and shrill commercialism, and as somehow less "authentic" in its cultural productions than ages past. The good news, one might say, is that from its very first days the legend encompassed banality, of either a political or a commercial sort. The trauma of the assassin's act had barely ebbed in the North before politicians turned the rumors of his escape to mundane use. Enid's entrepreneurs played off the ideal of the romantic southern gentleman by embalming a drifter's corpse and then displaying it. The legend's first general feature, then, is the support it lends to cultural theorists who see no separation between the profane and the sacred, or between "respectable" cultural expression and commercial exploitation. Further, as a memory of an important event in the American past, the legend defies the notion that memory in the present has become somehow fragmented and torn apart by the critical discourse of history. As both counterhistory and countermemory, the Booth legend demonstrates the persistent viability of what Pierre Nora called *lived memory*, but which he argues has disappeared in modern western societies, obliterated by the debunking propensities of modern historical narrative.[1] Izola Forrester's paean to the primacy of lineaments over records, Clarence True Wilson's insistence on the moral shape of the past and present, and Finis L. Bates's reliance on resemblance and personality to establish the truth of the past force us to consider how groups within modern culture continue to construct their vision of the past not in accordance with the dictates of historical discourse but through the constant presence of remembered places, faces, and things.

The legend's path over time also yields insight into the mechanics of cultural production in the modern United States. The interplay of written and oral sources, especially the somewhat surprising dependence of oral traditions on prior written accounts, is one facet of these mechanics. Another is the role played by a dedicated group in collecting, exchanging, and validating "evidence," whether artifacts or stories, in constructing the legend narrative. From its beginnings in oral culture and popular print, the legend reached what might be termed a period of "literary concentration" in the 1920s and '30s. This literary concentration included the establishment of a group of collectors (or, less decorously, "legend buffs") who exchanged evidence, theories, and correspondence, and who established the legend's archival community in the twentieth century. The internal circulation of information is also one of the distinctive features of conspiracy theorizing, first noted by Richard Hofstadter and more recently by Robert Goldberg.[2] Having reached this phase, the story continued to subsist at all levels, oral and literary, again suggesting that any theory attempting to explain an overall pattern of cultural development must recognize the specific modes of cultural production. It is not enough to say, for instance, that the commemorative activities of the past have yielded to a commercialized form of memory, such as the heritage tour. The legend resists this neat characterization because at the level of mechanics — the individual actions leading to the production of narrative and performance — it continues to draw upon a range of sources.

There is also an epistemological — or, perhaps more accurately, a historiographical — element that helps to define the legend's larger meaning. Along with kindred cultural productions, the Booth story directly confronts contemporary modes of historical understanding. The denunciations of contemporary conspiracy theorists make this obvious. Underneath their unkind words toward "traditional" historical practice, however, lies an inversion. For it is they, in the truest sense, who are the traditionalists. They are the ones attempting to recover a mode of knowledge discredited in the historical mainstream. Most people engaged in the contemporary professional study of history, along with most readers, have adopted an interpretive and/or a functionalist framework. In the first case, we view the past as a field for possible interpretations, none of which can ever be established as fully representing the event. These interpretations are evaluated for their "fit" and serve contemporary needs of a political, social, or cultural kind. We also examine the past for its usefulness to the present.

The functionalist examination of historical events aims to better the present, whether it be bridge design, military tactics, or social policy (to name a few examples), by applying the lessons of past experiences to present problems. Neither of these two frameworks claims to arrive at the whole truth of the historical event it analyzes. Nor does either seek what Yosef Yerulshalmi describes, in a very different context, as *meaning in history*.[3] Contemporary historians never claim to lay hold of the Truth (with a capital T) — understood as the total meaning of the past, and involving metahistorical agents such as "destiny," "progress," "providence," or "Idea." Dorothy Ross has examined the transformation of American historical understanding from the time when prevailing religious worldviews still conditioned most Americans to see their past, present, and future as a tableau upon which providential destiny was enacted. Only in the early twentieth century, with the dawning of the Progressive era, did historicism (historical causation determined solely by prior historical events), in her view, gain sway.[4] What the legend and allied conspiracy theories force us to realize is that many people continue to insist on seeing larger designs at work in the past, even if the designs are malevolent.

Whether this insistence, in the form of conspiracy theory, results in a "degraded" representation of present reality, as Fredric Jameson argues, is beyond the scope of this book. The relevant point for our purposes is that the legend, as a memory of the past opposed to the history of the event, seeks to impart *meaning* to Lincoln's assassination in ways that conventional histories no longer do. This is abundantly clear in the case of Methodist divine Clarence True Wilson, for whom Booth's escape and subsequent wandering symbolized the entire moral drama of post–Civil War America. There is a constant refrain in Booth legend and Lincoln conspiracy works, a constant hankering after the "whole story," that always entails the uncovering of something hidden (and almost always nefarious). In his classic exposition of conspiracy theory as an expression of right-wing political paranoia, Richard Hofstadter found this belief in hidden causes symptomatic of a social pathology. Without denying the pathological turn contemporary counterhistories can take (the example of Holocaust denial comes to mind), I believe that the larger motive in the case of the Booth legend is a desire to reinject the course of human events with purposeful agency. Charging the state with treason against the people becomes, ironically, one means of achieving this. At least there is an identifiable force to blame for the nation's ills. It is a situation akin to that suggested by Gordon Wood in explaining the prevalence of conspiracy belief in the Enlightenment era. Faced with the growing complexity of society and the growing impersonality of human relations in an expanding commercial world, eighteenth-century citizens found in conspiracy theory a means of restoring human, personal agency to the events about them.[5] Believers in Booth's escape, and those participating in the conspiracy theories surrounding Lincoln's death, seek to restore agency in history by asserting the operation of unseen forces in the president's death.

The question remains *why* a significant subgroup in American society insists upon uncovering the meaning of Lincoln's death (and Booth's escape), and why there is this desire to assign agency. The answer is suggested by Gene Smith's observation of the need people feel to be in touch with events that are past yet that still possess great power. Do the Booth bus tours (even if only a minority of the participants believe that Booth escaped) function as ritual therapy on a collective level? Could it be that Lincoln conspiracy theories function in a similar fashion, and that their rejection of conventional accounts stems from standard histories' inability to effectively communicate the trauma of the original event? Conventional histories relate the facts of the assassination (although conspiracy theorists deny that they do even this), but they cannot adequately evoke the sense of loss that originated in the moment of Lincoln's shooting. This loss has received amplifying shocks in its transit to the present, joining Lincoln with King and Kennedy in a linked event that refutes America's providential destiny. Historical discourse cannot capture the tragic weight, but memory and conspiracy theory do because both recover the event's emotional value, foregoing factual fidelity in the process. Lincoln's assassination and those that followed make up what trauma theorists describe as a "limit event." The dimension of the tragedy is incommensurate, incapable of being measured, and beyond narration through conventional means. It constitutes the negative sublime, and conspiracy theory is one available means to represent it discursively.[6] In order to achieve its effect, conspiracy narrative must operate on two levels simultaneously. The first asserts the revelation of complete truth, and hence meaning in history. The second takes away what the first gives by adopting rhetorical strategies including logical non sequiturs, overreliance on circumstantial evidence, and suggestive inferences to create indeterminacy. The contradiction here is only an apparent one, because while the goal may be to arrive at Truth, there is no intention of achieving closure, of "working through" the trauma. The final goal of Finis Bates, Izola Forrester, Otto Eisenschiml, Theodore Roscoe, and more recent promulgators is to keep the event alive, not quell it through final resolution. Like the biographical elaborations and sightings reports in the North immediately following the assassin's act, conspiracy narratives create uncertainty even as they offer total explanation. Consequently, the violation of historical discourse through which conspiracy theory operates is only a necessary secondary condition; criticism of its methods and sources can never put an end to its production.

If the final meaning of the legend were its contribution to a collective repetitive trauma syndrome in American culture, we might dismiss it as a harmless matter. The inevitable by-product of American political violence, it hardly seems deserving of the attacks leveled against it by historians and public officials, regardless of its antigovernment fulminations. But this is not its final meaning, at least not in my reading. In the introduction to this work, I noted what I felt was the legend's greatest significance as an object of study: the conflation of attitudes deemed "southern" with a broader regionalist discontent over the course of progress in modern America. This conflation was most pronounced during the interwar period when, as discussed in Chapter 6, the legend came to represent regionalist discontent at the same time it was popularized in mass-circulation periodicals. During the same period, a new element entered the legend equation — the revisionist interpretation of the Civil War; and as this study draws to a close, I have come to realize that its greatest significance as an object of study involves a different kind of conflation. Lincoln conspiracy theories, including the Booth legend, over the past half century have conflated the trauma of Lincoln's death with the revisionist interpretation of the Civil War. Just as Lloyd Lewis's modernist debunking of the legend enfolded an attack on Radical political efforts to achieve racial justice, so too have the successors to Eisenschiml reinscribed the revisionist message, hiding it within their reenactment of the trauma of the event.

Whether the contemporary crafters of Lincoln conspiracy theories are aware of the ideological content they pass along is a question I cannot answer. But there should be no doubt this content survives and continues to condition the public's (or at least the conspiracy public's) understanding of the Civil War and its aftermath. To accuse Edwin Stanton of zealotry remains an accusation against the efforts of the Radical wing of the Republican Party. And these Radicals stand in the judgment of historians now, as they stood then, for racial equality and the total dismantling of racist political and social structures in the United States. Alan Nolan laments the continuing power of the myth of the Lost Cause and its antiprogressive influence. So it is with current conspiracy versions of Lincoln's death. The injection of reactionary dogma into the traumatic memory of the assassination also distinguishes Lincoln conspiracy theories from more recent ones (at least for the time being), including theories of alien abduction and JFK's murder. It is this dimension, and not the perversion of historical sources, that most requires historians' attention. For while the legend may tell us much about how the popular history of America has been formed over the past century and a half, and while much about the legend remains innocuous, its intolerant messages must be made plain. The legend's greatest lesson to the present is how subgroups in American culture appropriate deeply symbolic events for harmful purposes. It is a process that is, unfortunately, ongoing; and vigilance is required lest the traumas of America's very recent past come in for similar treatment.

I would be remiss to close this study without mentioning the current fate of David E. George. In 1992, Nate Orlowek, a longtime legend believer and religious education director for a suburban Washington synagogue, spearheaded a drive to exhume Booth's actual remains from their resting place in Baltimore's Green Mount Cemetery. He was supported by several legend believers from around the country, and by two government-employed forensic anthropologists, whose interest in the case appears to have been more scientific than legend-born. Orlowek, contrary to the main drift of contemporary assassination theory, remained devoted to Finis L. Bates's turn-of-the-century account. He convinced NBC's *Unsolved Mysteries* to produce a fifteen-minute segment on the legend that featured the Bates version (it aired in September 1991 and occasionally reappears on cable channels). Despite his heterodoxy in the matter of legend versions, he shared the common attitude of modern-day theorists that "several generations of historians have not done their homework."[7]

When Green Mount Cemetery turned down his request, Orlowek turned to the courts and filed a petition for exhumation. His legal action set off a minor media blitz and aroused the attention of the Lincoln assassination community. Led by the Surratt Society, the Maryland historical organization devoted to preserving the history of Lincoln's murder, the assassination experts mobilized to block the exhumation through its monthly newsletter and by providing expert witnesses for the cemetery's counsel.[8]

Judging from the transcript of the court proceedings, which finally took place in May 1995, the hearings were anticlimactic after the months of media exposure and testimony preparation. This was due partly to the inexperience of Orlowek's attorney (it was his first case) and partly to legal precedents that discourage exhumation for other than compelling reasons. Additionally, there were technical difficulties that worked against the petitioners' case: Orlowek's team admitted that they could not locate Booth's grave precisely without employing ground-penetrating radar and possibly exploratory excavation. The presence of groundwater in the cemetery also militated against excavation. Even if Booth's remains were successfully recovered, the scientific advisers admitted that an accurate determination of the remains' identity would hinge upon the body's state of decomposition and their ability to recover suitable samples of mitochondrial DNA.[9]

Nor were Orlowek *et alia* able to provide a compelling historical argument for doubting that the remains in the cemetery were not Booth's (the aim of the petitioners, obviously, was to show they were not). His reliance on the Bates narrative made Orlowek an easy target for the historical experts called by the cemetery's counsel. The purplish prose and logical leaps employed by Bates could not withstand modern legal scrutiny. Orlowek's attorney's attempt to enlist the 1866 avowal of Senator Garrett Davis — "I have never seen myself any satisfactory evidence that Booth was killed" — met with an easy rebuff when William Hanchett, testifying on the cemetery's behalf, pointed out that the statement carried no weight unless considered in context.[10] But the nail in the coffin, some believe, was the testimony against exhumation by James Starrs, professor of law and forensics at George Washington University and the leading impresario of the newest brand of alternative history — historical exhumations. Beginning in 1989, when he dug up the remains of five victims of a nineteenth-century frontier cannibal, Starrs has adapted the methods and rationale of conspiracy theory to argue for the intervention of forensic science in setting history right. His other notable exploits include digging up Jesse James and his unsuccessful attempt to exhume the remains of Meriwether Lewis. Given Starrs's fondness for publicity and high-profile exhumations, the Booth petitioners might have expected him to support their project. This may in fact have been the problem: one individual close to the trial has suggested to me in conversation that Starrs ultimately shot the exhumation down because it wasn't his show.[11]

The failure of the petition (and the subsequent appeal) left the legend advocates only one recourse: locating the embalmed remains of the Oklahoma drifter. If George's mummy were found and subjected to modern scientific analysis, then the matter of Booth's survival could be definitively settled. But where was the body? It had disappeared in the 1940s and supposedly made its way east to Philadelphia in the 1950s or '60s. It was last spotted in 1976, at a sideshow in New Hope, Pennsylvania.[12] Unbelievably (or maybe inevitably), the body made its way to Silver Spring, Maryland, the very town Orlowek lived in when he was pushing for the exhumation. The facts I have been able to gather are word of mouth and unverified, but it appears that Booth now belongs to a collector of circus paraphernalia (one source also told me he works in a delicatessen — a savory thought!), who has threatened to throw the body in a dumpster if ever he is bothered by the legend believers. Orlowek, I have been told, attempted to approach the collector without success. Not everyone, however, accepts this version of the mummy's travels. Among the assassination experts are several who don't mind telling you that they do know, but are not divulging, the latest resting place of David E. George.

NOTES

INTRODUCTION

1. Historical accounts detailing the assassin's flight, other than those appearing in the few years immediately following Lincoln's murder, began with George Alfred Townsend's "How Wilkes Booth Crossed the Potomac," *Century Magazine*, April 1884; Prentiss Ingraham's "Pursuit and Death of John Wilkes Booth," *Century Magazine,* January 1890; and Victor Louis Mason, "Four Lincoln Conspiracies," *Century Magazine*, April 1896. Lincoln collector Osborne Oldroyd's *The Assassination of Abraham Lincoln* (Washington, D.C.: O. H. Oldroyd, 1901) was followed by numerous works. The brief summary provided here is based on Michael W. Kauffman, "Booth's Escape Route: Lincoln's Assassin on the Run," *Blue and Gray,* May 1990: 9–22, 38–61; and Edward Steers Jr., *Blood on the Moon: The Asssassination of Abraham Lincoln* (Lexington: University Press of Kentucky, 2001), 135–65, 183–206. Steers's account includes an analysis of the hard evidence produced over the years to make the case for Booth's escape.

2. For the adventures of real Confederates in Mexico after the war and their position between the French-imposed Emperor Maximilian and the Liberal Benito Suarez, see Andrew Rolle, *The Lost Cause: The Confederate Exodus to Mexico* (Norman: University of Oklahoma Press, 1965).

3. Tony Rice, "John Wilkes Booth," written by Mary Chapin Carpenter, on *Native American*, compact disc (Rounder Records Corp., 1988), Rounder CD 0248; Tom Pacheco, "John Wilkes Booth," on *Lost American Songwriter,* compact disc (Road Goes on Forever Records, 1999), TPDCD016; Clutch, "I Have the Body of John Wilkes Booth," on *Clutch,* compact disc (Atlantic Recording Co., 1995), 61755–2. Clutch's recording studio at the time was in Silver Spring, Maryland, perhaps explaining the song's inspiration.

4. Gene Smith, "The Booth Obsession," *American Heritage* 43, no. 5 (1992): 119. For a lighthearted rendition of the escape tour, see David Montgomery's article "Happy Boothday to You: In Which Our Intrepid Correspondent Rides, Rolls, and Rows His Way into History Chasing the Ghost of John Wilkes Booth," *Washington Post,* April 18, 1999.

5. William Hanchett, *The Lincoln Murder Conspiracies* (Urbana: University of Illinois Press, 1983), 3–4. Neely's statement appeared originally in "The Lincoln Theme since Randall's Call: The Promises and Perils of Professionalism," in *Papers of the Abraham Lincoln Association* (Springfield, Ill.: Abraham Lincoln Association, 1979), 1:41–42.

6. Thomas R. Turner, *Beware the People Weeping: Public Opinion and the Assassination of Abraham Lincoln* (Baton Rouge: Louisiana State University Press, 1982), 61–62.

7. The judgments, respectively, of assassination experts James O. Hall and William C. Davis. See Edward Colimore, "The Search for Lincoln's Assassin," *Philadelphia Inquirer*, April 28, 1992; and William C. Davis, "Caveat Emptor," in *Civil War Times*, August 1977, 34.

8. *Virginia Eleanor Humbrecht Kline and Lois White Rathbun, Petitioners, v. All Descendants of John Wilkes Booth, Known or Unknown, and Green Mount Cemetery, Respondents*, Baltimore City Circuit Court, Judge Joseph H. H. Kaplan presiding, case 94297044/CE187741, May 17–20, 1995, trial transcript, May 19, 1995, 42.

9. Telephone interview with the author, Aug. 23, 2000.

10. Lloyd Lewis, *Myths after Lincoln* (New York: Harcourt, Brace and Co., 1929), 399–407.

11. George S. Bryan, *The Great American Myth* (New York: Carrick and Evans, 1940), ix–xii.

12. Constance Head, "John Wilkes Booth as a Hero Figure," *Journal of American Culture* 5 (Fall 1982): 22, 27.

13. The concept that modern myths entail a form of "depoliticized speech" was first presented by Roland Barthes in *Mythologies* (Paris: Gallimard, 1952). More immediate to the subject at hand, Harold Hyman and William Hanchett have noted the relationship between national political developments, Lincoln's image, and the evolving theories of conspiracy surrounding Lincoln's assassination. See Hanchett, *Lincoln Murder Conspiracies*, and Hyman, "With Malice towards Some: Scholarship (or Something Less) on the Lincoln Murder" (Springfield, Ill.: Abraham Lincoln Association, 1978).

14. Michael Kammen, *Mystic Chords of Memory* (New York: Basic Books, 1991), 129. The demand for images joining Lincoln with Washington as equals, or nearly so, began immediately following the assassination and led to adulterations of existing works, including John Barralet's famous 1800 lithograph *Apotheosis of George Washington*. See Harold Holzer, Gabor S. Boritt, and Mark E. Neely Jr., *The Lincoln Image: Abraham Lincoln and the Popular Print* (New York: Charles Scribner's Sons, 1984), 192–205.

15. Gary W. Gallagher and Alan T. Nolan, eds., *The Myth of the Lost Cause and Civil War History* (Bloomington: Indiana University Press, 2000), 11, 12–14.

16. Ellen Carol DuBois, review of *The Civil War* by Ken Burns, *American Historical Review* 96, no. 4 (October 1991): 1140–42. DuBois notes the narrative predominance of Shelby Foote, whose "mellifluous southern accent"

was only superficially offset by that of African American historian Barbara Fields. The result, asserted DuBois, was a rendition of the war as a romantic tragedy in which the slaves appeared as "a vague suffering collectivity, a dusky Greek chorus who suffer under the lash but whose actions, resistance, and individual humanity are largely missing" (1141).

17. Charles Reagan Wilson, *Baptized in Blood: The Religion of the Lost Cause, 1865–1920* (Athens: University of Georgia Press, 1980), 12–13; Gaines M. Foster, *Ghosts of the Confederacy: Defeat, the Lost Cause, and the Emergence of the New South, 1865 to 1913* (New York: Oxford University Press, 1987), 6, 141–42. Rollin G. Osterweis's *The Myth of the Lost Cause, 1865–1900* (Hamden, Conn.: Archon Books, 1973), also analyzed Lost Cause expression in the postwar South. Wilson and Foster's contribution lies in considering how the various institutional, commemorative, and rhetorical activities served contemporary ideological needs, a crucial perspective for the current scholarly treatment of collective memory. Foster's work also highlights how scholars from two disciplines—sociology and history—have employed the concept of collective memory over the past twenty years. For sociologists, collective memory supports theories of social cohesion. An early study along these lines was W. Lloyd Warner's *The Living and the Dead: A Study of the Symbolic Life of Americans* (New Haven: Yale University Press, 1959.) Recent studies include several works by Barry Schwartz and Gary Fine. In the introduction to *Abraham Lincoln and the Forge of National Memory* (Chicago: University of Chicago Press, 2000), Schwartz addresses the distinction between the sociological analysis of collective memory and what he terms the "dominant ideology thesis" advocated by historians such as John Bodnar. While the line between social cohesion and dominant ideology is not a fixed one, as Foster's own work makes clear, I suspect that historians will remain uncomfortable with the sociologists' lack of attention to political and ideological factors. Truth be told, sociologists have prior claim to the term "collective memory," since it was French sociologist Maurice Hawlbachs who first coined it. Whereas sociologists continue to employ the term in its original sense to denote the group recollection of the past to foster social cohesion, historians have for the most part followed the lead of Pierre Nora and assume that collective memory exercises ideological functions. The benefit of the historical approach lies in its ability to allow for the presence of competing memories and oppositional commemorative practices. The historical treatment of memory also pays much closer attention to the conditions attending the production of memory "texts," such as ritual ceremonies, monuments, battlefield preservation, artwork, and written narratives.

18. Nina Silber, *The Romance of Reunion: Northerners and the South,*

1865–1900 (Chapel Hill: University of North Carolina Press, 1993). John Bodnar, *Remaking America: Public Memory, Commemoration, and Patriotism in the Twentieth Century* (Princeton: Princeton University Press, 1992), 38. David W. Blight, *Race and Reunion: The Civil War in American Memory* (Cambridge, Mass.: Belknap Press of Harvard University Press, 2001), 2.

19. Kammen, *Mystic Chords of Memory*, 120–24; Jim Cullen, *The Civil War in Popular Culture: A Reusable Past* (Washington, D.C.: Smithsonian Institution Press, 1995), 22–28.

20. Foster, *Ghosts of the Confederacy*, 57.

21. Kammen, *Mystic Chords of Memory*, 118.

22. Head, "John Wilkes Booth as a Hero Figure," 22.

23. Stephen Tatum, *Inventing Billy the Kid: Visions of the Outlaw in America, 1881–1981* (Albuquerque: University of New Mexico Press, 1982). Tatum notes in his introduction that the Kid's "persistent presence in our imagination demonstrates an appeal that crosses and recrosses any supposedly firm boundaries of the folk, the popular, and the artistic imaginations, or any conventional boundaries between history and legend" (6). The categories "folk" and "popular" have come under scrutiny in the past decade; still, Tatum's notion of boundary crossing is useful and informs my study. Booth's identity as a social bandit in the sense defined by E. J. Hobsbawm, Richard Maxwell Brown, and Richard White requires careful consideration. For now, suffice it to say that one of the principal loci for the modern legend—Granbury, Texas—also claims that Jesse James lies buried in its soil.

24. James E. Young, *The Texture of Memory: Holocaust Memorials and Meaning* (New Haven: Yale University Press, 1993), 2–3.

25. George Lipsitz, *Time Passages: Collective Memory and American Popular Culture* (Minneapolis: University of Minnesota Press, 1990), 211–31.

26. Ibid., 230; Bodnar, *Remaking America*, 13–14.

27. Michael Frisch, review of John Bodnar's *Remaking America* and Michael Kammen's *Mystic Chords of Memory, Journal of American History* 79, no. 2 (September 1993): 620; Alon Confino, "Collective Memory and Cultural History: Problems of Method," *American Historical Review* 102, no. 4 (December 1997): 1401–2.

28. Edward L. Ayers, "Narrating the New South," *Journal of Southern History* 66, no. 3 (August 1995): 555, 558, 556.

29. Practitioners of this approach also include scholars of American religion, who have argued for the presence of the "religious" in everyday life— the commingling of sacred and profane, symbolic and material, reasonable and irrational—by human beings intent on fashioning workable worldviews. Instead of seeing the world as disenchanted, these "lived religion" advocates find faith perpetuated in a range of ordinary activities.

For this reason, ordinary activities and everyday speech take on added importance in their work. See Robert Orsi, "Everyday Miracles: The Study of Lived Religion," in *Lived Religion in America: Towards a History of Practice,* ed. David Hall (Princeton: Princeton University Press, 1997), 6–8.

1. MAKING THE MUMMY

1. *Enid Daily Wave,* Jan. 14, 1903.

2. Ibid., Jan. 13, 1903.

3. Ibid.

4. *Enid Eagle,* Jan. 15, 1903.

5. W. B. Penniman, "The Story of a Mummy with a History," *Sunnyside,* July 15, 1909, 10–11; William G. Shepherd, "Shattering the Myth of John Wilkes Booth's Escape," *Harper's Magazine,* November 1924, 702–19.

6. *Enid Daily Wave,* Jan. 15, 1903; *Garfield County Democrat,* Jan. 29, 1903.

7. Shepherd, "Shattering the Myth," 716–17.

8. Penniman, "Story of a Mummy," 10.

9. Christine Quigley, *Modern Mummies: The Preservation of the Human Body in the Twentieth Century* (Jefferson, N.C.: McFarland and Co., 1997), 59.

10. Blaine V. Houmes, "Cashing in on the Mummy," *Surratt Courier,* November 1996, note 5.

11. *Enid Daily Wave,* Jan. 16, 1903.

12. *Garfield County Democrat,* Jan. 22, Feb. 26, 1903.

13. *Enid Eagle,* Jan. 29, 1903.

14. *Enid Daily Wave,* Jan. 17, 1903.

15. Ibid., Jan. 19, Jan. 20, 1903.

16. *Garfield County Democrat,* Jan. 22, 1903.

17. *Enid Daily Wave,* Jan. 15, 1903.

18. Ibid., Jan. 16, 1903.

19. Penniman, "Story of a Mummy," 10.

20. Historical Census Data for Oklahoma, U.S. Census Bureau, available at http://www.census.gov/population/cencounts/ok190090.txt (accessed Jan. 2, 2003).

21. *Garfield County Democrat,* Jan. 22, 1903.

22. *Enid Eagle,* Jan. 29, 1903.

23. *Daily Wave,* Jan. 21, Jan. 22, 1903.

24. *Enid Eagle,* Jan. 29, 1903.

25. *Garfield County Democrat,* Feb. 12, 1903.

26. Ibid., Feb. 26, 1903.

27. *Enid Eagle,* Feb. 19, 1903.

28. Finis L. Bates, *Escape and Suicide of John Wilkes Booth, Assassin of Abraham Lincoln* (Memphis: Pilcher Printing Co., 1907), 292–98.

29. *Enid Eagle,* Feb. 19, 1903.

30. *Garfield County Democrat,* Feb. 12, 1903.

31. Ibid., Feb. 19, Feb. 26, 1903.

32. Quigley, *Modern Mummies,* 80.

33. Anne Hodges Morgan and H. Wayne Morgan, eds., *Oklahoma: New Views of the Forty-Sixth State* (Norman: University of Oklahoma Press, 1982), 39–40.

34. James R. Scales and Danney Goble, *Oklahoma Politics: A History* (Norman: University of Oklahoma Press, 1982), 18–19.

35. D. Earl Newsom, "Milton W. Reynolds (Kicking Bird): The Man Who Named Oklahoma 'Land of the Fair God,'" *Chronicles of Oklahoma* 74, no. 2 (1996): 210. The first use of the term was in 1887, when Reynolds founded the *Geuda Springs (Kansas) Herald.*

36. Murray R. Wickett, *Contested Territory: Whites, Native Americans, and African Americans in Oklahoma, 1865–1907* (Baton Rouge: Louisiana State University Press, 2000), 46–66; Carl Coke Rister, *Land Hunger: David L. Payne and the Oklahoma Boomers* (Norman: University of Oklahoma Press, 1942).

37. The Run was the subject of Universal Pictures' 1992 film *Far and Away,* directed by Ron Howard and starring Tom Cruise and Nicole Kidman, with music by John Williams. Williams's soundtrack, which received more plaudits than the movie itself, included among its numbers "The Land Race."

38. Karen Dye, "Politics and Greed? Allotments and Town Building Schemes in the Cherokee Outlet," *Chronicles of Oklahoma* 73, no. 3 (1995): 308–21; Stella Campbell Rockwell, ed., *Garfield County Oklahoma, 1893–1982,* 2 vols. (Enid, Okla.: Garfield County Historical Society, 1982), 2:768–69.

39. Stan Hoig, *The Oklahoma Land Rush of 1889* (Oklahoma City: Oklahoma Historical Society, 1984), 189.

40. Rockwell, *Garfield County Oklahoma,* 1:12–13.

41. Ibid., 2:756–58; L. Edward Carter, *The Story of Oklahoma Newspapers, 1844 to 1984,* Oklahoma Horizons Series (Muskogee, Okla.: Western Heritage Books, 1984), 65–66.

42. Alvin O. Turner and Vicky L. Gailey, "The Best City in the Best County: Enid's Golden Era, 1916–1941," *Chronicles of Oklahoma* 76, no. 2 (1998): 116–18.

43. Robert G. Athearn, *The Mythic West in Twentieth-Century America* (Lawrence: University Press of Kansas, 1986), 43–45.

44. *Enid Eagle,* Oct. 22, 1902.

45. Ibid., Oct. 29, 1902. The *El Reno American* reported the cost.

46. *Enid Eagle,* Jan. 29, 1903.

47. Edward L. Ayers, *The Promise of the New South: Life after Reconstruc-*

tion (New York: Oxford University Press, 1992), 64. Douglas Hale notes that by 1907, in Oklahoma, a heady spirit of boosterism prevailed: speculation and the ethics of the main chance set the standards of behavior, and frontier optimism became the official creed. In Morgan and Morgan, *Oklahoma: New Views*, 32.

48. *Die Enid Post*, Jan. 23, 1903.

49. *Enid Daily Wave*, Sept. 18, 1902.

50. Rockwell, *Garfield County Oklahoma*, vol. 1; Marquis James, *The Cherokee Strip: A Tale of an Oklahoma Boyhood* (New York: Viking Press, 1945).

51. Wickett, *Contested Territory*, 54–59; Quintard Taylor, *In Search of the Racial Frontier: African Americans in the American West, 1528–1990* (New York: W. W. Norton and Company, 1998), 143–52; Morgan and Morgan, *Oklahoma: New Views*, 37, 39.

52. Scales and Goble, *Oklahoma Politics*, 3–19.

53. Wickett, *Contested Territory*, 175–204.

54. Worth Robert Miller, "Frontier Politics: The Bases of Partisan Choice in Oklahoma Territory, 1890–1904," *Chronicles of Oklahoma* 62, no. 4 (Winter 1984): 429–46; Miller, *Oklahoma Populism: A History of the People's Party in the Oklahoma Territory* (Norman: University of Oklahoma Press, 1987), 144. Garfield County was not the worst case of gerrymandering in Oklahoma. Neighboring Woods County, which had actually gone Populist in the 1894 elections, was chopped into six house and three council districts. According to Miller, "The only district entirely within the boundaries of the county contained the full extent of the Santa Fe Railroad through the county. Two townships had the misfortune to be completely excluded from the 1896 apportionment, and thus their voters were disfranchised" (ibid., 144).

55. Frank Luther Mott, *American Journalism: A History of Newspapers in the United States through 250 Years, 1690–1940* (New York: Macmillan, 1941), 469.

56. *Enid Daily Wave*, Oct. 20, 1902.

57. *Enid Eagle*, Dec. 5, 1902.

58. James, *Cherokee Strip*, 113, 182.

59. Richard Patterson, *Historical Atlas of the Outlaw West* (Indianapolis: Johnson Publishing Co., 1984), 127–51; Blake Gumprecht, "A Saloon on Every Corner: Whiskey Towns of the Oklahoma Territory, 1889–1907," *Chronicles of Oklahoma* 74, no. 2 (1996): 146–73.

60. Rockwell, *Garfield County Oklahoma, 1893–1982*, 2:788–89.

61. Richard Maxwell Brown, "Violence," in *Oxford History of the American West*, ed. Clyde A. Milner II, Carol A. O'Connor, and Martha A. Sandweiss (New York: Oxford University Press, 1994), 393–425.

62. Athearn, *Mythic West*, 45.

1. Angie Debo, *Prairie City: The Story of an American Community* (New York: Alfred A. Knopf, 1944), 9.

2. James Taylor, *Shocked and Amazed: On and Off the Midway* (Guilford, Conn.: Lyons Press, 2002); Howard Bone, *Sideshow* (Northville, Mich.: Sun Dog Press, 2001); Rachel Adams, *Sideshow U.S.A.: Freaks and the American Cultural Imagination* (Chicago: University of Chicago Press, 2001).

3. Christine Quigley, *Modern Mummies: The Preservation of the Human Body in the Twentieth Century* (Jefferson, N.C.: McFarland and Co., 1997), 59–87.

4. Andrea Stulman Dennett, *Weird and Wonderful: The Dime Museum in America* (New York: New York University Press, 1997), 12–13; Sidney Hart and David C. Ward, *New Perspectives on Charles Willson Peale: A 250th Anniversary Celebration,* ed. Lillian B. Miller and David C. Ward (Pittsburgh: University of Pittsburgh Press, 1991), 222–23.

5. "Kentucky Mummy," *Niles' Weekly Register* 9 (Sept. 30, 1815), 77; see also Harold Meloy, *Mummies of Mammoth Cave* (Shelbyville, Ind.: privately printed, 1968), 33–38.

6. Nathaniel Parker Willis, *Health Trip to the Tropics* (London: Sampson Low, Son and Co., 1854), 195; Meloy, *Mummies of Mammoth Cave,* 29–31.

7. John Farnham, in *Transactions of the American Antiquarian Society* 1 (1820): 355–61. Quoted in Meloy, *Mummies of Mammoth Cave,* 27.

8. Willis, *Health Trip to the Tropics,* 193–95.

9. S. J. Wolfe and Robert Singerman, "'As Cheap as Candidates for the Presidency': The Beginnings of Mummy Mania in America," paper presented at the Northeast Popular Cultural Association (NEPCA) meeting, Bridgeport, Conn., October 2001.

10. R. Jackson Wilson, "Thebes to Springfield: The Travels of an Egyptian Mummy," in *Padihershef, the Egyptian Mummy* (Springfield, Mass.: George Walter Vincent Smith Art Museum, 1984); William T. Alderson, ed., *Mermaids, Mummies, and Mastodons: The Emergence of the American Museum* (Washington, D.C.: American Association of Museums, 1992), 44–46, 60; Wolfe and Singerman, "As Cheap as Candidates for the Presidency."

11. "Description of an Egyptian Mummy now exhibiting in this City" (New York, ca. 1824), pamphlet v. 852, no. 11, American Philosophical Society Library, Philadelphia, Pa. This description is an abridged version of the earlier description published by Warren in Boston.

12. A. P. Searing, "Pamphlet Promoting Exhibition of Egyptian Mummy" (Ithaca, N.Y., ca. 1827), broadside collection, American Antiquarian Society, Worcester, Mass. S. J. Wolfe believes the assumption of female gender was typical for mummy descriptions during this period. Antebellum observers mistook the ornamentation and coiffure depicted on sarcophagi

and on the bodies as confirmation that the subjects were female. These assumptions could lead to hilarious results, as when George Gliddon unwrapped the body of a Theban priest's "daughter" in front of an audience in Boston and was laughed off the stage when it became apparent that she was a he. Interview with the author, July 28, 2002.

13. A Gardner, "Mummies," *Painesville (Ohio) Telegraph,* March 27, 1835, reprinted in John A. Larson, "Joseph Smith and Egyptology: An Early Episode in the History of American Speculation about Ancient Egypt, 1835–1844," in *For His Ka: Essays Offered in Memory of Klaus Baer,* ed. David P. Silverman, Studies in Ancient Oriental Civilization no. 55, Oriental Institute (Chicago: University of Chicago Press, 1994), 162–63.

14. "Proposal. Mr. Gliddon, having to make many arrangements . . ." broadside (Boston, 1850), BDSDS 1850, American Antiquarian Society, Worcester, Mass.

15. My thanks to Michael Kammen for pointing out that Howard Carter, the archaeologist who excavated Tutankhamen in 1922, toured the United States in the mid-1920s and is credited with launching the twentieth-century American fascination with all things Egyptian. Carter may well have influenced the design of the Booth mummy exhibit. Conversation with the author, Nov. 25, 2003.

16. Bruce Kuklick, in *Puritans in Babylon: The Ancient Near East and American Intellectual Life, 1880–1930* (Princeton: Princeton University Press, 1996), describes the establishment of the University of Pennsylvania's Near East studies and museum programs in the latter part of the nineteenth century.

17. In *Some Words with a Mummy* (1845), even Edgar Allan Poe made his mummy dignified and unthreatening. Shocked back to life among a gathering of gentlemen-naturalists, "Allamistakeo," a former count from ancient Thebes, debates the relative merits of modern America and ancient Egypt with his hosts, with democratic America coming out on the short end.

18. Dennett, *Weird and Wonderful,* 61–65; Michael Sappol, *A Traffic of Dead Bodies: Anatomy and Embodied Social Identity in Nineteenth-Century America* (Princeton: Princeton University Press, 2002), 274–312.

19. Edward L. Schwarzchild, "Death Defying/Defining Spectacles: Charles Willson Peale as Early American Freak Showman," in *Freakery: Cultural Spectacles of the Extraordinary Body,* ed. Rosemary Garland Thomson (New York: New York University Press, 1996), 82–83; Susan Pearce, "Bodies in Exile: Egyptian Mummies in the Early Nineteenth Century and Their Cultural Implications," in *Displaced Persons: Conditions of Exile in European Culture,* ed. Sharon Ouditt (Aldershot, Eng.: Ashgate Publishing, 2002), 54–71.

20. Su Wolfe of the American Antiquarian Society has compiled a data-

base of nearly 700 Egyptian mummies or parts thereof that entered the United States between 1800 and 1850. This does not include mummies that were imported for papermaking.

21. Edward Said, *Culture and Imperialism* (New York: Vintage Books, 1993), 62–63, 120; Brian Fagan, *The Rape of the Nile* (New York: Scribner's, 1975).

22. Sahina Ikram and Aidan Dodson, eds., *The Mummy in Ancient Egypt: Equipping the Dead for Eternity* (London: Thames and Hudson, 1998), 64–72; Wilson, "Thebes to Springfield," 33–35.

23. Ikram and Dodson, *The Mummy in Ancient Egypt*, 71–2; S. J. Wolfe and Robert Singerman, "Better Than Stealing Pennies from the Eyes of Dead Men: The Commercial Exploitation of Mummies in Victorian America," unpublished paper, 18; S. J. Wolfe, conversation with the author, July 31, 2002.

24. In the case of Native Americans, the collection, examination, and display of the dead remains an emotional and politically charged issue. Beginning in the 1960s, Indian rights activists began calling for the return of their ancestors, many being then held in museums of anthropology. Their searing indictment of Euro-American grave robbing eventually resulted in passage of the Native American Graves Protection and Repatriation Act (NAGPRA) in 1990. The act stipulates that institutions holding artifacts must respect tribal wishes regarding the disposition of artifacts and remains deemed "culturally affiliated" with the tribe in question. In some cases, museums have relinquished possession of materials gathered decades or even a century earlier. The largest repatriation of human remains in the twentieth century occurred in May 1999, when the Peabody Museum in Andover, Massachusetts, turned over the remains of nearly 2,000 Pueblo Indians to their descendants for reburial. NAGPRA has returned to Native Americans physical control over their material culture and ancestors after more than three centuries of usurpation. Naturally, these developments have caused much soul-searching among archeologists and anthropologists, whose professional forebears gathered thousands of Native American skeletons and skulls in the pursuit of "objective" science. See David Hurst Thomas, *Skull Wars: Kennewick Man, Archaeology, and the Battle for Native American Identity* (New York: Basic Books, 2000), 216–17; T. J. Ferguson, "Native Americans and the Practice of Archaeology," *Annual Review of Anthropology* 25 (1996): 63–79.

25. Speculation also gave a boost to archaeology in the new republic. Some modern archeologists consider the first dig conducted on scientific principles Thomas Jefferson's excavation of a mound on his Virginia property in 1784, which he described in *Notes on the State of Virginia* (1787). In the face of budding speculation that the Mound Builders were a lost race,

Jefferson concluded on the basis of his findings (the product, it should be noted, of his slaves' spadework) that the builders were the ancestors of living Indians. This was, however, the minority opinion at the time.

26. Robert Silverberg, *Mound Builders of Ancient America: The Archaeology of Myth* (Greenwich, Conn.: New York Graphic Society, 1968), 1–2.

27. Ibid., 85–88, 83–84, 135–51.

28. William Pidgeon, *Traditions of Dee-Coo-Dah, and Antiquarian Researches* (London: Sampson Low, Son, 1853; New York: Horace Thayer and Co., 1853), 19. Lloyd W. Smith Collection, Morristown National Historical Park (MNHP) Library, Morristown, NJ. (henceforth "Smith Collection, MNHP").

29. Ibid.

30. Silverberg, *Mound Builders,* 98–99.

31. Ibid., 51.

32. Ibid., 159–60.

33. Bruce R. Dain, *A Hideous Monster of the Mind: American Race Theory in the Early Republic* (Cambridge, Mass.: Harvard University Press, 2002), 123–24. Dain elsewhere mentions the display of mummies as part of the attention paid to "Egyptian majesty" in the 1820s. This majesty, he believes, was not usually tied to race. Nonetheless, ancient Egypt "would be especially useful for racial debate because it was mysterious and portentously vague, even frightening and tomblike, associated with the mysteries of death and fate" (107).

34. Edith R. Sanders, "The Hamitic Hypothesis: Its Origin and Function in Time Perspective," *Journal of African History* 10, no. 4 (1969): 521–24.

35. Dain, *Hideous Monster of the Mind,* 126–27.

36. Anon., "Mutability of Human Affairs," *Freedom's Journal,* April 6, 1827, quoted in Dain, *Hideous Monster of the Mind,* 129.

37. Stephen J. Gould, *The Mismeasure of Man* (New York: W. W. Norton, 1981), 61–62.

38. *New York Observer,* Jan. 16, 1847, 10–11.

39. Anon., "Ancient Egyptians," *New England Monthly* 5 (October 1833), available online at Cornell University Library Digital Collections, Making of America Collection: http://cdl.library.cornell.edu/moa/index.html (accessed Dec. 9, 2003).

40. Ariel (pseud.), "The Negro: What Is His Ethnological Status?" 2nd ed. (Cincinnati, 1867), 16, Available online at the Library of Congress, American Memory, *From Slavery to Freedom: The African-American Pamphlet Collection, 1824–1909,* http://memory.loc.gov/ammem/aapchtml/aapchome .html (accessed Oct. 10, 2003). The idea that mummies were constructed purposely to prove their white racial identity to posterity was proposed as

early as 1806 by English traveler W. G. Browne. See Dain, *Hideous Monster of the Mind*, 127.

41. Reginald Horsman, *Race and Manifest Destiny: The Origins of American Racial Anglo-Saxonism* (Cambridge, Mass.: Harvard University Press, 1980), 10–11; Ernest Lee Tuveson, *Redeemer Nation: The Idea of America's Millennial Role* (Chicago: University of Chicago Press, 1968), 140–41. As Horsman points out, the "religious myth of a pure English Anglo-Saxon church" was followed by the political myth of the free nature of Anglo-Saxon political institutions, as described in Tacitus's *Germania*. Thus was born the Teutonic germ theory and the importance of the Roman historian to future generations of historians and Anglo-Saxonists. Horsman goes on to say that the emergence of Anglo-Saxonism saw a shift in English collective memory over national origins, away from the Arthurian legends and toward the German forests.

42. The two passages describe the dispersal of the Hebrew people as foretold by prophets. In Daniel, the prophet hears a "man clothed in linen" specify the time this will happen: "when he [Yahweh] shall have accomplished to scatter the power of the holy people, all these things shall be finished." (Daniel 12:7). In Deuteronomy, Moses and the priests instruct the people on the duties of the covenant and predict their future history. Following invasion, "the Lord shall scatter thee among all people, from the one end of the earth to the other; and there thou shalt serve other gods, which neither thou nor thy fathers have known, even wood and stone." (Deuteronomy 28:64). Menasseh ben Israel's intentions in his interpretation of the dispersal were quite different from those of his Puritan lectors. He hoped to gain legal readmittance for the Jews in England (who had been banned by Edward I) and thus secure a sanctuary for Sephardic Jewry, whose position remained extremely tenuous in the Spanish realms.

43. Cecil Roth, *Essays and Portraits in Anglo-Jewish History* (Philadelphia: Jewish Publication Society of America , 1962), 91. *The Hope of Israel* and other texts by Menasseh ben Israel are available online at Case Western Reserve's Digital Library: http://www.cwru.edu/UL/preserve/stack/Menasseh.html (accessed Sept. 21, 2003).

44. J. F. Maclear, "New England and the Fifth Monarchy: The Quest for Millennium in Early American Puritanism," *William and Mary Quarterly*, 3rd ser., 32, no. 2 (April 1975): 243.

45. John Eliot, "The learned Conjectures of Reverend Mr. John Eliot touching the Americans, of new and notable consideration, written to Mr. Thorowgood," in Thomas Thorowgood, *Jews in America, or Probabilities that those Indians are Judaical, made more probable by some Additionals to the former Conjectures* (London: Henry Brome, 1660). MORR 9269, Smith Collection, MNHP.

46. Charles Crawford, "An Essay on the Propagation of the Gospel; In Which There Are Numerous Facts and Arguments Adduced to prove that many of the Indians in America Are descended from the Ten Tribes" (Philadelphia: James Humphrey, 1801), 28–29. Smith Collection, MNHP.

47. Elias Boudinot, *A Star in the West; or, A Humble Attempt To Discover The Long Lost Ten Tribes of Israel, Preparatory To Their Return To Their Beloved City, Jerusalem* (Trenton, N.J.: Fenton, Hutchinson, and Dunham, 1816), ii–iii. MORR 10498, Smith Collection, MNHP.

48. Boudinot, *Star in the West,* 297.

49. Horsman, *Race and Manifest Destiny,* 1.

3. NORTHERN ORIGINS

1. George S. Bryan, *The Great American Myth* (New York: Carrick and Evans, 1940), ix.

2. Ibid., xi.

3. Michael Kammen, *Mystic Chords of Memory* (New York: Basic Books, 1991), 455–73; Brett Gary, *The Nervous Liberals: Propaganda Anxieties from World War I to the Cold War* (New York: Columbia University Press, 1999).

4. Carolyn L. Harrell, *When the Bells Tolled for Lincoln: Southern Reaction to the Assassination* (Macon, Ga.: Mercer University Press, 1997); William Hanchett, review of Carolyn Harrell's *When the Bells Tolled for Lincoln, Journal of American History* 86, no. 4 (March 2000): 1790.

5. Thomas R. Turner, *Beware the People Weeping: Public Opinion and the Assassination of Abraham Lincoln* (Baton Rouge: Louisiana State University Press, 1982), 93–97. North Carolina native Catherine Edmonston's journal entry for April 20, 1865, remarked on the information vacuum thusly: "Epistolary by correspondence is at end & not a newspaper can we hope to see, so if like Athenians we seem constantly to hear or tell some new thing we must be pardoned!" Three days later she wrote: "Father . . . brought such a budget of news that I stand aghast and in my bewilderment know not what to credit & what to reject." Edmonston's father had reported that Lincoln was murdered and Mosby had taken Richmond. See *Journal of a Secesh Lady: The Diary of Catherine Ann Devereux Edmonston,* ed. Beth G. Crabtree and James W. Patton (Raleigh, N.C.: Division of Archives and History, 1979), 701–2. Virginia refugee Judith McGuire also commented on events in her diary for April 16, 1865: "Strange rumours afloat tonight. It is said, and believed, that Lincoln is dead, and Seward much injured . . . Of course, I treated it as a Sunday rumour; but the story is strengthened by the way in which the Yankees treat it. They, of course, know all about it, and to-morrow's papers will reveal the particulars." Judith McGuire, *Diary of a Southern Refugee during the War* (New York: Arno Press, 1972), 355–56.

6. Quoted in Michael Davis, *The Image of Lincoln in the South* (Knoxville: University of Tennessee Press, 1971), 99.

7. Turner, *Beware the People Weeping*, 25–52.

8. L. C. Baker, *History of the United States Secret Service* (Philadelphia: L. C. Baker, 1874), 525. It is doubtful that Baker penned these words, as his earlier memoir was ghostwritten by a journalist named Headley. Nonetheless, the sentiment appears genuine.

9. David B. Chesebrough, *"No Sorrow Like Our Sorrow": Northern Protestant Ministers and the Assassination of Lincoln* (Kent, Ohio: Kent State University Press, 1994).

10. Victor Searcher, *The Farewell to Lincoln* (New York: Abingdon Press, 1965), 56–59, 291; Merrill Peterson, *Lincoln in American Memory* (New York: Oxford University Press, 1994), 14–26; Edward Steers, *Blood on the Moon* (Lexington: University of Kentucky Press, 2001), 274–93.

11. *New York Times*, April 17, 1865; *New York World*, April 18, 1865.

12. *New York World*, April 18, April 19, 1865.

13. *New York Times*, April 19, 1865; *New York World*, April 19, 1865; *Official Records of the Union and Confederate Armies*, vol. 46, part 3 of *The War of the Rebellion: Series I* (Washington, D.C.: Government Printing Office, 1894), 801, 820, 870–71.

14. *New York Times*, April 16, 1865; *National Intelligencer*, April 16, 1865.

15. *Official Records*, 46:3, 838; Turner, *Beware the People Weeping*, 104.

16. *New York World*, April 18, 1865.

17. Ibid., April 24, 1865; reprinted from the *Chicago Times*, April 21, 1865.

18. Bryan, *Great American Myth*, 228–29.

19. *New York Times*, April 20, 1865.

20. Ibid., April 21, 1865.

21. Bryan, *Great American Myth*, 229.

22. William Hanchett, *The Lincoln Murder Conspiracies* (Urbana: University of Illinois Press, 1983), 62–63; "Investigation and Trial Papers Relating to the Assassination of President Lincoln," Microfilm ID M599, 16 rolls; 35 mm. (Washington, D.C.: National Archives and Records Administration), roll 1, ii–xii.

23. "Investigation and Trial Papers," roll 2, K13 (JAO) 1865.

24. Ibid., roll 2, M34 and F6 (JAO) 1865.

25. Ibid., roll 2, J11 (JAO) 1865; L. C. Baker, *History of the United States Secret Service* (Philadelphia: L. C. Baker, 1867), 547.

26. Turner, *Beware the People Weeping*; Hanchett, *Lincoln Murder Conspiracies*, 7–19.

27. Baker, *History of the United States Secret Service*, 545.

28. "Investigation and Trial Papers," roll 2, H70 (DAO) 1865.

29. Baker, *History of the United States Secret Service,* 545–48; "Investigation and Trial Papers," roll 2, J11 (JAO) 1865.

30. Baker, *History of the United States Secret Service,* 548.

31. *Voices from the Pulpit of New York and Brooklyn* (New York: Tibbals and Whiting, 1865).

32. Hanchett, *Lincoln Murder Conspiracies,* 59; Chesebrough, *"No Sorrow Like Our Sorrow,"* 41–52.

33. Gary A. Fine, *Difficult Reputations: Collective Memories of the Evil, Inept, and Controversial* (Chicago: University of Chicago Press, 2001), 34–35.

34. Ibid., 40–43.

35. *"Right or Wrong, God Judge Me": The Writings of John Wilkes Booth,* ed. John Rhodehamel and Louise Taper (Urbana: University of Illinois Press, 1997), 154.

36. *National Intelligencer,* April 18, 1865.

37. Ibid., April 20, April 21, 1865.

38. *New York World,* April 18, 1865.

39. George Alfred Townsend, *The Life, Crime, and Capture of John Wilkes Booth* (New York: Dick and Fitzgerald, 1865).

40. Booth may have had Jewish ancestry. Gene Smith reports anecdotal evidence that the actor was descended from a Spanish Jewish silversmith named Botha. Smith also relates that Booth's father claimed from time to time that he was Jewish. Gene Smith, *American Gothic: The Story of America's Legendary Theatrical Family—Junius, Edwin, and John Wilkes Booth* (New York: Simon and Schuster, 1992), 18.

41. *New York World,* April 28, 1865.

42. Ibid.

43. Ibid., April 18, 1865.

44. Ibid., April 28, 1865.

45. Fine, *Difficult Reputations,* 33–35.

46. Robert E. McGlone, "John Brown, Henry Wise, and the Politics of Insanity," in *His Soul Goes Marching On: Responses to John Brown and the Harpers Ferry Raid,* ed. Paul Finkelman (Charlottesville: University Press of Virginia, 1995), 214.

47. *New York World,* April 18, 1865.

48. *National Intelligencer,* April 21, 1865.

49. Fine, *Difficult Reputations,* 39–40.

50. *New York Times,* April 22, 1865.

51. *New York World,* April 28, 1865.

52. *New York Times,* April 26, 1865.

53. Bryan, *Great American Myth,* 385.

54. Constance Head, "John Wilkes Booth as a Hero Figure," *Journal of American Culture* 5 (Fall 1982).

55. Henry Nash Smith, *Virgin Land: The American West as Symbol and Myth*, 2nd ed. (Cambridge, Mass.: Harvard University Press, 1970), 103–6. For an in-depth treatment of popular literature during the Civil War see Alice Fahs, *The Imagined Civil War* (Chapel Hill: University of North Carolina Press, 2001).

56. Constance Head, "John Wilkes Booth in American Fiction," *Lincoln Herald* 82, no. 3 (1980): 454–62.

57. Frank L. Klement, *Dark Lanterns: Secret Political Societies, Conspiracies, and Treason Trials in the Civil War* (Baton Rouge: Louisiana State University Press, 1984).

58. Dion Haco, *J. Wilkes Booth, the Assassinator of President Lincoln* (New York: T. R. Dawley, 1865), 28.

59. Ibid., 22.

60. *The Body in the Barn: The Controversy over the Death of John Wilkes Booth* (Clinton, Md.: Surratt Society, 1993).

61. Benjamin P. Thomas and Harold M. Hyman, *Stanton: The Life and Times of Lincoln's Secretary of War* (New York: Alfred E. Knopf, 1962), 420–21; Turner, *Beware the People Weeping*, 121–22; *New York Times*, April 28, 1865; *New York World*, April 29, 1865.

62. *National Intelligencer*, April 28, 1865. The second quote is a paraphrase from *Hamlet*, i.v.77: "Cut off even in the Blossomes of my Sinne, Unhouzzled, disappointed, unnaneld."

63. *New York World*, April 29, 1865.

64. Ibid.

65. Paul Newman, "Remembering Erostratus," *Third Stone: The Magazine for the New Antiquarian*, no. 38 (Summer 2000): 31–32.

66. Bryan, *Great American Myth*, 276–77.

67. James G. Randall, "The Newspaper Problem in Its Bearing upon Military Secrecy during the Civil War," *American Historical Review* 23, no. 2 (January 1918): 303.

68. Menaham Blondheim, "'Public Sentiment Is Everything': The Union's Public Communications Strategy and the Bogus Proclamation of 1864," *Journal of American History* 89, no. 3 (December 2002): 869–99; David T. Z. Mindich, "Edwin M. Stanton, the Inverted Pyramid, and Information Control," *Journalism Monographs* 140 (August 1993).

69. U.S. House Committee on the Judiciary, *Impeachment of the President: Report*. 40th Cong., 1st sess., HR 40–7, serial set 1314 (Washington D.C.: Government Printing Office, 1867–68), 409; Bryan, *Great American Myth*, 291, 293; Thomas and Hyman, *Stanton*, 421n2.

70. Head, "John Wilkes Booth as a Hero Figure," 21. Head notes that these relics continue to be sought by collectors, many of whom reside in northern states, to this day.

71. Burton Kendrick, *Lincoln's War Cabinet* (Boston: Little, Brown and Co., 1946), 241; Thomas and Hyman, *Stanton,* p. 27n7, 41. Thomas and Hyman are skeptical regarding the story of Stanton's daughter's remains, but they acknowledge that a series of deaths, including those of Stanton's first wife, his daughter, and his brother, affected him deeply and that he did engage in certain morbid excesses. Stanton's political opponents made use of his personal tragedies in their efforts to discredit him. Upon his death in 1869, some even claimed he slit his own throat, as had his brother before him, out of remorse for his role in the alleged judicial murder of Mary Surratt. Among those engaging in the posthumous vilification of Lincoln's war chief was Manton Marble, editor of the *New York World.* See Thomas and Hyman, *Stanton,* 638–41.

72. Bryan, *Great American Myth,* 291; *New York World,* Feb. 16, Feb. 18, 1869.

73. Searcher, *Farewell to Lincoln,* 60.

74. David T. Valentine, ed., *Obsequies of Abraham Lincoln, in the City of New York, Under the Auspices of the Common Council* (New York: Edward Jones, 1866), 127–28.

75. Ibid., 130–40, 145. For processions as civic spectacles in nineteenth-century America see Susan G. Davis, *Parades and Power: Street Theater in Nineteenth-Century Philadelphia* (Berkeley: University of California Press, 1988), and Mary Ryan, "The American Parade: Representations of the Nineteenth-Century Social Order," in *The New Cultural History,* ed. Lynn Hunt (Berkeley: University of California Press, 1989).

76. James McPherson, *Battle Cry of Freedom: The Civil War Era* (New York: Ballantine Books, 1988), 609–11.

77. Valentine, *Obsequies of Abraham Lincoln,* 151.

78. Gary Laderman, *The Sacred Remains: American Attitudes towards Death, 1799–1883* (New Haven: Yale University Press, 1996).

79. Michael C. Kearl and Anoel Rinaldi, "The Political Uses of the Dead in Contemporary Civil Religions," *Social Forces* 61 (1983): 697–99.

80. Herbert Mitgang, ed., *Abraham Lincoln: A Press Portrait* (Chicago: Quadrangle Books, 1971), 455.

81. Merrill D. Peterson, *Lincoln in American Memory* (New York: Oxford University Press, 1994), 21, 27.

82. John R. Gillis, ed., *Commemorations: The Politics of National Identity* (Princeton: Princeton University Press, 1994), 8.

83. John Bodnar, "Pierre Nora, National Memory, and Democracy: A Review," *Journal of American History* 87, no. 3 (December 2000): 951–63.

84. Paul Finkelman, "Manufacturing Martyrdom: The Antislavery Response to John Brown's Raid," in *His Soul Goes Marching On: Responses to John Brown and the Harper's Ferry Raid,* ed. Paul Finkelman (Charlottesville: University Press of Virginia, 1995), 47.

85. Lewis O. Saum, *The Popular Mood in America, 1860–1890* (Lincoln: University of Nebraska Press, 1990). In Chapter 4, titled "The Dying of Death," Saum explores this transformation and concludes that the war, along with scientific naturalism, worked to deconsecrate death and by the end of the century led to a growing denial of death.

86. Lloyd Lewis, *Myths after Lincoln* (New York: Harcourt, Brace and Co., 1929), 350–56; Kammen, *Mystic Chords of Memory*, 102–3; David W. Blight, *Race and Reunion: The Civil War in American Memory* (Cambridge: Belknap Press of Harvard University Press, 2001), 68–71. The first organized observance took place in Charleston, South Carolina, on May 1, 1865, when African Americans and northern abolitionists led by James Redpath, former correspondent for the *New York Tribune,* paid homage to those who had died in Charleston's Race Course prison. The memory of the African American contribution to the holiday's beginnings quickly faded, however, as white majorities in the North and South appropriated the ceremony for different ends.

87. Blight, *Race and Reunion,* 72.

88. *Congressional Globe,* 39th Cong., 1st sess., July 28, 1866, 4292.

89. *Virginia Eleanor Humbrecht Kline and Lois White Rathbun, Petitioners, v. All Descendants of John Wilkes Booth, Known or Unknown, and Green Mount Cemetery, Respondents*, Baltimore City Circuit Court, Judge Joseph H. H. Kaplan presiding, case 94297044/CE187741, May 17–20, 1995, case trial transcript, May 19, 1995.

90. *Congressional Globe,* 39th Cong., 1st sess., July 28, 1866, 4292.

91. Baker, *History of the United States Secret Service,* 508; Bryan, *Great American Myth,* 289–90.

92. *New York World,* April 29, 1865.

93. Ibid., April 28, 1865.

94. Leonard F. Guttridge, "Identification and Autopsy of John Wilkes Booth: Reexamining the Evidence," *Navy Medicine* 84, no. 1 (January–February 1993): 20. Assassination expert Steve Miller remains unconvinced by Guttridge's argument, citing the reports of numerous witnesses that Booth spoke the lines attributed to him. For instance, one Private Parady, in a letter to his parents on April 28, 1865, said that Booth muttered, "Tell Mother, Tell Mother," an utterance that actually supports both conclusions.

95. Otto Eisenschiml, *Why Was Lincoln Murdered?* (New York: Grosset and Dunlap, 1937), 122–29.

96. Hanchett, *Lincoln Murder Conspiracies,* 83.

97. David Balsiger and Charles E. Sellier, *The Lincoln Conspiracy* (Los Angeles: Schick Sunn Classic Books, 1977), 10–13.

98. Baker, *History of the United States Secret Service,* 592–93.

99. *Congressional Globe,* 40th Cong., 1st sess., March 26, 1867, 363.

100. Jean Baker, *Mary Todd Lincoln: A Biography* (New York: W. W. Norton, 1987), 250.

101. *Congressional Globe,* 40th Cong., 1st sess., July 8, 1867, 515.

4. THE SOUTHERN LEGEND

1. William Hanchett, review of Carolyn Harrell's *When the Bells Tolled for Lincoln, Journal of American History* 86, no. 4 (March 2000): 1789–90. As Hanchett points out in his review of Carolyn Harrell's study, the available sources reveal principally the reaction of southern whites, as literacy and access to the written word by the freedmen were limited. In the case of the legend, this is not a problem, as there is no evidence that African Americans supported the story. They had demons enough in real life to feel a need to invent one. This lack of a legend among African Americans, in fact, is among the best arguments against viewing it solely as a folk mythology. To do so leads to the question, whose folk? This is not to say the freedmen did not have their own legends. In the postwar period, stories of Lincoln visiting the slaves in disguise to ascertain their condition and provide succor was one of the most popular.

2. Carolyn L. Harrell, *When the Bells Tolled for Lincoln: Southern Reaction to the Assassination* (Macon, Ga.: Mercer University Press, 1997), 69–70.

3. Ibid., 76–79; R. L. Reid, "Louisiana and Lincoln's Assassination: Reactions in a Southern State," *Southern Historian* 6 (1985): 20–27.

4. Michael Davis, *The Image of Lincoln in the South* (Knoxville: University of Tennessee Press, 1971), 99–101; Thomas R. Turner, *Beware the People Weeping: Public Opinion and the Assassination of Abraham Lincoln* (Baton Rouge: Louisiana State University Press, 1982), 96–97. From Sarah Morgan Dawson, *A Confederate Girl's Diary* (Bloomington: University of Indiana Press, 1960), April 22, 1865, 437–38.

5. Harrell, *When the Bells Tolled for Lincoln,* 34–37.

6. John M. Barr, "The Tyrannicide's Reception: Responses in Texas to Lincoln's Assassination," *Lincoln Herald* 91, no. 2 (1989): 58–64; Harrell, *When the Bells Tolled for Lincoln,* 84–86.

7. Martin Abbott, "Southern Reaction to Lincoln's Assassination," *Abraham Lincoln Quarterly* 7, no. 3 (September 1952): 126–27.

8. E. B. Armand, "Our Brutus," sheet music, Robert Cushman Butler Collection of Theatrical Illustrations (Pullman: Washington State University Libraries, 1868), 5.

9. Both quotes from Barr, "The Tyrranicide's Reception," 60.

10. Robert J. Duncan, "John Wilkes Booth's Motive," *McKinney (Texas) Courier-Gazette,* Nov. 13, 1986; Kent Biffle, "Booth Papers Lend Credence

to Tall Tales," *Dallas Morning News*, Oct. 4, 1998. Available online at http://www.granburydepot.org/z/biog/biffle_b.htm (accessed Dec. 30, 2002). In his article, Duncan relayed the family oral tradition of Ben Carlton Mead, Texas folklorist and artist. Mead had heard the story from his Aunt Julia's family, who were, so tradition had it, related to Beall by marriage. My thanks to Mr. Duncan for providing me a typescript copy of the *Memoir of John Yates Beall: His Life; Trial; Correspondence; Diary* (Montreal: John Lovell, 1865). Portions of this lengthy work were produced in the effort to have the rebel partisan's sentence commuted. Unfortunately, the work's preface indicates publication occurred sometime after July 1865; Beall was hanged in February.

    11. *New York Times*, April 21, 1865. The reports, from *Times* correspondent J. R. Hamilton, were dated April 16 and 18 and issued from Richmond, Virginia, where many journalists covering the war had converged following the city's surrender on April 3. Hamilton's slant in his reporting was on the loyal sentiment among southerners in Richmond, and that the assassination did not appear to be the workings of a conspiracy involving the rebel government. The Beall theory, while it proved to be based on a case of mistaken identity between John Wilkes and a Captain Booth, was significant while it lasted because it "will be able to satisfy us and the world that this monstrous villainy did not come from any political southern organization." This attempt at depoliticizing the murder was not the same as that practiced by the northern dissident papers. In the first place, the *Times* devoted no ink to demonizing the assassin and continued to view him, in true Union fashion, as the agent of some larger plot. Second, the *Times* had its own favorite conspiracy candidates: seditious northern secret societies. In an editorial dated April 26, but penned four days earlier, the *Times'* correspondent noted, "When the time comes for revelations, such startling facts will be revealed as will make people shudder. It will then be seen that all the talk about 'Knights of the Golden Circle,' 'Sons of Liberty,' 'American Knights,' &c., was not without foundation."

    12. Mildred Lewis Rutherford, "The Assassination of Abraham Lincoln," *Miss Rutherford's Scrap Book: Valuable Information about the South,* January 1924, 8, 6.

    13. Anon., *Private Confession of John Wilkes Booth* (Birmingham, U.K.: n.p., 1865), 4, 5, 6, 12.

    14. Bertram Wyatt-Brown, *Southern Honor: Ethics and Behavior in the Old South* (New York: Oxford University Press, 1982), 34, 38–39, 53, 55–57.

    15. R. H. Crozier, *The Bloody Junto; or, The Escape of John Wilkes Booth. A Novel.* (Little Rock, Ark.: Woodruff and Blocher, 1869), 6, 9, 18.

16. Ibid., 12–13, 14, 15.

17. Ibid., 140.

18. Ibid., 143.

19. Drew Gilpin Faust, *Mothers of Invention: Women of the Slaveholding South in the American Civil War* (New York: Vintage Books, 1996), 251–54.

20. George S. Bryan, *The Great American Myth* (New York: Carrick and Evans, 1940), 324–32. In his summary of the legend literature, Bryan lists the four main stories, to be reviewed shortly. In addition to these are several others: the *St. Louis Democrat* (n.d.) carried the story of an Alabama refugee who encountered a beggar said to be Booth while in Washington; the *Buffalo Courier* (n.d.) related the story of a man who visited its office claiming hard proof the assassin yet lived; the *Chicago Evening Post* (n.d.) related the story of Louisville, Kentucky, prison inmate Sterling King, who claimed he was the fugitive; and the *Richmond Examiner* (n.d.) published an editorial on the possibility of the assassin's yet living. These accounts were collected by an employee(s) of the Library of Congress in the 1860s and '70s in the *Lincoln Obsequies Scrap Book,* a collection of press clippings from the assassination, the funeral, and events following. The *Scrap Book* may be seen in the Library's Rare Books Room. Another collection of sightings tales may be found in Box 12, Folders 674–676, David Rankin Barbee Papers, Georgetown University Library Special Collections, Washington, D.C. (henceforth cited as the Barbee Papers).

21. *New York Times,* Jan. 12, 1867. The raider *Shenandoah* sank nearly a dozen ships after Lee's surrender before finally surrendering in August 1865. Its exploits made headline news in the northern press. As Bryan noted in *Great American Myth*, p. 324, there was no evidence that a man named Tolbert had skippered this ship or any other in the Confederate Navy; *Lincoln Obsequies Scrap Book,* 96–97.

22. *Beloit (Wisconsin) Daily News,* April 19, 1898.

23. Finis L. Bates, *Escape and Suicide of John Wilkes Booth, Assassin of Abraham Lincoln* (Memphis: Pilcher Printing Co., 1907), 226–27. A copy of Gay's statement is in Clarence T. Wilson, "Trailing Lincoln's Assassin," Tms 3, 164, Wilson Collection, Methodist Archives, Drew University, Madison, N.J. (henceforth cited as the Wilson Collection).

24. Clarence T. Wilson, "Trailing Lincoln's Assassin," Tms 3, Wilson Collection.

25. Andrew Rolle, *The Lost Cause: The Confederate Exodus to Mexico* (Norman: University of Oklahoma Press, 1965), 135–42.

26. Cyrus B. Dawsey and James M. Dawsey, eds., *The Confederados: Old South Immigrants in Brazil* (Tuscaloosa: University of Alabama Press, 1995), 15–17.

27. Gaines M. Foster, *Ghosts of the Confederacy: Defeat, the Lost Cause, and*

the Emergence of the New South, 1865 to 1913 (New York: Oxford University Press, 1987), 18–19.

28. T. H. Alexander, "I Reckon So," *Nashville Tennessean,* Jan. 24, 1932.

29. Bryan, *Great American Myth,* 326–28; *New York Herald,* April 26, 1903.

30. T. H. Alexander, "Booth, Lincoln Assassin, Lived, Died in Tennessee, Heroine's Son Declares," *Evening Tennessean,* Jan. 22, 1932.

31. Statement of J. C. Burrus, April 23, 1921, Folder 2129–6–1:03, Wilson Collection.

32. Bates, *Escape and Suicide,* 228. Thrailkill's full statement is also found in the Wilson Collection, "Trailing Lincoln's Assassin," Tms 3, Chapter 9.

33. C. L. Bass to C. T. Wilson, Feb. 25, 1925, Folder 2129–6–1, Wilson Collection.

34. This version of the poem found among Wilson's papers, Box 10, Folder 10, E. H. Swaim Collection, Georgetown University Library Special Collections, Washington, D.C. (corrected by author for punctuation and grammar).

35. Mary Kate Durham, quoted by Mary Saltarelli, "Was Granbury Legend Honest Abe's Assassin or Just a Phony Booth?" *Ft. Worth Star-Telegram,* Fall 1994. For an account of latter-day Granbury's promotion of legends, see "The Ballad of Jesse and John," *Economist,* Dec. 2, 1995.

36. T. T. Ewell, *Hood County History* (Granbury, Texas: Junior Woman's Club, 1956 [reprint]; Granbury: F. Gaston, 1895); James M. Day, "Shadows of John Wilkes Booth," Forty-Eighth Annual Meeting of the Texas Folklore Society, Houston, March 27–28, 1964. Mr. Day was kind enough to provide me with a copy of his unpublished paper.

37. Mrs. J. D. Rylee, Granbury, Texas, January 8, 1937, "American Life Histories: Manuscripts from the Federal Writers' Project, 1936–1940," American Memory, Historical Collections from the National Digital Library, Library of Congress. Available at http://memory.loc.gov/ammem/wpaintro/wpahome.html (accessed Dec. 29, 2002).

38. Izola Forrester, *This One Mad Act: The Unknown Story of John Wilkes Booth and His Family* (Boston: Hale, Cushman and Flint, 1937); Joyce Knibb and Patricia Mehrtens, *The Elusive Booths of Burrillville: An Investigation of John Wilkes Booth's Alleged Wife and Daughter* (Bowie, Md.: Heritage Books, 1991).

39. Turner, *Beware the People Weeping,* 97. Bingham also served in the U.S. House of Representatives following the war and angrily denounced Benjamin Butler's insinuations of a government conspiracy on the floor of the House. See *Congressional Globe,* 40th Cong., 1st sess., March 26, 1867, 363–66, for the text of his remarks.

40. Mark Neely Jr., Harold Holzer, and Gabor S. Boritt, *The Confederate*

Image: *Prints of the Lost Cause* (Chapel Hill: University of North Carolina Press, 1987), 99–106; Michael Kammen, *Mystic Chords of Memory* (New York: Basic Books, 1991), 118–19.

41. "Her Story Is True: W. D. Kenzie Corroborates the Statements of Mrs. Christ as to the Escape of J. Wilkes Booth," *Beloit (Wisconsin) Daily News,* April 20, 1898.

42. Steve Miller, "Ripples from the Hanson Hiss Article," *Surratt Courier,* 21:7 (July 1996).

5. FINIS L. BATES AND THE "CORRECTION OF HISTORY"

1. Garfield County Democrat, April 2, 1903; Christine Quigley, Modern Mummies: The Preservation of the Human Body in the Twentieth Century (Jefferson, N.C.: McFarland and Co., 1997), 80; Stella Campbell Rockwell, ed., *Garfield County Oklahoma, 1893–1982* (Enid, Okla.: Garfield County Historical Society, 1982), 1:60–61.

2. Francis Wilson, *John Wilkes Booth: Fact and Fiction of Lincoln's Assassination* (Boston: Houghton Mifflin, 1929), 249.

3. Izola Forrester, *This One Mad Act: The Unknown Story of John Wilkes Booth and His Family* (Boston: Hale, Cushman and Flint, 1937); Otto Eisenschiml, *In the Shadow of Lincoln's Death* (New York: Wilfred Funk, 1940), 53–88.

4. Helen Jo Banks, "The Enid Booth Legend" (master's thesis, Oklahoma Agricultural and Mechanical College, 1953), 31.

5. William G. Shepherd, "Shattering the Myth of John Wilkes Booth's Escape," *Harper's Magazine,* November 1924, 705.

6. The record of Barbee's legend involvement may be found in the David Rankin Barbee Papers, Georgetown University Library Special Collections, Washington, D.C. (henceforth cited as the Barbee Papers). Barbee corresponded widely with other assassination buffs; and although he disdained the legend, he had his own pet theories. On his belief that Bates may have been Conover, see Otto Eisenschiml to Barbee, letter dated May 7, 1934, Box 12, Folder 669, Barbee Papers.

7. F. L. Black, "David E. George as J. Wilkes Booth," *Dearborn Independent,* April 25, 1925.

8. *The Body in the Barn: The Controversy over the Death of John Wilkes Booth* (Clinton, Md.: Surratt Society, 1993), 47.

9. David Rankin Barbee to Walter Prescott Webb, letter dated February 4, 1941, Box 12, Folder 674, Barbee Papers.

10. *Enid Daily Wave,* Jan. 21, May 29, June 1, 1903.

11. *Enid Eagle,* June 4, 1903; *Enid Daily Wave,* June 1, 1903.

12. *Die Enid Post,* June 5, 1903; *Garfield County Democrat,* June 11, 1903.

13. W. B. Penniman, "The Story of a Mummy with a History," *The Sunny-side,* July 15, 1909, 11.

14. *Enid Daily Wave,* June 2, 1903.

15. *Enid Daily Wave*, May 28, 1903; *Garfield County Democrat*, June 4, 1903; *Enid Eagle,* June 4, 1903.

16. Bates also provided a depoliticized version of his talk to the *Commercial Appeal* on his return to Memphis. See Frank Bell, "The Suicide of John Wilkes Booth. Escaped from Federal Authorities and Lived a Wanderer under Many Aliases. First Publication of Thrilling Narrative," *Memphis Commercial Appeal*, June 21, 1903. The newspaper version contained no mention of Andrew Johnson's involvement (as discussed later in the present chapter).

17. Finis L. Bates, *Escape and Suicide of John Wilkes Booth, Assassin of Abraham Lincoln* (Memphis: Pilcher Printing Co., 1907), 12.

18. Ibid., 28.

19. Ibid., 30.

20. Ibid., 42.

21. Ibid., 45, 74. Bates's personal history likely entered into his formulation of St. Helen's/Booth's political rationale. Born in 1852, Bates was the son of a Bolivar County, Mississippi, plantation owner. Too young to have participated in the war, he joined with other members of his family in the migration to Texas following defeat. He took up residence in Hood County, which was on the frontier's edge in the late 1860s, and stayed there until 1878. Returning to redeemed Mississippi, he established residence in Carroll County, and practiced as a lawyer in nearby Greenville. Sometime after 1890, he moved to Memphis, Tennessee, and thus participated in the second migratory wave of white Mississippians, this time to the urban centers of the New South.

22. Ibid., 74.

23. Ibid., 70.

24. Ibid., 98.

25. Ibid., 117, 119.

26. Ibid., 62–63.

27 .Ibid., 180–81, 210–12, 218.

28. Ibid., 254–55.

29. Ibid., 261.

30. Ibid., 263.

31. Nina Silber, *The Romance of Reunion: Northerners and the South, 1865–1900* (Chapel Hill: University of North Carolina Press, 1993).

32. *Enid Daily Wave,* June 4, 1903.

33. *Enid Eagle,* June 11, 1903; *Garfield County Democrat,* June 11, 1903.

34. *Garfield County Democrat,* June 11, 1903.

35. Bates, *Escape and Suicide*, 28.

36. Robert Alan Goldberg, *Enemies Within: The Culture of Conspiracy in Modern America* (New Haven: Yale University Press, 2001).

37. *Enid Daily Wave*, Aug. 17, 1903.

38. *Garfield County Democrat*, June 18, 1903.

6. THE LEGEND IN THE ERA OF LINCOLN'S COMMEMORATION

1. Stella Campbell Rockwell, ed., *Garfield County Oklahoma, 1893–1982* (Enid, Okla.: Garfield County Historical Society, 1982), 1:60–61. Enid resident Lewis King remembers that he and other neighborhood children were spooked by the body's presence and went up in the hayloft to gaze down upon George in his open casket.

2. "Assassination of Lincoln Is Recalled by Niece of John Wilkes Booth," *New York World*, Jan. 11, Jan. 18, 1925; "When Did John Wilkes Booth Die?" *Literary Digest*, Dec. 25, 1926, 40–41.

3. William Parker Campbell, *John Wilkes Booth: Escape and Wanderings until Final Ending of the Trail by Suicide at Enid, Oklahoma, January 12, 1903*, Travelers Series No. 7 (Oklahoma City, 1922); Bernie Babcock, *Booth and the Spirit of Lincoln: A Story of a Living Dead Man* (Philadelphia: J. B. Lippincott, 1925); Lloyd Lewis, *Myths after Lincoln* (New York: Harcourt, Brace and Co., 1929); Francis Wilson, *John Wilkes Booth: Fact and Fiction of Lincoln's Assassination* (Boston: Houghton Mifflin, 1929); Izola Forrester, *This One Mad Act: The Unknown Story of John Wilkes Booth and His Family* (Boston: Hale, Cushman and Flint, 1937); Otto Eisenschiml, *Why Was Lincoln Murdered?* (New York: Grosset and Dunlap, 1937); Asia Booth Clarke, *The Unlocked Book: A Memoir of John Wilkes Booth by His Sister* (New York: G. P. Putnam's Sons, 1938); Philip Van Doren Stern, *The Man Who Killed Lincoln* (New York: Literary Guild, 1939); George S. Bryan, *The Great American Myth* (New York: Carrick and Evans, 1940); Otto Eisenschiml, *In the Shadow of Lincoln's Death* (New York: Wilfred Funk, 1940); Stanley Kimmel, *The Mad Booths of Maryland* (New York: Dover Publications, 1940).

4. William Hanchett, *The Lincoln Murder Conspiracies* (Urbana: University of Illinois Press, 1983), 135.

5. Michael Kammen, *Mystic Chords of Memory* (New York: Basic Books, 1991), 375–443; Robert Dorman, *Revolt in the Provinces: The Regionalist Movement in America, 1920–1945* (Chapel Hill: University of North Carolina Press, 1993).

6. John Crowe Ransom, "Reconstructed but Unregenerate," in *The American Intellectual Tradition: A Sourcebook*, 3rd ed., ed. David A. Hollinger and Charles Capper (New York: Oxford University Press, 1997), 2:210.

7. Ibid., 2:213.

8. Leslie Traylor to David Rankin Barbee, January 8, 1954, Box 12, Folder 674, David Rankin Barbee Papers, Georgetown University Library Special Collections, Washington, D.C. (henceforth cited as the Barbee Papers).

9. Alva Johnston, "'John Wilkes Booth' on Tour," *Saturday Evening Post,* Feb. 10, 1938, 34, 36. Except as noted, my account of the mummy's travels draws from Johnston's account.

10. William Shepherd to Finis L. Bates, August 22, 1922, Box 2, Folder 1, E. H. Swaim Collection, Georgetown University Library Special Collections, Washington, D.C. (henceforth cited as the Swaim Collection).

11. F. L. Black, "David E. George as J. Wilkes Booth," *Dearborn Independent,* April 25, 1925; "Identification of J. Wilkes Booth," *Dearborn Independent,* May 2, 1925.

12. Kammen, *Mystic Chords of Memory,* 355–56.

13. Otto Eisenschiml to David Rankin Barbee, May 13, 1934, Box 12, Folder 669, Barbee Papers.

14. Johnston, "'John Wilkes Booth' on Tour," 36.

15. The rounded line of the ceiling in the carnival exhibit (Figure 1) suggests that the exhibit was installed inside a railroad car, and could be easily moved. According to recent maps, a railroad spur reaches Declo.

16. Thomas E. Cheney, "Facts and Folklore in the Story of John Wilkes Booth," *Western Folklore* 22, no. 3 (1963): 171.

17. "Kansas Diary Gives New Evidence in Circumstances of Lincoln's Death," *Kansas City Journal-Post,* Feb. 7, 1932.

18. Whether or not Wilkerson collected the reminiscences of the Texas judge in the manner described in the *Saturday Evening Post* article (as relayed here) must remain open to question. Correspondence indicates that Wilkerson wrote the judge sometime after the Texas tour, and the judge replied in writing with his recollections. See Walter F. Schenck to James N. Wilkerson, letter dated January 10, 1929, Box 2, Folder 16, Swaim Collection.

19. Orlando Scott to Leslie Traylor, letter dated May 6, 1945, Box 2, Folder 15, Swaim Collection; *Baltimore Post,* Dec. 21, 1931.

20. Johnston, "'John Wilkes Booth' on Tour," 16.

21. Merrill D. Peterson, *Lincoln in American Memory* (New York: Oxford University Press, 1994), 262.

22. Roland Ostman, "Photography and Persuasion: Farm Security Administration Photographs of Circus and Carnival Sideshows, 1935–1942," in *Freakery: Cultural Spectacles of the Extraordinary Body,* ed. Rosemary Garland Thomson (New York: New York University Press, 1996). Many of the photographs featured in Ostman's article are now viewable online at the Library of Congress American Memory project, available at http://memory.loc.gov/ammem/fsahtml/fahome.html; search on keywords "carnival"

and "sideshow" (accessed Feb. 12, 2003). The illustrations of the traveling crime show near Fayetteville, North Carolina, indicate how the Booth exhibit probably traveled during the same era. As the national road network expanded in the 1920s, and as the Depression forced more and more people on the road in search of work and new beginnings, traveling exhibits of this kind were probably familiar sites across America. Evangelical Protestantism also adapted itself to the motor age: witness the image of a proselytizer's panel truck parked in front of the U.S. Capitol, included in Colleen McDannell's own traveling exhibition, "Picturing Faith: Religious America in Government Photography, 1935–1943," reviewed in the *Journal of American History* 83, no. 3 (December 2001): 1016–19.

23. Peterson, *Lincoln in American Memory*, 29.

24. Ibid., 27.

25. Jim Cullen, *The Civil War in Popular Culture: A Reusable Past* (Washington, D.C.: Smithsonian Institution Press, 1995), 42.

26. Peterson, *Lincoln in American Memory*, 85, 285, 311.

27. David W. Blight, *Race and Reunion: The Civil War in American Memory* (Cambridge, Mass.: Belknap Press of Harvard University Press, 2001), 2, 369–70.

28. Thomas Dixon Jr., *The Clansman: A Historical Romance of the Ku Klux Klan* (New York: Doubleday and Co., 1905), 50. Text available online at the University of North Carolina Chapel Hill Libraries' Web project "Documenting the American South: Library of Southern Literature," http://docsouth .unc.edu/dixonclan/menu.html (accessed Feb. 22, 2003).

29. Peterson, *Lincoln in American Memory*, 256, 299; James G. Randall, "Has the Lincoln Theme Been Exhausted?" *American Historical Review* 41, no. 2 (January 1936): 270–94; Claude G. Bowers, *The Tragic Era: The Revolution after Lincoln* (Boston: Houghton Mifflin, 1929).

30. Eisenschiml, *Why Was Lincoln Murdered?* 82.

31. Ibid., 137.

32. Ibid., 161.

33. Ibid., 4.

34. Ibid., 311–12, 357.

35. Ibid., 367.

36. Paul M. Angle, "Sunday Book Review," *New York Times*, March 28, 1937; C. R. Wilson, *American Historical Review* 43 (January 1938): 421–22; Paul H. Buck, *Saturday Review of Literature* 20, March 27, 1938. Buck's own study stressed the effect of "extremism," both North and South, in preventing the formation of a common nationalism following the war, and the gradual supplanting of this extremism by moderation after 1880. In his analysis the extremist elements included the northern Protestant churches, who remained "sectional bodies, an antagonistic element in the

integration of national life"; the Negro, "a rock separating the current of national life in angry currents"; and, of course, the Republican Party, the party of sectional strife, especially in its Radical guise: "The Reconstruction program originated by Radicals became the test of party loyalty with hatred of the white South and distrust of Democrats as fixed tenets of the creed." Paul H. Buck, *The Road to Reunion, 1865–1900* (Boston: Little, Brown and Co., 1937), 66, 67, 72, 87. Buck is considered the first student of Civil War collective memory. Despite his strong revisionist bias (slavery, he describes in his preface, was a "not inhumane institution"), he captured the problematic—past, present, and future—for any evaluation of regionalism in America. During the antebellum period, he argued, the North and South diverged from their common, inherited "Americanism." The North, undergoing the threefold revolution of democracy, nationalism, and industrialism, was on the march "toward new and untested objectives." The South, owing to the expansion of the slave plantation system, hewed to the older traits of the "American character." The imperative commitments of this slave society were "patriotism of locality, loyalty to agriculture and to an aristocratic structure of society, and adherence to stability in folkways" (ix). Throwing out the two middle terms leaves *localism* and *folkways*, keywords in the contemporary scholarly discussion of countermemory. See George Lipsitz's discussion of the contrast between marginal, "local" memory and the universalizing, totalizing kind of dominant historical narratives in Chapter 5 of his book *Time Passages*. The point is not that marginal groups agree with the cultural systems of their former oppressors, but to recognize, as noted in the introduction to this study, that terms like "local" and "folk" do not necessarily carry positive moral valuations. Also, and more important for the aims of this study, the divergent character of regionalist subcultures in America calls into question the simplistic equation whereby American culture is divided into a progressive mainstream that is assumed to be racially tolerant, upscale, urban, and secular and its assumed opposite.

37. Peterson, *Lincoln in American Memory,* 302.

38. Edgar Lee Masters, *Lincoln: The Man* (New York: Dodd, Mead and Co., 1931). A good indication of how Masters's biography was received comes from the correspondence between Otto Eisenschiml and David Rankin Barbee. Barbee held to the older southern viewpoint and loathed Lincoln. He contemplated writing a book on the assassination and wrote Eisenschiml of his plans. The Chicago conspiracy theorist replied with this advice: "Do not unnecessarily indulge in attacks on Lincoln, unless it is a part of the story. Since Edgar Lee Masters' debacle, the publishers are shy on this subject." Eisenschiml to Barbee, June 12, 1937, Box 12, Folder 669, Barbee Papers.

39. Peterson, *Lincoln in American Memory,* 251–55 (quotation on 251).

40. Lewis, *Myths after Lincoln*, 405.

41. Ibid., 402–3, 406.

42. Roland Barthes, *Mythologies* (Paris: Gallimard, 1952).

43. Given that *Myths* was originally published eight years before *Why Was Lincoln Murdered?* makes it likely that Eisenschiml drew his portrait of Stanton and the Radicals from Lewis. Along with Carl Sandburg, Lewis and Eisenschiml were three of the most influential nonhistorians writing on the topic during this time, and all three hailed from Chicago. Lewis went on to write *Sherman: Fighting Prophet* (1932) and *Captain Sam Grant* (1952). Sandburg would become best known for his million-word biography of Lincoln, published between 1936 and 1944. The connections between Chicago-area writers on the Civil War became manifest with the forming of the previously mentioned Chicago Civil War Roundtable (CCWR) in 1940. The first body of its kind, the CCWR inspired the formation of dozens of similar groups across the country. Its monthly meetings mixed in-depth lectures on Civil War topics by devoted lay scholars with male camaraderie and (according to the retrospective account of its founder) ample liquid refreshments. See Barbara Hughett's history of the organization, *The Civil War Round Table: Fifty Years of Scholarship and Fellowship* (Chicago: Civil War Roundtable, 1990).

44. Lewis, *Myths after Lincoln*, 11–12.

45. Ibid., 21, 57–60.

46. Ibid., 79, 80.

47. Lewis's modernist analysis of the gender transformation of American culture from frontier masculine to antebellum, small-town effeminate and finally to modernist urban masculine finds its contemporary scholarly rendition in the work of Ann Douglas, whose *Feminization of American Culture* (1979) and *Terrible Honesty: Mongrel Manhattan in the 1920s* (1993) argue in much greater detail for a similar progression. Like Lewis, Douglas in her earlier work found the clergy of the established eastern denominations a source of feminization, a result of their attempts to maintain political and cultural relevance in the age of masculine Jacksonian Democracy.

48. Lewis, *Myths after Lincoln*, 106, 107.

49. Barry Schwartz, *Abraham Lincoln and the Forge of National Memory* (Chicago: University of Chicago Press, 2000), 248, 256–57, 264.

50. F. Lauriston Bullard, *Lincoln in Marble and Bronze* (New Brunswick, N.J.: Rutgers University Press, 1952), 228–41; Peterson, *Lincoln in American Memory*, 210–11.

51. Schwartz, *Abraham Lincoln and the Forge of National Memory*, 267.

52. Cullen, *Civil War in Popular Culture*, 38, 41.

53. Carl Sandburg, *Abraham Lincoln: The War Years* (New York: Harcourt, Brace and Co., 1939), 333.

54. Lewis's analysis was not completely inaccurate. Beginning in the 1920s, the FBI began keeping files on Booth's alleged escape, based on letters sent to the Department of Justice (DOJ) by a few "concerned citizens." In 1923, director William Burns instructed Herbert Hoover to go over a copy of Bates's opus, which had been sent to the Bureau by a correspondent from Enid, Oklahoma, who asked for the opportunity to "prove our proofs" regarding Booth's survival. According to the correspondent, Warren Harding and Charles Evans Hughes also received copies of the book. Around the same time the DOJ received another letter from a "concerned citizen" in Excelsior Springs, Missouri, that bears quoting in its entirety for its confirmation of Lewis's take on village existence: "There is a man here named Booth, who claims to know John Wilkes Booth, the assassin of Lincoln, not only is not dead but wrote him a letter 15 years ago, and says everyone is crazy who that claims Booth was killed. He is dark complexioned and in some ways resembles the Booth tribe. He lives in rear of this house and is a mysterious fellow and does not explain what he was corresponding with the killer of Lincoln for." FBI, Freedom of Information Act (FOIA) Reading Room, "John Wilkes Booth," letter dated May 8, 1922, to William Burns, available online at http://foia.fbi.gov/booth/booth1.pdf (pp. 2–3; accessed April 1, 2003).

55. Constance Head, "John Wilkes Booth as a Hero Figure," *Journal of American Culture* 5 (Fall 1982).

56. Susan M. Stabile, *Memory's Daughters: The Material Culture of Remembrance in Eighteenth-Century America* (Ithaca: Cornell University Press, 2004), 4.

57. My reading of Forrester's family account as standing for a larger national discourse has been influenced by Lynn Hunt's *The Family Romance of the French Revolution* (Berkeley: University of California Press, 1987). While I do not intend submitting Forrester's work to the detailed psychoanalytic and literary analysis Hunt applied to French cultural texts, I have assumed Hunt's basic premise, and the basic premise of much contemporary feminist scholarship, regarding the parallel between representations of the family and of the nation.

58. Michael Lemanski in the *Norwich (Connecticut) Bulletin,* Jan. 16, 2003, online at http://www.norwichbulletin.com/news/stories/20030106/localnews/715804.html (accessed March 22, 2003). For more on the Burrillville Booth legend, see Joyce G. Knibb and Patricia A. Mehrtens, *The Elusive Booths of Burrillville: An Investigation of John Wilkes Booth's Alleged Wife and Daughter* (Westminster, Md.: Heritage Books, 1991).

59. Forrester, *This One Mad Act,* 4, 118, 6, 15–16, 119.

60. Ibid., 121, 123.

61. Ibid., 131.

62. Ibid.

63. Ibid., 20, 50.

64. Ibid., 95–96, 107, 91, 75–76.

7. CLARENCE TRUE WILSON AND THE "THINGS THAT ARE TO BE"

1. "Dr. Clarence T. Wilson Saw Booth's Body Lately," press release to the *International News Service,* Feb. 21, 1925, in the Clarence True Wilson Collection, Methodist Collection, Drew University, Madison, N.J. (henceforth cited as the Wilson Collection). For a recent reinterpretation of Bakhtin's theory of the carnivalesque as it applies to contemporary American carnivals and sideshows, see Bruce Caron and Jeff Brouws, *Inside the Live Reptile Tent: The Twilight World of the Carnival Midway* (San Francisco: Chronicle Books, 2001).

2. David Hall, ed., *Lived Religion in America: Toward a History of Practice* (Princeton: Princeton University Press, 1997); Robert Orsi, "Everyday Miracles: The Study of Lived Religion," in Hall, *Lived Religion in America,* 3–21.

3. The only published biography of Wilson is Robert Dean McNeil's *Valiant for Truth: Clarence True Wilson and Prohibition* (Portland: Oregonians Concerned about Addiction Problems, 1992).

4. See, for example, Robert T. Handy, *Christian America: Protestant Hopes and Historical Realities* (New York: Oxford University Press, 1971); George Marsden, *Religion and American Culture* (San Diego: Harcourt Brace Jovanovich, 1990); Mark A. Noll, *History of Christianity in the United States and Canada* (Grand Rapids, Mich.: W. B. Eerdman's, 1992). Two recent works include Gaines M. Foster, *Moral Reconstruction: Christian Lobbyists and the Federal Legislation of Morality, 1865–1920* (Chapel Hill: University of North Carolina Press, 2002), and Philip Hamburger, *Separation of Church and State* (Cambridge, Mass.: Harvard University Press, 2002).

5. Leo Ribuffo, *The Old Christian Right: The Protestant Far Right from the Great Depression to the Cold War* (Philadelphia: Temple University Press, 1983), 3–5.

6. James H. Moorhead, *World without End: Mainstream American Protestant Visions of the Last Things, 1880–1925,* Religion in North America, 28 (Bloomington: Indiana University Press, 1999), 94–96. Wilson described the rising fundamentalist and premillennialist movement in the post–World War I period as "vagaries and crude literalisms . . . being built up now into a system of doctrine under the term "Pre-Millenialism." *The Voice of the Board of Temperance, Prohibition, and Public Morals*, December 1920: 2 (hereafter cited as the *Voice*).

7. Ribuffo, *Old Christian Right,* 5; Michael Barkun, *Religion and the Racist*

Right: The Origins of the Christian Identity Movement (Chapel Hill: University of North Carolina Press, 1997).

8. The record of Wilson's legend involvement may be found in the Wilson Collection and the E. H. Swaim Collection, Georgetown University Library Special Collections, Washington, D.C. (henceforth cited as the Swaim Collection). On Wilson's lecturing on the legend, see *Voice*, April 1922: 4. For the *True Confessions* article and Wilson's publishing rejections, see Box 3, Folder 6, Swaim Collection. For Leslie Traylor's legend involvement, see Box 2, Folder 15, Swaim Collection. For Wilson's collection of oral legend accounts from Enid, see Box 10, Folder 10, Swaim Collection, and "Trailing Lincoln's Assassin," Tms 2, 180–83, Wilson Collection. C. T. Wilson to Mrs. Bates, letter dated March 5, 1924, Wilson Collection.

9. W. P. Campbell to Blanche Booth, letter dated April 28, 1924, Wilson Collection.

10. *Literary Digest,* Nov. 13, 1926, 33–34 ; "The Methodist Board of Temperance, Prohibition, and Public Morals," *Christian Century,* Dec. 24, 1930, 1582–85.

11. Marsden, *Religion and American Culture,* 172–73.

12. Charles Merz, "The Methodist Lobby," *New Republic,* Oct. 13, 1926, 213.

13. James D. Bernard, "The Methodists," *American Mercury,* April 1926, 430; Washington Pezet, "The Temporal Power of Evangelism: The Methodists in National Politics," *Forum,* October 1926, 482–91 (see Wilson's reply in the next issue, 668–81); Merz, "The Methodist Lobby," 213–15; "Are the Methodists Seeking Temporal Power?" *Literary Digest,* Nov. 13, 1926, 33–34; Ray T. Tucker, "Prophet of Prohibition," *North American Review,* August 1930.

14. *Voice,* January 1925; *New York Times,* March 22, 1926, 2; *Congressional Record—House,* 69th Cong., 1st sess., March 24, 1926, 6178. Wilson was not unique in his intemperate approach to the cause. For the Methodist penchant of justifying the means by the ends during this period see Robert Moats Miller, "Methodism and American Society, 1900–1939," in *The History of American Methodism,* ed. Emory Stevens Bucke (New York: Abingdon Press, 1964), 328–406. Miller quotes the Methodist reformer William "Pussyfoot" Johnson: "I had to lie, bribe, and drink to put over prohibition in America."

15. Clarence T. Wilson, *The Things That Are to Be: Pulpit Discussions in Eschatology* (Cleona, Pa.: G. Holzapfel, 1899), 150; Christine L. Heyrman, *Southern Cross: The Beginnings of the Bible Belt* (New York: Alfred Knopf, 1997).

16. David Hempton, "Methodist Growth in Transatlantic Perspective, ca. 1770–1850," in *Methodism and the Shaping of American Culture,* ed. Nathan O. Hatch and John H. Wigger (Nashville: Kingswood Books, 2001), 58.

17. Ray T. Tucker, "Prophet of Prohibition," *North American Review* 230, no. 2 (August 1930): 129–36.

18. Dorothy Ross, "Historical Consciousness in Nineteenth Century America," *American Historical Review* 89, no. 4 (October 1984): 909–28.

19. Gordon Wood, "Conspiracy and the Paranoid Style: Causality and Deceit in the Eighteenth Century," *William and Mary Quarterly* 3rd ser., 39, no. 3 (July 1982): 411.

20. C. T. Wilson, *Trailing Lincoln's Assassin*, Tms 3, Wilson Collection.

21. Ibid., 6, 72. Wilson may deserve credit as the first conspiracy theorist to implicate Lafayette Baker in the crime of Lincoln's murder. See Chapter 8 for more on Baker.

22. Hans L. Trefousse, *Andrew Johnson: A Biography* (New York: W. W. Norton, 1989), 189.

23. Wilson, *Trailing Lincoln's Assassin*, Tms 3, p. 16, Wilson Collection.

24. Ibid., foreword.

25. Deets Pickett, Clarence True Wilson, and Ernest Dailey Smith, eds., *Cyclopedia of Temperance, Prohibition, and Public Morals* (New York: Methodist Book Concern, 1917), 81.

26. Clarence T. Wilson, "The United States in Prophecy: Isaiah's Vision of Our Country," *Christian Faith and Life,* October 1934, 270.

27. Clarence True Wilson, *Dry or Die: The Anglo-Saxon Dilemma,* 2nd ed. (Topeka, Kans.: The Temperance Society, 1913), 113.

28. Wilson, *Trailing Lincoln's Assassin,* Tms 3, 210.

29. "A Grave and Menacing Situation," *Voice,* February 1926: 1.

30. Wilson, *Dry or Die,* 166–67.

31. *Voice,* February 1922: 1–2.

32. *New York Times,* April 21, 1926. The full text of Wilson's testimony before the committee is in *National Prohibition Law,* Hearings before the Subcommittee of the Committee of the Judiciary, U.S. Senate, 69th Cong., 1st sess., vol. 2 (Washington, D.C.: Government Printing Office, 1926).

33. *Voice,* April 1922: 4; January 1925: 3. The climax of the Board's attack on the alien peril and its role in derailing prohibition came when the *Voice* interviewed Henry Ford on the Jews and the liquor traffic. See *Voice,* September 1923.

8. THE LEGEND IN THE PRESENT TENSE

1. Leonard F. Guttridge and Ray A. Neff, *Dark Union: The Secret Web of Profiteers, Politicians, and Booth Conspirators That Led to Lincoln's Death* (Hoboken, N.J.: John Wiley and Sons, 2003).

2. Robert Alan Goldberg, *Enemies Within: The Culture of Conspiracy in Modern America* (New Haven: Yale University Press, 2001), 49.

3. This ironic quality was noted most recently by James McPherson in his review of *Dark Union* (discussed later in the present chapter), and most famously by Richard Hofstadter in his classic essay, "The Paranoid Style in American Politics" (1964), in which he described the conspiracy theorist's meticulous cataloguing of evidence followed by an unsupported leap of reasoning to untenable conclusions. See Richard Hofstadter, *The Paranoid Style in American Politics and Other Essays* (New York: Vintage Books, 1967).

4. See, for example, George S. Bryan, *The Great American Myth* (New York: Carrick and Evans, 1941); Stewart Holbrook, "Phonies of the Old West," *American Mercury* 68 (February 1949): 230–35; and Stanley Kimmel, *The Mad Booths of Maryland* (Indianapolis: Bobbs-Merrill Co., 1940). Lloyd Lewis's *Myths after Lincoln* (originally published in 1929) appeared in a Reader's Club Edition in 1941, and in a diminutive softback Armed Forces Edition in 1940.

5. Guttridge and Neff, *Dark Union,* 17.

6. Ibid., 63.

7. Ibid., 98.

8. Ibid., 98–99.

9. Ibid., 99.

10. Ibid., 52.

11. Ibid.

12. Ibid., 53.

13. Ibid., 17.

14. Edward Steers, Jr., and Joan L. Chaconas, "*Dark Union*: Bad History," *North and South* 7, no. 1 (January 2004): 12–30.

15. James M. McPherson, "Fact or Fiction?" *Perspectives: Newsmagazine of the American Historical Association* 42, no. 1 (January 2004): 11.

16. David Vancil, "Response to James McPherson, Edward Steers, Joan Chaconas, and Jane Singer," posted to the Indiana State University Cunningham Memorial Library Web site, Jan. 27, 2004. Alas, the original version is no longer available, and has been replaced by one more in keeping with archival practice, accessible at http://library.indstate.edu/level1.dir/ cml/rbsc/neff /response2.html (accessed March 21, 2004). The revised response was also posted to the History News Network (HNN) Web site sometime around March 8, 2004, and may be viewed at http://hnn.us/articles/printfriendly /3871.html. Copy of the original response in the author's possession.

17. Vancil, "Response," Jan. 27, 2004.

18. Leonard Guttridge, "In Defense of *Dark Union,*" *History News Network*, March 8, 2004, online at http://hnn.us/articles/printfriendly/3873.html (accessed March 21, 2004).

19. Michael E. Hill, "Morrow Adds Depth to John Wilkes Booth," *Washington Post,* April 12, 1998.

20. William Hanchett, *The Lincoln Murder Conspiracies* (Urbana: University of Illinois Press, 1983), 5.

21. Ibid., 186–93.

22. Robert H. Fowler Jr., "Was Stanton behind Lincoln's Murder?" *Civil War Times,* August 1961.

23. Ibid.

24. Thanks to Steve Miller for chasing down this bit of Lincoln lore.

25. Robert H. Fowler, "Author Presents New Evidence in Lincoln Murder Conspiracy," *Civil War Times Illustrated*, February 1965: 4–11.

26. Goldberg, *Enemies Within*, 128. After three years of investigating the assassinations of John F. Kennedy and Martin Luther King Jr., the committee issued a final report in January 1979. It concluded that "scientific acoustical evidence establishes a high probability that two gunmen fired at President John F. Kennedy" and that "on the basis of the evidence available to it," Kennedy "was probably assassinated as a result of a conspiracy." But, it added, "The committee is unable to identify the other gunman or the extent of the conspiracy." U.S. House of Representatives, Select Committee on Assassinations, *Final Report,* 95th Cong., 2nd sess., 1979; available online at the National Archives and Records Administration (NARA) at http://www.archives.gov/research_room/jfk/house_select_committee/committee_report.html (accessed Dec. 16, 2003).

27. Lawrence VanGelder, "Film: *Lincoln Conspiracy,*" *New York Times*, Oct. 6, 1977; "Paperback Bestsellers," *New York Times,* Oct. 23, 1977; Ray Walters, "Paperback Talk," *New York Times,* Dec. 4, 1977.

28. David Balsiger and Charles Sellier Jr., *The Lincoln Conspiracy* (Los Angeles: Schick Sunn Classic Books, 1977), 9.

29. Ibid., 12.

30. Ibid., 13.

31. The information in this section was obtained by the author via a Freedom of Information Act (FOIA) request addressed to the National Park Service, National Capitol Region, dated Jan. 6, 2004. Records obtained include correspondence by principals involved in the matter and a typescript summary of the affair by Richard E. Sloan, titled "The Case of the Missing Pages." I do not know if this article was ever published. Sloan was formerly editor and publisher of the *Lincoln Log,* a newsletter devoted to the study of Lincoln's assassination.

32. FBI FOIA Electronic Reading Room, available online at http://foia.fbi.gov/booth.htm (accessed Feb. 19, 2004).

33. Haynes Johnson, "Now, About Those 18 'Missing Pages' in Booth's Diary," *Washington Post*, Aug. 3, 1977; Jack Anderson and Les Whitten, "FBI Probes Lincoln Assassination," *Washington Post*, Aug. 3, 1977.

34. Harold Hyman, "With Malice towards Some: Scholarship (or Something Less) on the Lincoln Murder" (Springfield, Ill.: Abraham Lincoln Association, 1978), 14–15. For mention of the block ticket sales to school groups and honorary degrees, see Hyman's review of William Hanchett's *The Lincoln Murder Conspiracies*, "Hitting the Fan(s) Again: Or, Sic Semper Conspiracies," *Reviews in American History* 12, no. 3 (September 1984): 388.

35. Hyman, "With Malice towards Some," 7, 5, 6.

36. Vaughan Shelton, *Mask for Treason: The Lincoln Murder Trial* (Harrisburg, Pa.: Stackpole Books, 1965), 7.

37. Guttridge and Neff, *Dark Union,* 210.

38. The last of the Catholic conspiracy books was Emmett McLoughlin's *An Inquiry into the Assassination of Abraham Lincoln* (New York: Lyle Stuart, 1963).

39. The complete list, from *The Shadowlands* Web site, http://theshadow lands.net/mystery.htm (accessed Dec. 18, 2003):

1. Lincoln was elected in 1860 and Kennedy in 1960, exactly one hundred years later.

2. Both men were deeply involved in civil rights for African Americans.

3. Both men were assassinated on a Friday, in the presence of their wives.

4. Each man's wife had lost a child while living at the White House.

5. Both men were killed by a bullet that entered the head from behind.

6. Lincoln was killed in Ford's Theater; Kennedy was killed while riding in a Lincoln convertible made by the Ford Motor Company.

7. Both men were succeeded by vice-presidents named Johnson who were southern Democrats and former senators.

8. Andrew Johnson was born in 1808 and Lyndon Johnson in 1908, exactly one hundred years later.

9. The first name of Lincoln's private secretary was John; the last name of Kennedy's private secretary was Lincoln.

10. John Wilkes Booth was born in 1839 (according to some sources) and Lee Harvey Oswald in 1939, exactly one hundred years later.

11. Both assassins were Southerners who held extremist views.

12. Both assassins were murdered before they could be brought to trial.

13. Booth shot Lincoln in a theater and fled to a warehouse; Oswald shot Kennedy from a warehouse and fled to a theater.

14. The names *Lincoln* and *Kennedy* have seven letters each.

15. The names *Andrew Johnson* and *Lyndon Johnson* have thirteen letters each.

16. The names *John Wilkes Booth* and *Lee Harvey Oswald* have fifteen letters each.

17. A Lincoln staffer, a woman named Kennedy, told Lincoln not to go to the theater. A Kennedy staffer, a woman named Lincoln, told Kennedy not to go to Dallas.

40. As discussed in Chapter 5, the Booth legend served at the beginning of the twentieth century as one of the first expressions of this kind of theory, one locating the source of the threat against American ways not in immigrants, Catholics, plutocrats, or other "alien" presences, but from within. Conspiracy theories alleging the corruption of government go back at least to the dissenting Englishmen of the eighteenth century (as discussed in Chapter 5 of Bernard Bailyn's classic, *The Ideological Origins of the American Revolution*). In the postrevolutionary American context, however, the shift in suspicion from outside groups, or select groups having undue influence on government, to government itself appears to be a later development. See David Brion Davis, *The Fear of Conspiracy: Images of Un-American Subversion from the Revolution to the Present* (Ithaca: Cornell University Press, 1971), for a good account of the development of conspiracy theory in American history. See also Goldberg, *Enemies Within,* for a survey of more recent theories, including that of the overarching Master Conspiracy featuring the "Insiders" bent on establishing a "New World Order."

41. Mark Fenster, *Conspiracy Theories: Secrecy and Power in American Culture* (Minneapolis: University of Minnesota Press, 1999), 68–74; Fran Mason, "A Poor Person's Cognitive Mapping," in *Conspiracy Nation: The Politics of Paranoia in Postwar America,* ed. Peter Knight (New York: New York University Press, 2002), 40–56; Timothy Melley, "Agency Panic and the Culture of Conspiracy," in *Conspiracy Nation,* 57–81; Gregory S. Camp, *Selling Fear: Conspiracy Theories and End-Times Paranoia* (Grand Rapids, Mich.: Baker Books, 1997).

42. As I write these sentences, in May 2004, the United States and the world are stunned by the revelations of prisoner abuse by American military personnel at the Abu Ghraib prison in Iraq. On May 11, 2004, in apparent retaliation, Iraqi insurgents beheaded an American contract worker. Despite official pronouncements that the few enlisted personnel so far indicted were acting on their own responsibility, many Americans strongly suspect they were directed by superiors to act as they did. As a former soldier, I am compelled to inject a personal note here and express my deep distress at the abuses and the risks to which these abuses have exposed all Americans serving in Iraq. More to the point of this study, I think it highly probable that the Iraq conflict (or, more properly, the way the conflict is being managed by U.S. political and military leaders) will result in

renewing Americans' distrust toward their government. If so, and if future developments follow the pattern of the past, we can expect the renewed production of conspiracy theories implicating the state.

43. Guttridge, "In Defense of *Dark Union.*"

44. Hanchett, *Lincoln Murder Conspiracies*, 218.

CONCLUSION

1. Pierre Nora, "Between Memory and History: *Les lieux de mémoire,*" *Representations* 26 (Spring 1989): 7–25.

2. Robert Alan Goldberg, *Enemies Within: The Culture of Conspiracy in Modern America* (New Haven: Yale University Press, 2001), 50.

3. Yosef Hayim Yerushalmi, *Zakhor: Jewish History and Jewish Memory*, foreword by Harold Bloom (Seattle: University of Washington Press, 1996), 14–15.

4. Dorothy Ross, "Historical Consciousness in Nineteenth Century America," *American Historical Review* 89, no. 4 (October 1984): 909–28.

5. Gordon S. Wood, "Conspiracy and the Paranoid Style: Causality and Deceit in the Eighteenth Century," *William and Mary Quarterly,* 3rd ser., 39, no. 3 (July 1982): 401–42.

6. For a fuller and more theoretically informed discussion of limit event, the negative sublime, and repetitive trauma syndrome, see Dominick La-Capra's *History and Memory after Auschwitz* (Ithaca: Cornell University Press, 1998). My thanks to Professor LaCapra for stimulating my thinking in this area in the course of a presentation I gave to Cornell's history faculty in November 2003.

7. Edward Colimore, "The Search for Lincoln's Assassin," *Philadelphia Inquirer*, April 28, 1992. See also Robert A. Erlandson, "Unearthing the Truth about Booth," *Baltimore Sun*, March 15, 1992.

8. For the Suratt Society's involvement, see the *Surratt Courier* for March 1994, and the January, March, May, and June 1995 issues. The record of the society's efforts on behalf of the cemetery's counsel may be found in its files, which director Laurie Verge was kind enough to allow me to look at, but which I am not at liberty to divulge, permission having been denied by the cemetery's counsel, Francis J. Gorman. See also Michael W. Kauffman, "Booth Mystery Solved or Crackpot Theory?" *Washington Times*, Dec. 3, 1994, and "Historians Oppose Opening of Booth Grave," *Civil War Times Illustrated* 34, no. 2 (1995): 26–30, 71–78. For the judge's verdict see Greg Pierce, "Judge Won't Allow Booth Exhumation," *Washington Times*, May 27, 1995.

9. *Virginia Eleanor Humbrecht Kline and Lois White Rathbun, Petitioners, v. All Descendants of John Wilkes Booth, Known or Unknown, and Green Mount Cemetery, Respondents*, Baltimore City Circuit Court, Judge Joseph H. H.

Kaplan presiding, case 94297044/CE187741, May 17–20, 1995. For the appeals decision, see 110 Md. App. 383 (1996).

10. *Congressional Globe*, 39th Cong., 2nd sess., July 28, 1866, 4292. As noted earlier, the context shows that Davis was engaged in lighthearted banter on the last day of the congressional session and that the real object of his comments was Lafayette Baker's reputation, not the possibility that Booth had escaped. For Hanchett's cross-examination see *Kline and Rathbun v. Green Mount*, May 19, 1995, 59–62.

11. Amanda Ripley, "Bone Hunter," *Washington City Paper*, March 13, 1998, available online at http://www.washingtoncitypaper.com/archives/cover/1998/cover0313.html (accessed Feb. 20, 2004).

12. Colimore, "Search for Lincoln's Assassin."

INDEX

Hofstadter, Richard, 208, 214–215
honor
    Booth's punctilious sense of, 88
    as justification for Booth's act,
        104–105
    southern primal, 106
Hood County, 6, 150, 242n35
Hope of Israel, 65
House Select Committee on
        Assassinations, 202, 255n26
Humphrey, Hubert, 203
Hyman, Harold, 204–205, 222n13,
        237n71, 256n34

"I have taken my last drink, boys"
        (poem), 116
I'll Take My Stand (Ransom), 144
imagination, northern popular, 13,
        72–77
Indiana State University, 196
Indian Territory, 34. *See also*
        Oklahoma Territory
Isenberg, J. L., 25, 44–45
Israel/Israelites, 49, 65, 186, 190,
        232n42

Jackson, Andrew, 9, 164
JFK. *See* Kennedy, John F.,
        assassination of
Johnson, Andrew, 8, 91, 98,
        129–130, 166, 185
Johnson, Haynes, 204

Kammen, Michael, 11, 147, 229n15
Kennedy, John F., assassination of,
        202–207
Kenzie, Wilson, 120
King Jr., Martin Luther, 202, 207
Knights of the Golden Circle, 8,
        85, 170, 240n11
Ku Klux Klan, 188

Lewis, Lloyd, 9, 18, 154–164, 198,
        249n43, 249n47
Lincoln, Abraham
    assassination of, 7, 8, 71–74,
        102–103, 191–192, 207
    commemoration, 155–160, 207
    condoned cotton trade, 193
    desanctification during Civil
        Rights era, 199
    diverging remembrance of, 156
    divided reputation in North
        before death, 78
    elevated to national deity, 143
    portrayed as racial
        moderate/conservative,
        143, 156
    promises to release Beall on
        Booth's appeal, 105
    remains exhibited in northern
        cities, 92–94
Lincoln, Mary Todd, 92, 95, 99
Lincoln Conspiracy, The (Balsiger
        and Sellier), 98, 201
Lincoln Memorial, 156, 166
Lincoln Memorial University,
        204
lived religion, 177, 224n29
Lost Cause, 11–16, 158, 206
Lost Tribes, 59, 64. *See also*
        Anglo-Israelism,
        Anglo-Saxonism

Maione, Michael, 8
Mammoth Cave, 51
Mask for Treason (Shelton), 201
master conspiracy narrative, 192
Masters, Edgar Lee, 162, 248n38
Maury, Matthew Fontaine, 112
Maximilian, 4, 112
MBTP. *See* Methodist Episcopal
        Board of Temperance

phrenology, 26, 84
Pidgeon, William, 59
politics of insanity, 82
Pomeroy, Brick, 118
popular death displays, 48, 50
postmillennialism/
    premillenialism, 177–178
Potter, Andrew, 196, 202
preachers, influence on northern
    public opinion, 165–166
Private Confession of J. Wilkes Booth,
    105–106
Prohibition, 178, 182. *See also*
    Eighteenth Amendment
Protestant reform movement,
    177–178
Puritans, 65

Radicals, radical Republicans,
    98–99, 135, 159–160, 165,
    166, 193, 195, 208, 218
Randall, James G., 91, 157, 198
Ransom, John Crowe, 144
reconciliationist, 11–12, 157
Reconstruction, 8
regionalism, 143–145, 168
    central problematic of, 247n36
revisionism, 143, 157–158, 162,
    201, 210–211, 217, 247n36
Ribuffo, Leo, 178
Rock Island Railroad, 21, 35–36
Roscoe, Theodore, 199
Ross, Dorothy, 183–184, 215
Rutherford, Mildred, 104, 162

Sandburg, Carl, 154, 167–168,
    249n43
Saturday Evening Post, 6, 151
Schwartz, Barry, 166, 223n17
Scopes Monkey Trial, 143
Scott, Dr. Orlando, 150

Sellier Jr., Charles, 201
Seward, William H., 108
Shelby, Jo, 112
Shelton, Vaughan, 201
Shepherd, William, 123, 146, 198
Silber, Nina, 12, 16
Silverberg, Robert, 58
Smith, Gene, 7, 216, 235n40
Smith, George, 22, 25
Smith, Gerald L. K., 179
Smith, Joseph, 53
social bandits, 13, 154, 224n23. *See
    also* outlaws
Sons of Liberty, 8
Southern Agrarians, 143
southern legend
    defining characteristics of,
        101, 120
    expressing cultural/political
        disobedience, 107
    and gender, 110
    geographic provenance, 118–119
    initial conditions giving rise to,
        71, 102–107, 233n5
    oral and retrospective quality of,
        115, 117
    representation of Booth,
        116–117
    sited in places of public
        transience, 110
Stabile, Susan, 170
Stanton, Edwin, 8, 73, 89–93,
    158–160, 193, 237n71
Starrs, James, 219–220
Steers Jr., Ed, 196, 221n1
St. Helen, John, 6, 117, 125,
    128–131
St. Louis Exposition, 32, 126, 139
Stone, Kate, 104
Stone, Oliver, 207
Stoneman, Austin, 157

Suarez, Benito, 4, 112
Surratt, Mary, 23, 28, 107
Surratt Society, 7, 124, 219, 258n8

T. B. Road, 132
This One Mad Act (Forrester), 141,
      151, 169–170
Thorowgood, Thomas, 65
Thrailkill, Levi, 115
Tolbert, Captain, 6, 110
Townsend, George Alfred, 72, 80,
      105–107
Traditions of Dee-Coo-Dah
      (Pidgeon), 59
"Trailing Lincoln's Assassin,"
      179, 186
trauma, 13, 75–78, 206, 216, 258n6
Traylor, Leslie, 179
Turner, Frederick Jackson, 34
Turner, Thomas, 118
Tutankhamen, 55
Tyler, Lyon G., 162
Tyrell, Judge A. W., 103, 118

unreconstructedness, 13, 107,
      135, 162
Unsolved Mysteries, 7, 123, 218

Vancil, David, 196
Vietnam, 202, 204
Voice, The, 182, 187–189

Ward, Frederick Townsend, 6, 111
Ward, Nahum, 51

Warren, John Collins, 53
Warren Commission, 202
Washington, George, 9, 93
Watergate, 202, 204
Web of Conspiracy (Roscoe), 199
white militia movements, 15
white supremacist, 11–12, 157
Why Was Lincoln Murdered?
      (Eisenschiml), 91, 151,
      158–161
Wilkerson, J. N., 118, 149, 246n18
Willis, Nathaniel Parker, 51
Wilson, Charles Reagan, 12,
      223n17
Wilson, Clarence True, 6, 176,
      251n6
   Anglo-Israelism and
      Anglo-Saxonism of, 179,
      187
   heads MBTP, 181
   involvement with Booth legend,
      179–180, 252n8
   nativist and antimodernist
      outlook, 181
   rhetorical style, 183
Wilson, Woodrow, 157
Wolfe, Su, 53, 228n12, 229n20
Wood, Gordon, 184, 215
Wood, William P., 194
WPA Oral History Project, 118,
      150
Wyatt-Brown, Bertram, 106

Zekiah Swamp, 3